The War
Our Doorstep

The War on Our Doorstep

London's East End
And how the Blitz Changed it Forever

HARRIET SALISBURY

in association with the Museum of London

EBURY
PRESS

3 5 7 9 10 8 6 4

First published in 2012 by Ebury Press, an imprint of Ebury Publishing

A Random House Group company

The Random House Group Limited Reg. No. 954009

Addresses for companies within the Random House Group can be found at www.randomhouse.co.uk

A CIP catalogue record for this book is available from the British Library

The Random House Group Limited supports The Forest Stewardship Council (FSC®), the leading international forest certification organisation. Our books carrying the FSC label are printed on FSC® certified paper. FSC is the only forest certification scheme endorsed by the leading environmental organisations, including Greenpeace. Our paper procurement policy can be found at www.randomhouse.co.uk/environment

Printed and bound by CPI Group (UK) Ltd, Croydon, CR0 4YY
ISBN 9780091941505

To buy books by your favourite authors and register for offers visit www.randomhouse.co.uk

To my mother, Elisabeth Salisbury,
who was born within the sound of Bow Bells

Contents

Foreword

The word 'history' is a lot more complicated than it first seems
to be and this book takes us right to the heart of the maze. When
I was at school and university in the 1950s and 60s, History was
owned by historians. These were for the most part men who had
attended private schools and Oxford or Cambridge University
and they tended to write either grand narratives about long eras
– France in the nineteenth century or the like – or biographies of
major figures: prime ministers, dictators, generals.

But out of sight, other histories were being written. A few
people were painstakingly putting together histories of men
and women they called labourers and trying to tell the story
of crafts, trades, associations and unions. Some were docu-
menting accounts of their particular immigrant groups. From
all walks of life, people began studying their streets, villages,
towns and localities and wrote pamphlets and booklets and
attended local meetings to talk about it.

Eventually, these tendencies – personal, local, 'from below'
and migrant histories were being seen as a movement and this
hooked up with new ways of describing ourselves in the
present. Key to it all were testimonies – written and oral by
people in the positions in society that had mostly been written
'about' and not 'by'. This is the territory on which memoirs
and what has come to be called life-writing meets diaries,
recorded interviews, radio and TV documentaries, which allow
'ordinary people' to speak, and archives of people's accounts
of events and experience.

Over the years, the Museum of London began collecting

various collections of testimonies that were relevant to London. Created from the Museum's archives, this book comes directly out of this oral history movement and touches on all these strands about ordinary people – labourers, unions, migration, women, ordinary families. *The War on Our Doorstep* immediately leads us to the heart of that great historical question: what was it like? To be clear, I'm not someone who thinks that the old-style history I was brought up with is necessarily redundant. For us to understand why and how things happened, we need grand narratives, we need accounts of how wars were made, how wealth was made and lost, how this or that group of people became powerful, how people were organised to make and distribute the things we need and use. That said, if we want to know how these things felt, just as you and I might feel it, if we want to understand the motives and desires of people, then we had better listen to the things that people say about these matters. Otherwise the danger is that you end up retelling myths, the received legends as often made up about other people as those made up by the people themselves.

I was on the receiving end of some of these. My parents were East Enders; my mother was born in 1919 in Stepney and lived there till she was eighteen. My father was also born in 1919 but in the USA, came to Whitechapel when he was two years old and having met my mother, also stayed till he was eighteen. All their sixteen great-grandparents were born in Poland, Russia or the Austro-Hungarian Empire and either they or their children were the first generation migrants into the East End of this book. As a child, growing up in the suburbs of north-west London, for me the East End was a place of the past, talked about again and again, sometimes lovingly, sometimes laced with danger, fear and on occasions dislike. It was a place where my parents had met and grown to love each other. It was also a place where they had engaged in a movement to defend their right to live there, to fight for better housing, jobs for all and ultimately a better society for all. As part of that, they had been offered and used the free education and free cultural facilities of local libraries, museums and historic sites which enabled them to go on to higher education and work in a profession.

They both spent a good deal of time thinking, talking and writing about how their own home cultures of Judaism and secular eastern European Jewishness intermingled in the East End with other migrants – Caribbean, Indian; older genera-tions of migrants, Irish, in particular – and whether there was something specifically London or 'Cockney' and how all this related to people – many of whom they admired – who were seen as trying to 'do good': doctors, teachers, priests, preach-ers, rabbis, politicians and the like.

Mysteriously for me as a child, this East End was in an obvious sense invisible because it was in that other country called 'the past'. But it was also invisible in a less obvious sense, on the rare occasions we visited it, because it wasn't there! That was of course just a perception moulded by my parents' own highly subjective view of their East End. They meant that *their* East End wasn't there. A new East End was – and always is – being made. And for over thirty years, I lived along its northern frontiers in Hackney and have spent many hours working in schools there as a visiting writer.

What is particularly moving and important about this book – in addition to its way of telling history – is how its voices embrace, challenge and enrich my sense of the East End: both in its mythic form which I'd learnt from my parents' accounts but also in my life and work in and around the area.

So, we all have pictures in our heads of what things were like in the past and education seems to gather about it a rosy glow of children in rows listening obediently while stern but fair teachers taught everyone to read, write and do maths. Gracie Smith says:

'I had no schooling, or very little schooling. I didn't have a rough upbringing, I was just the eldest of the family and of course I was expected, if Mother worked, to help my mother. I started work at ten years of age – sweeping snow, scrubbing doorsteps, helping Mother out – I went out with the barrow, or helped out the winkle man on Sundays.'

It doesn't fit the prevailing image of twentieth-century childhood, does it?

Again, the word 'blitz' has come to mean the bombing of London during the Second World War, but held in the collective memory of East Enders is the earlier bombing during the First World War, which included the bombing of an infant school in Poplar. Stan Bryan:

'The biggest shambles that I ever saw was after that Zeppelin raid – dear, oh dear, there was six inches of fat and sugar all along that factory road, along the side of Tate and Lyles. September 7th, at two minutes to five. I always remember it because I was working that day till five o'clock, and the siren went at five to five, so we all dashed down to the office but the timekeeper wouldn't let us out. I always thank him now because if he had let us out, I'd a been down at the shelter at Pier Road, or the one up the tunnel, I'd have been dead and buried by now.'

Perhaps I could finish with one of my parents' many stories. In 1936, the leader of the British Union of Fascists, Oswald Mosley had a plan to march with several thousand fellow fascists through the East End, along Cable Street. This was an area largely lived in by Jews and included the people in my parents' families. It's not hard to see that Mosley wanted to do this in order to make a public and theatrical point about entitlement. He and the fascists, he was suggesting, were entitled to be in Cable Street – which as human beings they were, of course – but, he appeared to be saying, the Jews were not. It was an old method used by any group intent on threatening another.

What happened next can only be described as a form of

uprising. Hundreds of thousands of people, mostly local, assembled in the streets leading into Cable Street, barricades were put up while Mosley was asked by the police to wait on the borders of the City of London and the East End until, ultimately, he was told to leave. He did not march through the East End.

My parents would tell us their version of this story at various times – at tea-time, on holidays, on car journeys. They told us about how 'mosleyites' would attack people and threaten them. And then this day in October 1936, when their streets were packed, it was dangerous and violent. They ended up fighting the police because the police said it was their job to clear the way for Mosley to march. In fact – and this is the point where the story got exciting to us as children – our parents, idealistic seventeen-year-olds, found themselves in one of the little streets that lead into Cable Street. In front of them was a barricade, and then, behind them was a mounted policeman. He was charging towards them, with his stick raised. They were caught on the wrong side of the barricade!

Before he could do whatever he thought he was going to do, a door in one of the small terraced houses opened and the pair of them were pulled inside. They were safe.

I always liked that story. For a start I was always glad that my parents come out of it safely. I liked the way that they felt they were defending something that was right to defend: where and how they lived and worked. I liked the way that this was something that brought hundreds of thousands of people together to 'win the day', but particularly I liked the fact that this was a story with something ironic or even absurd about it. They were on the 'wrong' side of the barricades! That's the personal part, that part of history that has no place in the big story; the story inside the story.

There! That's my contribution to this book of stories inside stories.

Michael Rosen, 2012

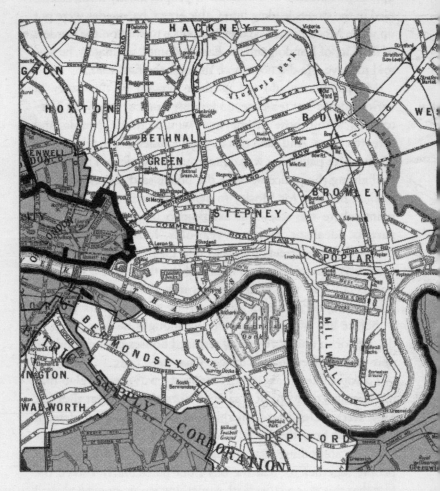

London's East End – from a map showing areas served by the Electric Lighting and Power companies of London, at a time when the East End had no electricity. Published by Geo. D. Atkin and Co. c.1920

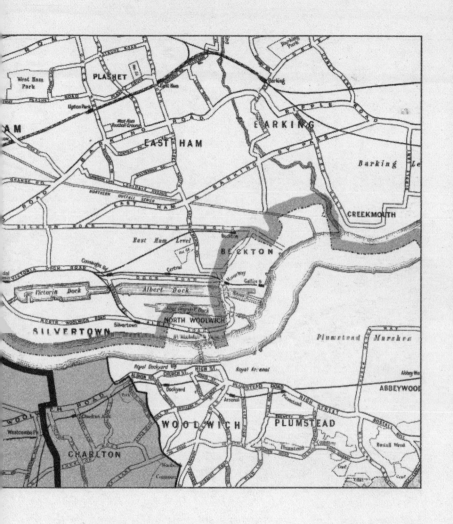

Introduction

Where and What is the East End?

London has an East End and a West End, although nobody ever speaks of a north or south end. The West End of London has always been posh; the top end of the city, for the rich and powerful. Westminster, where kings and queens were crowned, began as an island and for centuries remained very much a separate entity, aloof and apart from the noise and smells of the masses. Even in the twenty-first century, people talk of 'going up the West End'. It is part of London, but the smart bit; you go up west to be dazzled by bright lights, gaze in awe at famous landmarks and spend more than you can afford in restaurants, department stores, theatres and cinemas.

The East End, by contrast, has never been anything other than down-to-earth and downmarket. You go 'down the East End'. The East End is about lively gatherings of people, usually loud, usually eating or drinking, or both. It is markets rather than landmarks; whelks and jellied eels, public houses, backchat, a bit of a flutter, grabbing a bargain, having a laugh, and spontaneously bursting into song.

Or rather, that is what the East End was. These days, it is rare to hear anyone talk of 'going down the East End'. There are a few places that could be described as typical East End: some old pubs, and pie and mash shops; a few narrow alleyways in Whitechapel; Brick Lane and Petticoat Lane markets. But trying to conjure up from these what the East End used to be like is like standing by a puddle in the basin of a once-great lake and attempting to get an idea of how it must once have been. Without the sights, the smells, the teeming life, the abundance of colourful, noisy, exotic inhabitants, it is just an area, a place on a map. At some point during the late twentieth century, the real East End, the place you could visit, seems to have faded away.

So where was the East End? Unlike west London, the East End was never separate and apart. The heart of London is the Square Mile, the centre of commerce and finance since the Middle Ages, once protected and defined by city walls and gates (remnants of these fortifications can still be seen at London Wall, including a circular bastion by the Museum of London). On the eastern boundary wall is Aldgate, where Geoffrey Chaucer once lived in the custom officer's apartments above the ancient gate. When you left the City at Aldgate, right by the Aldgate pump, you were in the East End. Nobody ever moved to the East End for peace and quiet; they came because it was right by the City, one of the best places to find work in the numerous trades that support and underpin any large metropolis.

So it is easy to pinpoint where the East End starts – where it stops is far less certain. The East End could be said to carry on until you arrive at a place where no one claims to be an East Ender. How far east is the East End? Traditionally, after Aldgate, it takes in Whitechapel, Bow, Stepney, the Isle of Dogs, Bethnal Green and Poplar. But the development of the East End was always about work, and the main source of work was the river. The original East Enders were descended from the shipbuilders, mast and oar makers, yardmasters, pilots, riggers, coal whippers, ship chandlers, glassblowers, potters, ropemakers and all the other trades based on and around the ancient wharves of the Thames. These workers did not just follow the emergence of the docks, they helped create them; labourers were drawn in, particularly from Ireland, to dig the canals and basins alongside which their descendants were to be found generations later. So as the wharves became docks and the docks kept on expanding, the East End's migration of workers annexed areas further and further eastwards: Wapping and Shadwell, East Ham and Canning Town. If you are considering the history of the docks, you have to include Tilbury as a working outpost of the East End.

The River Thames is traditionally the East End's southern boundary, although this is not universally accepted. London's docks were not all on the north banks of the river, which means that dockers will cheerfully refer to 'the East End, north and south of the river'. London's first dock, the Howland Great Wet Dock, opened in the late seventeenth century on the south of the river – it later became Greenland Dock, part of the Surrey Commercial Docks. The trades of the river – the dockers, lightermen, stevedores and porters – were carried out on both sides, and many people who considered themselves East Enders lived in Bermondsey and Rotherhithe, close to the Surrey Docks. To them, it would seem odd if those doing the same job, living in similar circumstances, in the south, were excluded from a community to which those on the north emphatically belonged.

How far north? While dozens of cabinetmakers' workshops were a vital part of industry at one end of Hackney, further north, towards Tottenham, was countryside until the late nineteenth century. This made the middle of Hackney a sort of buffer zone between the slums and sawdust of Shoreditch, and the leafy estates in the north. The East End's endless sprawl did not go unnoticed; Prime Minister William Gladstone, on being invited to admire the seclusion of his friend Samuel Morley's estate near today's Springfield Park, is said to have responded, 'But Morley, Shoreditch is coming.' And by Shoreditch, he meant the noise, poverty and squalor of the East End.

The East End is more a set of customs, common values and even peculiarities of speech than a line on a map – and much of these shared values are to do with the trades and industries that attracted and maintained the East End's working-class population. London is not the only city to have an East End; many European cities have poor areas to the east of their centre, as well as wealthier ones in the west. This is because the northern hemisphere's prevailing winds blow from west to east, taking smoke and smells with them. If they mostly blew the other way, the poor areas with their unattractive and noxious industries would all be in the west, leaving the East Enders with the lion's share of clean air. The Metropolitan Building Act of 1844 prohibited 'harmful trades' within London, and so, for instance, Samuel Silver's waterproof clothing works gave its name to Silvertown, and Henry Tate and Abram Lyle both set up refineries nearby which later merged to form Tate & Lyle. Arnold Hills , the owner of the Thames Ironworks, went on to build a football ground for his workers in West Ham that spawned the East End's most famous sporting club.

The Importance of the Thames

Long before there were any 'harmful trades', London's growth was shaped by the wide blue ribbon of the 215-mile River Thames which becomes tidal at Teddington and enters Greater London at Thames Ditton. It is almost certainly the river that has given rise to the terms East End and West End – and it turns out that there is a South End, where the river finally reaches the sea. Flowing through the city, like the prevailing winds, from west to east the Thames became browner and murkier as it progressed, making the westerly reaches infinitely more attractive.

If you look at a map, you will see that the Thames in the West End has bridges crossing it at regular intervals. From Battersea up to Tower Bridge, the focus is on keeping the flow of people and traffic moving back and forth over the river. Corralled into embankments in the nineteenth century, the western Thames is harnessed to flow swiftly and neatly through its designated course in central London, creating pleasing backdrops for scheduled monuments. Beyond Tower Bridge, the river seems to wriggle free of constraints, twisting into its signature loop around the Isle of Dogs, after which it starts to swell; wild, wide and open. It is no longer an easily fordable water feature. With no linking bridges, the far side of the river ceases to appear close, like the other side of the road; it looks more like another country. This is not a river for pedestrian crossings (at least, not until the arrival of technology that could bore tunnels underneath the river in the nineteenth century), it is a river for boats, a major artery carrying traffic to the heart of London, with the convenience of bridges abandoned to the cause of the all-important river traffic.

When England began amassing its empire, any ship bringing dutiable imports into London had to unload at one of the twenty legal quays authorised by Elizabeth I between the centre of London and Tower Bridge; these were later supplemented by sufferance quays further east, and on the south bank of the river. London's earliest docks were for building and repairing ships rather than unloading cargo, but eventually a system of enclosed docks was built – largely to prevent huge losses of revenue through theft. In 1800, the value of floating property on the river was estimated at £75 million, with river pirates, night plunderers, scuffle hunters, mudlarks and a host of other criminals making off with easy pickings as ships moored in the river waiting for a space on the limited quays. The West India Dock Act of 1799 authorised two parallel docks which sat across the top of the loop that almost encircles the Isle of Dogs; this was followed by the London Docks at Wapping, where wine, port, dried fruit, ivory, wool, spices and tobacco were stored in warehouses behind high walls, and the East India Dock, where valuable goods such as silks and carpets were sped swiftly to safe warehouses at Cutler Street in the City, along the newly built Commercial Road. As the nineteenth century progressed, these enclosed docks were supplemented by the extension of the Surrey Docks, St Katharine Docks, the Royals (Victoria and Albert), and Millwall Docks. This both enabled and fuelled an explosion in river-borne cargo, which led to London becoming the world's greatest and busiest port. London's East End was right at the heart of this great engine of commerce.

All alone I went a-walking by the London Docks one day,
For to see the ships discharging in the basins where they
* lay,*
And the cargoes that I saw there, they were every sort of
* kind,*
Every blessed brand of merchandise a man could bring
* to mind;*
There were things in crates and boxes, there was stuff in
* bags and bales,*
There were tea-chests wrapped in matting, there were
* Eastern-looking frails,*
There were balks of teak and greenheart, there were
* stacks of spruce and pine,*
There was cork, and frozen carcasses, and casks of
* Spanish wine,*
There was rice and spice and coco-nuts, and rum enough
* was there*
For to warm all London's innards up and leave a drop
* to spare.*

Nitrates by Cicely Fox Smith

Cicely Fox Smith's 1920 poem conjures up some idea of the extent and importance of London's docks in the nine-teenth and early twentieth centuries. It is hard to imagine now, when office blocks and airplanes punctuate skies that once bristled with masts, and the few remaining pieces of dockside machinery look like modern art sculptures reflected in the still waters. But the 1901 census listed more than three hundred ships in the various London docks (the census counted only ships with crew on board). The fifty ships in the Pool of London and St Katharine Docks included four-masted barques that plied the wool trade from Australia, and ships that brought Norwegian ice to London. In the East and West India Docks were fifty-six large vessels, one of which laid the cables under the Atlantic for the Eastern Telegraph Company, as well as Thames pleasure steamers laid up for the winter. Among the seventy craft in the Surrey and Millwall Docks were vessels that carried Jewish immigrants from the Baltic, and Scandinavian timber boats from Norway. Referencing the poem above, the largest was a four-masted steel barque, the *Lindfield*. She transported nitrates mined in the deserts of Chile, initially for use in making fertiliser; later, during the First World War, in the manufacture of the explosives that would have such a devastating effect on the East End. More than a hundred ships waited in the Royal Victoria and Royal Albert Docks (the final Royal, the King George V Dock, was yet to be built), including the *Lady Jocelyn*, built for East India trade, then employed to carry troops and emigrants, then refrigerated cargo, before finally, in the dock strikes, becoming a floating barracks for strikebreakers. In 1901, there were only twenty-nine ships further downriver at the Tilbury Dock – its day was yet to come.

The Voices of the East End

The War on our Doorstep is the story of the East End as told by East Enders; a story of a camaraderie born of poverty and hardship, of children who forged lifelong allegiances to each other and to the streets where they grew up. It tells how this close-knit community hung together through the heaviest aerial bombardment Britain has ever seen during the six years of the Second World War and how they were betrayed by the promise of progress when successive well-meaning policies, plans and schemes finished off the destruction that the Blitz had started.

The pages to follow are packed with voices from those very streets. They were recorded by a variety of oral history projects, now held by the Museum of London, some of them dating back more than thirty years, to a time when the availability of simple, affordable recording equipment meant that academics and study groups could tape and preserve memories that would otherwise have been lost. This gave labour and social historians a tool for amassing information about groups and individuals – particularly women, the poor and members of minority social and ethnic groups – whose accounts were often left out of traditional written histories. These tapes, either transcribed or re-recorded to preserve the precious originals, form a valuable archive of memory. To put on a pair of earphones and listen to the distinctive cadences, rhythms and laughter of someone born in the 1890s is an extraordinary experience, and one that I hope will be recreated as the pages of this book reveal the many and varied personalities whose voices I have been privileged to encounter.

Drawn from a number of sources, the original interviews had a variety of agendas, often to do with patterns of work or living conditions in particular areas. Few of the interviewees were recorded for the purposes of providing a neat comprehensive history of the East End. This has meant that in arranging the material, some considerations and constraints had to be taken into account. As so many interviewees had vivid memories of their childhoods in the early years of the twentieth century, Part One of this book, entitled 'Life in the East End before the Second World War' is full of childhood memories from home life, through school, to the working lives of young girls and apprentices and their subsequent journeys into the wider world.

Many aspects of these early experiences remained the same from the later decades of the nineteenth century right through to the 1930s, interrupted only by the strange, vivid and terrifying events of the First World War which seemed to prefigure the Blitz, with Zeppelin air raids, blackouts, rationing and shelters. The struggle against poverty and oppression, and the fight for better pay and conditions runs through this period of the East End's history, from the Victorian era of the Matchgirls' Strike to the General Strike of 1926, until a greater enemy appeared in the form of Hitler and his territorial ambitions.

When considering the Second World War and the East End, the question that fascinated me was not 'What happened?', but 'Who did it happen to?'. We have all heard of the Blitz spirit but there are varying explanations of how this phrase came about. It has been attributed to contemporary government propaganda and to later wishful nostalgia, as well as to a genuine and spontaneous reaction to the experience of having your family, home and neighbourhood bombed. With a clearer idea of who the people of the East End were, and where and how they lived, I hope readers will be able to draw their own conclusions about the hearts and minds of East Enders during those terrible years.

The changes that took place in the East End may have begun with Hitler's bombs but they continued for many years, influenced by politics, labour relations, modern ideas about architecture and planning and the very basic human desire for a better and more comfortable life. The final section of this book gives the East Enders' view of the reshaping of post-war east London.

Most of the interviewees are identifiable, and brief biographies at the back of the book explain their connections with the East End. Many were born there, some arrived as immigrants, some came for work, but all can tell us something about East End life in the days when there was still plenty of life in the East End.

PART 1

Life in the East End before the Second World War

Charles Booth's poverty survey lists the residents of this street in Bethnal Green as costermongers, fish-curers and thieves. Some of the children have bare feet, yet despite its slum status, and a width of only nine feet, Little Collingwood Street has an air of cheerful neighbourliness. John Galt, 1900–1907

CHAPTER 1

At Home in the East End

My Father's House

'In my father's house are many mansions.'

– JOHN, 14:2

In the early twentieth century, the King James's Bible would have been familiar to most children, either from church attendance or from copying out verses at school. The words of John 14:2 must have struck a chord with many young East Enders, as most lived in properties that contained several separate households. The phrase would have suggested a heavenly father whose living arrangements were much like their own fathers' – just on a grander scale.

Home, for a typical East End family, would be one or two rooms with a shared kitchen, or in some cases a cooker on the landing, and a shared outside toilet. Within the same building would be other families, each living in a room or two. In Whitechapel, Jewish families would fill whole houses with relatives, but in other areas it was more usual to share with strangers.

Many of the larger East End houses had once been middle-class homes – not mansions, but respectable single-family houses. As public transport improved with the introduction of tram lines and rail systems, affluent inner-city dwellers moved outwards from the centre to leafy suburbs springing

3

up around the edges. The houses they left were soon let, divided, and sublet again, providing homes for London's expanding population, which grew from about one million at the start of the nineteenth century, to 6.5 million by the start of the next.

One of the first municipal housing schemes, offering purpose-built flats in multi-storey buildings, without lifts, made an appearance around 1900 when the Boundary Estate scheme replaced a notorious East End slum, the Old Nichol, known as the Jago, on the edge of Bethnal Green. Here, houses and workshops had been packed into every alley and courtyard, creating a dense maze where sunlight barely penetrated. But such programmes of slum clearance could exacerbate the problem of overcrowding, as the new estates provided fewer housing units than the buildings they replaced, and rents for the new homes could not be afforded by the original tenants. A national survey in 1936 showed that the worst overcrowding in the country was in east and central London.

For most East Enders, 'home' was a set of rooms, rather than a building, and families tended to be loyal to their area but unsentimental about houses. It was common to move around to be closer to a job, or in search of cheaper rooms, or to keep one step ahead of the bailiffs by doing a 'moonlight flit'.

When I was a younger boy, I couldn't bear the thought of living in a house without another family – I mean, there was us, we only had two rooms, little kitchen, that's all we had. And the woman upstairs, she had seven or about nine kids. There was an old couple downstairs. Was about forty of us in there.

Henry Corke

At one time there were nine people in the flat. We used to use the doors which had been taken off the cupboards, laid on chairs and made up as beds. Nobody complained; the superintendent didn't mind because everybody was doing the same.

Miss M

My earliest memories are when we lived in a three-storey house, two rooms on each floor, my eldest uncle and his family on the ground floor, another uncle and family on the first floor, another on the second floor, which was my aunt's family. My dad and mum and three of us children on the top floor. There were fourteen children in the house and we grew up almost like sisters and brothers.

Vicki Green

The houses were cold. There was some three-storey houses in Louder Street – a three-storey house would probably be shared by about four or five families, some of them in one room. In the early days we lived in Louder Street, I remember that was a three-storey house and the woman who paid the rent of the house, she was looked upon as the landlady, but actually she was the main tenant and she'd sublet – by that means she lived rent-free. We had the top two rooms, then the back room was another woman on her own; on the next floor there'd be two more families, and on the bottom floor another two.

Jack Banfield

Number five Wilson Street was a little old house, built in the nineteenth century. The back kitchen floorboards seemed to be perished. If you went out there in the dark, you trod on hundreds of black beetles. Oh, it was a terrible place.

Charles Lisle

We had two rooms and a small kitchenette; there were three toilets in the yard. Altogether, there must have been eighty to ninety people living in the whole block, who shared these three toilets and a communal dustbin. The place was foul – people used to stand on the toilet seats to avoid sitting on them, there were newspapers saturated with urine all over the place – it's a miracle that everybody didn't die of some dire disease there.

You had a gas meter that used to take shillings, and if you ran out of shillings or ran out of money, then you just couldn't have any light or gas for cooking. There was a large bed in the bedroom and a child's cot, and a sofa that we used to open in the sitting-room, in which four of us used to sleep, head to toe. I and the brother who was younger than me by thirteen months, my brother Pinny, were the two in the family who wet the bed, so we were the two who had to sleep in the cot. And we were very tall kids, and I remember that my legs used to stick out of the bars of the cot – about half of my leg used to stick out.

Emanuel Litvinoff

The Jago was demolished about 1890, because it became – it was utterly, oh, what I am describing was high-class living, compared to conditions in the Jago. I mean, they were great big houses, and nobody had more than one room, and there'd be families of fourteen, fifteen – up to twenty, living in these tiny little places, no oilcloth, no floor covering, one room, filthy, starving, and most of them lived on burglaries or sneak-thieving, or whatever, even the kids. Girls generally were the slavies – while the mother and father were out boozing, the kids had to do all whatever had to be done at home, sweeping up, scrubbing floors and whatever, and boys were out pinching, stealing – even if it was only a couple of potatoes, or a few carrots, you know, they brought them home.

When the council destroyed the Jago, they didn't make any provision whatever for the people who lived there, and so they had to spread out into Hoxton and Highbury and the other parts of Bethnal Green, and that's how Hoxton became such a slum. Because the Jago moved in and brought its slummery with it.

Louis Dore

I left Limehouse when I was about five, in 1933, and we left there because it was slum clearance and my father being in bad health, they advised my mother to go and live at Downham. Most of them from Padstow Place went to Jonskill House where they built two big blocks of flats. We weren't happy about it; in fact, we ran away from home twice, my brother and I. Downham was a marvellous place, it was beautiful and clean, the houses and flats were very, very nice, there was grass there, something we'd never seen, didn't even know existed, but the thing was, we missed the community spirit of Limehouse. Although we were still very young, we still loved the community spirit.

Mary Partlett

My remembrance of home was one back room, two chairs and a big tin box where my old man kept whatever he was saving, and we used to sit in there. I remember we had no sheets, and my father used to go out and bring in newspapers – we laid on newspapers, or we laid on the placards they used to put on the boards in those days. That was my sheets.

Jack Dash

The first house I remember is Queen's Road, Plaistow – a big, double-fronted house. We lived in there with other people – families up and downstairs. The house next to the Silk Mills was empty and, as kiddies, we went out and we found a purse, a little chain purse, you know, and in it was half a crown. So we spent it on tins of milk, condensed milk, and went in this empty house and we were sucking at the tins of milk. Somehow we got upstairs and somebody had locked us in and we couldn't get out. It was some time before we managed it – someone was playing a game. Eventually, someone came and got us out.

Charles Lisle

My brother Bill got married to the girl who lived opposite – I dunno what her family did but they didn't work in the docks. Anyway, when brother Bill got married, he was ever so posh, because he had all the upstairs to himself, you know, the three rooms that we, all the rest of us, had.

Us three boys had the bed in the little back room, there was Mum and Dad in the big bed in the big front room upstairs, alongside it was a chest of drawers – that's where young Beryl was; in the tiny single bed to the right of Mum and Dad's bed was where Percy, Nancy and Edna used to sleep. The two girls slept one end of the bed and Percy slept the other end.

Dennis Pike

There was an open grate with a coal fire and some of the cooking was done on this, the rest being done on a single gas ring – then called a 'blue light' for want of a better name – on the landing outside. Our lighting was by gas – this was well before electricity.

There was no lighting on the stairs at all, so when we went downstairs to the toilet, two floors down, we used to have to go with a candle, and I was petrified. I've always hated the dark. One of my cousins went to the toilet with the candle, put it on the seat, and set her nightdress alight.

Sunday mornings, my aunts and my mother used to go down into the backyard on the ground floor to do the washing. There was a big copper which they put wood under and lit it to heat the water in the copper, and they used to do their washing. And of course there was nowhere to dry the washing so we used to have washing lines on the staircase and every Sunday, when we'd go up and down the stairs, there was wet sheets flapping in our faces. It was a very primitive life.

Vicki Green

The sink was always in the backyard, we never used to have running water inside the house. There's always a single tap in the backyard and the sink was under it. So if you went into somebody's house and there was a wash sink in the kitchen – they were well off.

Jack Banfield

We lived in two rooms on the second floor and my brother and I used to sleep in the garret but I liked the garret because it overlooked the rooftops and the soaring steeple of Christ Church Spitalfields. I was always charmed because there would be a carolling of the bells and it would waft across the skyline, that, and the chanting, because on a Sunday there used to be Hebrew classes in the Brick Lane Talmud Torah, and they would be reciting by heart in Hebrew and it would waft across and blend with the sound of the bells.

Jack Miller

The coalies carried their shovels from job to job and had stands by all the docks. One stand was in Wapping, and one was outside The Swan pub at Stepney station. I lived next door to The Hastings Arms in Cable Street and that was a regular call for the coalies, and they would stand their shovels and plates against our street railings which meant when we looked up from our basement kitchen they blocked out some of the light. My mother knew these men had done a hard day's work and never complained.

Alexander Gander

When I was eleven, the business went broke and the family had to move into two rooms in Old Montague Street in the heart of Whitechapel – not a salubrious street at all. Whitechapel was dirty, noisy, smelly – a great wide road, the widest main road in London at that time, carrying six lines of traffic each side, going very fast, east and west. And off this great wide major highway opened a whole network of tiny slummy narrow turnings, full of old Victorian tenements that should have been demolished before the century started. And that was where the people lived.

Charles Poulson

This poor old girl, she'd get the chair from somewhere and perhaps she'd find an old fender from somewhere on a heap of rubbish and go into this room so she only had half a crown, but they used to manage on that, see – a loaf of bread would last them a week. But some of them would get a pennyworth of gin – you know, in the pub – they'd bought a pennyworth of gin and there'd be some old piano in the corner and someone playing... it's heaven to them, see? And of course, the half-crown would go, and so they'd have what you'd call the brokers in: 'Poor old Mrs So-and-so, she's gonna have the brokers in, she was just thrown out on the streets.' Then in would come these men with the top hats and tail coat, they'd go up and open a window and throw out the bits and pieces, all out on the road. And the old girl would come down and sit on the doorstep and men would try to sell these – tuppence for a chair, everything was so cheap in them days – and get the money back that was owing to them.

Hilda Bunyon

We were living in Canning Town; we've never moved out from an area of say five mile from the docks. In those days we'd do what you call 'moonlight flittin'' because you'd pack up when you owed a few bob rent, put your things on an old barrow for tuppence or threepence which you hired and you'd move to somewhere else.

Stan Rose

Our Daily Bread

When social researcher and philanthropist Charles Booth finished his survey of London's poor in 1903, he concluded that more than a third of the population of the East End lacked adequate nourishment and were at all times 'in want'. At this time, the staple diet of the poor was bread and margarine. The main drink was tea made with condensed milk, which was cheaper than fresh and lasted better, as well as serving as milk and sugar in one; a large tin cost tuppence ha'penny. Shopping for food was done daily, as workers were paid by the day and food could be bought in tiny quantities, so the poorest families could manage to buy a day's supply of tea, milk or jam.

The First World War accustomed London to its first experience of food shortages and rationing. Parks and gardens were dug over so home-grown produce could help the war effort. The docks provided opportunities for pilfering, as did the markets, which were also a source of cheap damaged produce. Street traders arrived with both regular and seasonal delicacies to sell house-to-house, and Bawley boats, which trawled the river estuary for brown shrimp, would come upstream to sell their catches. Local dairies continued to have cows on the premises right up until the Second World War.

Many workers went home for a midday meal, and there were many cookshops, often with the phrase 'A good pull-up for carmen' in their windows – this meant they provided a bucket of water and a place to tie up horses outside, and cheap, filling food inside. The only non-working day was Sunday, when the whole family gathered around the table, and if the family budget could stretch to roast meat it would be cooked in the local baker's oven for a small sum.

———•———

We used to shop every day – we didn't have no fridges. Six children and then my mother, that was seven. Every day you'd buy your butter, every day you'd buy your milk. My mother used to boil the milk up in the summer so it shouldn't go sour.

Miss H

My uncle's shop sold everything and it was never closed, because it was near the docks. And the men used to go in for the odd day's work, and they used to come out about seven in the evening, and it used to be crowded out around then. They could go and buy a loaf of bread, or perhaps two penn'orth of ham, a ha'porth of jam in a cup; they'd take a cup for a ha'porth of condensed milk – all little bits and pieces like that. His till used to get full up of ha'pennies and farthings – sometimes pennies; not much over a penny used to go in there.

Alice Humm

You never really went hungry because there was the lanes. Brick Lane and Petticoat Lane – there were always the stalls. In the East End there was always something you could nick – there was a tradition of scrumping apples or oranges. You used to go down Spitalfields, the market, and there was always stuff lying around that they were throwing away, that they couldn't sell.

Alfie Bass

This East End market, with its costermongers' carts and the man carrying a basket on his head, is the kind of place most housewives did their daily shopping. The smart clothes and the girls' white pinafores suggest this photograph was taken on a Sunday. c1900

All the Welshmen had diaries in those days. You had your own cow – they all had their names, Bessy, say – and you used to go in there, the women used to go to the cowshed for a gossip, and they'd say, 'Joe, when you gonna milk Bessy?' You know, 'cos they wanted it for their children, 'cos they liked Bessy's milk.

Mrs P

Another trick was to go to Spitalfield Market looking for 'specks' after the market had finished. There used to be crates of fruit that might have been smashed up, and we'd go through them, cut the bad parts out and take them home to our parents. There used to be a fruit man across the road who used to sell 'specked' apples and oranges; he used to cut the bad parts off and sell them so much a bag. Another man used to sell penny lucky bags – the crap he used to put in there for a penny!

Mr U

In the First World War, a lot of shops with German-sounding names were raided by looters, who were out simply for loot – they hadn't got very great feelings against the Germans, they were just out to get anything. It was a time of great poverty in the East End. If you're hungry, stealing is not such a great thing. They used to get a small boy in the crowd, give him a brick, and say 'Throw it through that window', and as soon as the glass was broken, the mob used to move in. They would clear the premises, whatever they were, butchers or bakers or whatever. I was aware there was a lot of that going on. My dad said to me, 'Don't you have anything to do with that.' They used to gather, to work up courage sort of thing, and he said, 'If you see that happening, you come home straight away.'

Cyril Demarne

I remember in 1917, on my birthday, which was the twenty-seventh of December, and it had been snowing, lining up outside

Teapot Jones's provision ship in Chrisp Street in the hopes of obtaining a quarter of a pound of margarine. We were at the end of the queue but before we got anywhere near the door, the supply of margarine had run out so we had to go home without that. But having got home, we learned that another had some barrels of condensed milk, which came from America, opened up. So we went around there with a couple of jugs and watched with interest as the jugs were put underneath the tap in the bung of the barrel and the condensed milk slowly came out. The jug, by the way, had already been weighed and was on a pair of scales and I think the limit was a half a pound.

Tom Stothard

There was a 'Dig for Victory' campaign. The whole of Millwall Park, which I remember as being something of about eighteen acres, was dug up. The soil, which was rich alluvial soil, produced enormous crops. It was absolutely wonderful soil. My father, who was then a Metropolitan policeman and an ex-farmer, was absolutely amazed by it – he said, 'If I had a farm with this sort of soil, I'd make my fortune.'

Laurie Landick

The tablecloth, more often than not, was a newspaper – Sundays, you had a tablecloth, Sunday's dinner, when all the family was there. The rest of the week, the family would never sit down to dinner, because there were bits and pieces who'd come in at different times of day and you'd have what was there for you. How they managed to feed us, I don't know. There was always a good stew or something, at least one good meal a day, from nothing. Marvellous how people used to cater there.

Jack Banfield

I used Bawley boats quite frequently during and after the war, going down past All Hallows and places like that, fetching shrimps and winkles and when they had their nets out, I can recollect they used to have a basket up on top of the mast to let people know that they've got the trawl out. You used to get a bag of coal and give them a bag of coal and they'd give you a bucket of shrimps or something like.

Dick Allington

We lived on very basic foods. Invariably, I'd have bread and marge. Very fond of condensed milk on my bread and marge in those days. Occasionally, Mum could afford me to go around to the pie and mash shop in the High Street, opposite Bow Church.

Albert Patten

At an orphanage, you're merely a number, you're not anybody in your own right. I was G101, and that was it. And, of course, it was during the First World War and the food was very plain. In fact, I can't bear the sight of suet pudding now. We used to have it five days a week.

Doris Salt

Teatimes, if we were lucky, Mum would send us over for a penny tin or a three-halfpenny jar of fish paste to put on the bread and butter. If they sent me, I always come back with bloater paste, because it was very very strong indeed – you didn't get a lot of it anyways, but when you got bloater paste, you knew you had something. My brother Reg didn't like it very much; if he went, he'd get salmon and shrimp.

Dennis Pike

One of us would be sent round to the corner shop to buy a pennyworth of tea, sugar and milk. This was done by the shop-keeper, on a piece of greaseproof paper, putting two slabs of condensed milk, one of tea and one of sugar, wrapping it up

– at least you got the paper free – and coming home and making as large a pot of tea as possible for the family, supplemented by probably bread and jam. I can't actually say that we went hungry – perhaps because semi-hunger was a way of life.

Bill Crook

Sunday lunch – my mother used to put it all in a big dish and she used to take it up to this baker's to be baked, as did lots of the women, because living in one room you didn't have a cooker.

Mary Partlett

They baked their own cakes and, having no oven, took their cakes to the local baker's yard, where he'd charge a penny for cooking it, having stuck a cloakroom ticket on the tin and given us the other half. On Friday morning, before Shabbat, they'd make a tray of biscuits – I remember it was a large black tray – and get it baked in the same way.

Vicki Green

My mother used to put us to bed five o'clock. We had nothing to eat. We were starving. We literally starved, and that's not a lie. My mother had to put us all to bed 'cos we were hungry. Breakfast was a hard bit of bread and we'd have to take that off to school. When we came home, cold bananas. Our sister always says to me, 'If I ever see a banana again, I'll scream!' I like bananas, yet we had such an awful lot of them.

Miss H

I can remember a particular occasion that stands out in my mind. We were all standing outside this wharf and they were loading crates or oranges and 'accidentally on purpose' one of the dockers dropped one of the crates and I can remember filling knickers with oranges – we wore navy blue knickers, fleecy lined, and I can remember the girls filling our knickers with oranges, about treble the size hips, wobbling home with all the oranges. The boys, of course, put theirs in their pockets.

Lucy Collard

I knew the wharf where me father used to go for work, and that was Middleton's of St Brides, see. So we'd go round and he'd say, 'Yes, we're working till seven o'clock, fetch me a jug of tea.' So then I'd take a jug of tea, wait outside the back gate, and then when the jug came out, there'd be some bananas in it, ripe bananas for us to have for our tea. So he'd give me sixpence: 'Take that home to your mum.' That sixpence would buy the tea for the rest of us. The way of shopping there was the most expensive way of shopping: penny packet of tea, quarter of sugar, two ounces of margarine. Jam, we'd take a cup.

Jack Banfield

On the Isle of Dogs there was a few shops – pawn shops in particular, it was the biggest shop there – fish and chip shop and butchers and grocers and that, greengrocers. But everybody used to go to Chrisp Street up in Poplar, you used to have a market there and Friday nights it used to be open till about nine and ten o'clock. And in those times, if you dealt with a butcher all the year round, he'd give you a rabbit or something like that. Chicken was a rarity – you used to have a chicken Christmas. Didn't get it any other time. And if you'd dealt with that butcher, he'd give you a rabbit.

Robert Stapleton

A tricycle used to come round. On the front of it was like a heated paraffin stove, with windows round it, and my dad wouldn't get up till he'd been round, 'cos he knew the time. My mum used to call him but he wouldn't get up, the old man.

Stickler for time, but he wouldn't. And the old bloke used to come round: 'Piieees… all hot!' And when I grew up, I thought, I'm going to have a pie every night. Of course, by the time I grew up, he wasn't there, was he?

Dennis Pike

On Sundays we had the muffin man. He used to carry a tray of muffins on his head and ring a bell, call out, 'Lovely fresh muffins.' Also a man came with a barrow, he used to call out, 'Fine large shrimps, winkles and watercresses.' There was the Indian toffee man, thinking back, he must have been a Sikh, because the Indian toffee man always wore a turban. Indian toffee was very much like candy floss; he had this tin box he carried in front of him, it was all ready made up and he would just put a stick in and twirl it around this stick. At the corner of Hind Street was the 'okey-pokey man. 'Okey-pokey was ice cream, and he would be there with his ice cream in the summer and in the winter it would be chestnuts; he would have a sort of brazier thing on a barrow.

Lucy Collard

It was a sister came round, full of tears, and you often wondered why people cried in those days, didn't you? What I found out was that her husband never given her any money, he was always in the pub, but always demanded food and something on the table when he came in. And she was going to get a good hiding.

My gran said, 'Oh, we'll sort him out.' So she sent the dog, old Bill, round to Coppins – Coppins was the pork butchers in Chrisp Street where you used to send the dog, used to go round and beg, and he'd come back with a wacking great bone or something. The dog would carry it all the way back to Leven Road from Chrisp Street. Well, Gran would stew it up and make a good stew of it.

He went round there one day and he come back with a string of sausages, and he'd dragged them all round the gutters from Chrisp Street – all the way round to Leven Road. He never ate them, he just dragged them. My gran picked them up, washed them, wrapped them up in newspaper: 'Take them home and cook them for his tea.' I was always a little bit worried eating round my gran's after that.

Len Faram

Brewer's Quay used to have General Steam Navigation boats that used to run to Holland – Rotterdam and Amsterdam. And they used to fetch Dutch produce: cheese, butter, eggs. Opposite Brewer's Quay in Lower Thames Street was a coffee shop. If you was fortunate enough to get work at Brewer's Quay, the routine was always, when they were doing the eggs, two of you would slip away for breakfast, come back and two more would go. That was the routine, see, because you'd probably left home at six o'clock in the morning and you hadn't had anything to eat. So you'd take half a dozen eggs in your pocket to the coffee shop, you'd give them to the proprietor, you'd get a rasher of bacon and one of the eggs, a mug of tea and two slices of bread. So it was tit for tat. I can remember one morning there was a hell of a hullaballoo there and they said, 'What's he grumbling about, then?' And apparently, what had happened, he's said, 'I'm using all me own so-and-so eggs!' He said, 'They're coming in here, they're not fetching any eggs. They're getting the breakfast, but I'm using me own eggs!'

Jack Banfield

In Sickness and Health

With more than a million people packed into crowded accommodation, many in extreme poverty, disease was a constant threat. Medical officers examining recruits for the First World War found that 37.4 per cent of Londoners had either a physical disability, or weakness due to past disease, against a national average of 31.5 per cent. Growing children were especially vulnerable to the effects of a poor diet combined with cold, dirt, and polluted air. The common diseases of infancy were scarlet fever and tuberculosis (often called consumption), as well as diphtheria, measles, chickenpox and whooping cough. Both children and adults were vulnerable to epidemics, such as the outbreak of Spanish influenza in 1918 which killed about forty million worldwide. Nearly every East End household was affected by this, and funeral processions filled the streets each day.

With no free health provision, if you did fall ill the expense of calling a doctor could weigh heavily on an overstretched household budget. An infectious illness meant a trip to hospital in a horse-drawn vehicle, known as the fever cart, followed by a long stay in an isolation ward – this allowed the patient's immune system time to gain strength and fight off the infection. For long-term illnesses, or just a failure to thrive, country air was recommended, and various charities stepped in to take children out of the East End into a healthier environment – it would seem neither doctors nor parents had qualms about sending a small child, unaccompanied, to an unknown family to recuperate.

Food poisoning was always endemic, caused a sick headache and, at the very worst, *ptomaine*, an all-embracing word used by doctors, if you could afford the shilling charge to visit one. Usually my mother would be the diagnostician, and bicarbonate of soda was the panacea, though occasionally senna tea could be administered. If your condition seemed dire enough to warrant a visit to the doctor, he'd make you up one of two remedies: white mixture or black mixture. The white mixture was fairly innocuous, causing you to 'go' without too much discomfort, but if you got the black, known as blackjack, then you knew that you were in for a bad time.

Practically all children had whooping cough, measles and rickets and chickenpox successively, but those maladies were quite normal and acceptable. And the more spots you had, especially chickenpox spots, the more amusement was provided for the rest of the family. 'How's your belly off for spots?' was a common enquiry.

Then there was the fever cart. When this arrived at any house everybody would run home and all doors would be closed until he'd gone. The fever cart was a four-wheeled carriage with covered windows. As a child, we didn't know what particular fever was being dealt with, all we knew was that whatever it was, it was catching and that anybody taken away would almost certainly not come back; they were taken to the infirmary and the infirmary was where you died, like in the sanatorium. You knew what you died of in the sanatorium – galloping consumption.

Louis Dore

I had a lot of illness when I was little and I caught the dreaded diphtheria, which usually carries you off, but I can remember – I must have been only about six – being carried down the stairs by two men, ambulance, and I was sent away to a fever hospital. And I spent nine months in there and I only saw my mum and dad once 'cos they didn't let you go in. And I had to see them through a glass window. And they had gowns on and hoods because I was infectious.

That was the only time I got a slap from a nurse. I done something and she slapped me, I can remember that. I think it was something to do with I'd made a mess. I think it was something to do with the bed not being neat and tidy and I'd spilt something. But I did get a slap.

Joanna Roberts

The first time I ever went away from home, being nosey, I poked my head inside an ambulance taking away one or two of my friends with scarlet fever. Lo and behold, I got scarlet fever. I ended up in Dartmouth Fever Hospital. I can just recollect going by boat down there, to the isolation ward – I was about five years old, maybe younger.

Dick Allington

Just before I was sixteen, I went into Plaistow Fever Hospital. I think it was just before Christmas, 1915, and I stayed there through it. I had quite a good time in there – I didn't have it too bad, the fever, but on the point of coming out a chap came in – one of a family of twenty-two – a great big fella. He'd got the diphtheria, and I sat with him purposely to catch diphtheria. Just to stay in there longer, 'cos I quite enjoyed meself. I was helping the nurses and all that. The war was on and when you turn a tap on, it's just like an aeroplane coming over, and we used to do it to frighten the nurses.

Charles Lisle

Now, my mother had lost half her family round the thirteen and a half age and I was the next one running up to it. Course, everyone was watching me – schoolteachers, the priests, the neighbours – 'cos I was getting near thirteen. Me mother was always a worrier. That's enough, she'd lost them all, I was the next one on the list. I gets to thirteen, I used to go to bed every night, and think, well – this time next week – that's how it got, didn't care no more.

And then I get not far off thirteen and a half and all of a sudden me mother starts putting two coppers into the school holiday fund, so I ended up with two weeks down in Devizes. I was fourteen when that came on, 'cos I'd left school then, and after that, I had about a month down in Kent hop-picking.

Charles Beck

All of us, bar Beryl, that's the youngest one, we all went away with suspected impetigo. Nancy had it, but they used to clear the lot. Used to take all the kids away. Doctor Lauderdale, good man he was, he said, 'Do you want me to send an ambulance, or what?' Dad said, 'No, I'll take them up by tram.' So we all went into Millers Hospital.

Dennis Pike

Unfortunately, I lost my mother when I was ten. We were sent on holiday, and when I came back, she was dead and buried. That restricted my health and everything for about six months. I stopped growing and I lacked on my education.

Kevin Chandler

The doctor we had, he used to charge two and six a visit. Well, he knew he was in an area where he wasn't gonna be made a millionaire. So if you called the doctor out, and my mum used to have a lot of heart attacks and she died when I was fourteen, but we used to call him out and he'd say, 'Well, if you can't pay today, send one of the girls up with the money next week,' or something like that.

Robert Stapleton

The nearest dentist was in Upper North Street, Poplar. It used to be free with no cocaine, a shilling with cocaine and two shillings with gas. Most of the people couldn't afford this shilling. I've had three out with nothing. Yeah, it makes you holler. I've sat in there, wife's been with me – 'cos I've met her since I was a kid, see, we've always been together. We'd sit in there and you'd hear 'em holler, shouting inside, say, 'It don't ache no more' and you'd come out. You'd often see a dockie come, 'Oh, I've got the toothache,' come up North Street. He'd come back, carry on with his work, tooth out, nothing!

Walter Dunsford

My dad died in 1918, when I was thirteen – he died of a stomach complaint, during the terrible influenza epidemic when it was estimated that Spanish flu was responsible for the deaths of more people in the world than were killed in all sides during the war. My family were almost unique in the East End in that nobody died as a result of the flu – but I hardly knew of a family that was not so visited. As soon as it got light, you would see the funeral processions, all horse-drawn in those days, going through the streets until dusk. Sundays as well.

Cyril Demarne

I wasn't very strong in the chest as a child and I was sent to the nearest chemist, a chap named Hogwood in Plough Road. You could send to this chemist and get a pennyworth of bronchitis mixture. I was sent there once for three penn'orth of bronchitis mixture, and he took my bottle and the three pence. He came back a minute or two later and said 'You got a cork?' I said, 'Yes.' He said, 'Where is it then?' And I patted me chest and I said, 'It's down here.'

He give me a funny look and he said, 'How did it get down there, then? Did you swallow it?' I said, 'No, it's been there all the time.' 'Righto,' he said, 'let's have another go. What have you done with the cork that goes in the top of this bottle?' They way we used to speak, it was cockney, and to me, when he said cork it was corf. It was the perfect answer in my opinion. But I thought that when he went away he was having a sort of loud smile to himself.

Norman Grigg

I'd had nerve trouble, and I went to the Princess Elizabeth Hospital for Children in Stepney. My mother was asked if she would let me go away for a holiday, for a month's holiday, and I went to Welwyn Garden City to the home of Richard Hughes, who wrote *High Wind in Jamaica*. I thought it was very strange because they were vegetarians, and of course, you know, East Enders were great meat eaters. I thought it was really strange that we had just vegetables and nut cutlets and that sort of thing.

The thing that stands out in my head about going there is Sir Bernard Spilsbury lived nearby and we were invited to tea at his place. We went to tea and I thought the man there had something wrong with his hands – sores on his hand, because in those days, you used to wear cotton gloves if you had something like dermatitis. We had tea out in the garden and I know there were strawberries and cream, and there was a butler serving and he wore white gloves. And Mrs Hughes kept saying to me, 'Lucy, why aren't you eating – why, dear?' And I thought to myself, well, I can't very well, you know. I didn't like to say to her 'Because he's got dermatitis'. But I thought to myself, well, he's probably made the sandwiches and you can't very well make sandwiches with gloves on, so I sat there all through that tea and all I did was drink. And Mrs Hughes just couldn't understand it, why everybody was tucking in, and I was saying 'No thank you, no thank you'.

Lucy Collard

Pawnshops, Welfare and Boot Clubs

In the mid-nineteenth century, when the Poor Law established the first nationwide system of financial aid in the form of workhouses, Whitechapel had one of the largest in the country, with seven hundred inmates. Destitute families had to move into what were essentially penitentiaries, where they were separated, men from women, and women from children, and had to undertake hard labour in return for food. The law specified living conditions must always be worse than those experienced by the poorest labourer outside. The workhouse system lingered on until 1948 – although by then, they housed only elderly people – and the fear of the workhouse remained strong. It was one reason poor people did not dare claim even benefits to which they might have been entitled.

In the period of high unemployment between the wars, the government introduced relief for the unemployed in the form of means-tested 'out of work donations' (the original 'dole'). Means tests delved into all areas of a family's finances, and were resented for their intrusiveness and insensitivity. It was partly in response to this system's unfairness that the National Unemployed Workers' Movement organised hunger marches such as the Jarrow March.

A more enlightened form of help existed in Jewish areas, where the Jewish-run Boards of Guardians provided assistance in the form of loans, advice and help finding employment. Applicants were not treated like criminals, although they were expected to follow the guardians' advice, whether they agreed with it or not.

Most London boroughs ran some sort of scheme to provide clothes, particularly boots, for the poorest children. However, when it came to putting food on the table, families usually relied on the local pawnbroker to tide them over when there was no money. If you had something – anything, including bedding and clothes – that you could pawn, it meant that you could feed your children for one more day.

If your family couldn't take you in, when you got to seventy, I think it was, you either starved or went to the workhouse. Well, I lived right near the workhouse, and they used to give them a black bonnet and a black shawl, black cloth boots, and I suppose they had some sort of bed to lie on, but they had to work sewing mail bags and things like that, and they gave them soup in the middle of the day and perhaps a slice of bread in the evening, and they stayed there for the rest of their lives. Once a month they were allowed out for a day to see if anyone would give them anything, and they used to come and sit on your doorstep and people would give them a halfpenny or farthing, you know.

Hilda Bunyon

When there was no welfare state, all you could have was what they called the means test. You know, a man would come round, the local man, like, and say, 'Sell this, sell this and sell that.' All you was allowed to keep was a table, bedding, linen, knives and forks. But every Monday morning, that used to be bundled up and put in the pop shop. The clock – all the lot – used to go regular. All in a parcel, same as last week – wouldn't even look at it, they knew you so well. You know, just pin it up and give you your ticket and go down and get it.

Henry Corke

The means test, if you applied for financial relief, or any kind of relief, they sent down a relieving officer and he looked in your house, and for example, if you had an upright grand piano, he'd tell you to sell it before you qualified for help. Well, it was a silly question, because although the piano was worth about thirty bob, no one down the street had thirty bob, so you couldn't sell it.

John Cleary

My mother had a suit – my dad was dead, but that suit still went in and out. We always laughed about that suit – he was dead but that suit went in and out of the pawnbrokers – in on Friday, out on Monday. Everything went in, including the candlesticks, but we always had the candlesticks out for Friday night. My mother would never have done without the candlesticks. She never got her wedding ring back, though – she bought another wedding ring. When my sister first brought a young man in, we said, 'He'll think that you're not married – you got six kids and not married.' So we went out and bought her a ring.

Miss H

Monday morning was the great time for going to the pawnbrokers. If you were too dignified to be seen at the pawnbrokers, then you gave the clothes to be pawned to one of what we called 'the regulars' who would just take it along for a penny or two, and pawn it for you on a Monday morning and get it out on a Friday night or Saturday morning. It was a regular way of life. The only thing that was pawned was the boots and the suit of the father. Invariably, somehow or other, you got that out.

Bill Crook

We used to have what they called a tally man come down and my mother was one of them and there were other women and my mother would probably buy my sister and I a coat and we'd wear it Sundays – you could only wear your best coat on a Sunday. But you'd wear it Sunday and then Monday they'd take it to the pawn shop, you see, and that would help them out with the food all the week, and then they'd have to struggle and try and get them out – and if they couldn't get them out, well, you just left your coat and that was the finish of it.

Mary Partlett

We were really poor; we used to go to free breakfast, free dinner, and we used to have free boots. They used to give you boots to wear, and sometimes you'd have one big one and one small one, so one hurt like hell and the other one used to slip off your feet.

Eileen Gibbons

We used to belong to a boot and shoe club in Bethnal Green Road. We used to pay a shilling a week at school – sometimes sixpence a week, it was all according – then when you had enough for a pair of shoes, they'd give you a chit and you'd go and get the boots or the shoes.

Dolly Cooper

Once me father said to me, I think I was about ten, and he said, 'You're not going to school tomorrow,' and I said, 'Oh, that's good, why?' and he said, 'You're coming with me up the relieving officer's.' So we went up there and he said, 'Now, the man's going to give you a pair of boots; when he asks you what size you take, you gotta say seven.' Well, I didn't take a seven, I only took a four. So I says, 'But I only take a four,' and I got a wallop from me dad, 'cos that's how they did things then. So when the officer says to me, 'What size boots you take?' I said 'Seven' and he give me a funny old look but he give me the boots – they were called parish boots because they didn't have a toecap. And when I got home with my dad, the boots were for my brother – he was fifteen and he had a job to go to and he didn't have no boots to go to work with. I had the boots eventually, when he was finished with them.

John Cleary

At school, I put in for a thrift form. I got a corduroy suit and a pair of boots and I came home so proud of that suit. And in the evening, my father came home and saw it. 'Where d'you

get that from?' 'From school,' I said. 'I signed the thrift form.'
'Well, you can take that back.' Charity, he wouldn't have.
Literally nothing to eat, but charity, he wouldn't have.

Mr P

Not all of the lads, but some of the boys'd come to school
with no boots. The local council did give you free boots but at
one time, some of the poor mothers used to pawn them,
because it's far better to have a dumpling stew than a pair of
boots – you couldn't eat your bleeding boots. But then the
council started renting them, and on the side of the boot,
they'd stamp in 'County Borough of West Ham' so you
couldn't take them up to redeem them in the pawn shop.

Maurice Foley

I remember my father deliberately getting the manhole cover
shifted and slipping down it and breaking his leg and then
appealing to the Board of Guardians for succour to help out
the family – which he got. I remember that, he did it deliberately – but that is what he was driven to.

Jack Dash

The Jewish Board of Guardians was a great help to all of us.
They used to give you an interest-free loan, and I remember
one of my regular jobs was to go to the Board of Guardians
– we had a £10 loan every year and we used to pay about two
shillings a week off. That went on for years; we just took it
out for Passover or for any particular holiday that was on, a
festival holiday. We might be lucky to get a change of clothes
or a new hat, or new dresses for the girls – like on the credit
or the tally business. But we never believed in that – anything
we used, we paid cash for.

Mr U

My mother went to the Board of Guardians. Twelve bob a week. Six children. Oh, the Board of Guardians, they were terrible. Then they wanted to take away Becky and Hymie – Morrie was too young – to Norwood, the orphanage, the Jewish orphanage. My mother said, 'If four'll starve, six'll starve. If I have a piece of bread for four, I'll have a piece of bread for six. I'm not giving anybody away. However it'll be,' she said. 'We're all happy together.' So they stopped the money.

Miss H

Uninvited Guests

The lack of washing facilities and overcrowding meant that living accommodation was shared, inevitably, with a number of parasites – bedbugs, fleas and lice. There were also moths, which might seem benign, but were a problem because their larvae could eat through what was often the most valuable item owned by a working man, his good suit. Unlike most possessions, a good suit could be pawned, and indeed it was often safer in the charge of 'Uncle', as pawnbrokers would take care to protect their pledges.

Every now and again rooms that had become too lousy would be shut up and cleansed with highly toxic sulphur candles. Even the boats in the docks were not immune and had to be fumigated periodically. Some cargoes also brought in their own exotic stowaways, such as weevils or the copra bug. Copra is dried coconut kernels, imported for use as animal feed, and the copra bugs were similar to house dust mites, and their bites caused terrible itching.

There was a widespread belief that bugs disappeared after the war, and certainly the destruction of the worst of the slums helped, along with the development of less noxious, but effective, insecticides. However, the greatest change after the war

© Museum of London

Notes with this photograph reveal the children's father is in prison, their mother at work, leaving Grandfather in charge. In poor homes, bugs lurking behind wallpaper were ineradicable. The close-cropped hair of one of the boys suggests treatment for headlice. c1900–1910 was greater access to washing facilities – until the 1930s, most shared tenancies did not even have their own water supply, but depended on a shared tap, and all water had to be heated over a hearth or open fire.

Bugs were a fact of life and it's little wonder that the first warm evenings of the year found residents sitting outside in the streets rather than staying indoors to be bitten. Perhaps the impact of bugs was not entirely negative, as they could be said to have made a vital contribution to make to the sociability of the East End.

———————

Sundays would be the day we'd start to clean the beds and the pictures. What I mean by cleaning the pictures was in those days we was running alive with bugs. We used to take the pictures off the wall and take them outside, and take your bed, what they called a bug-trapper, the old wire spring type, you used to get bugs down there. So we used to have to take that out, pour paraffin and set light to it. And that was the kind of task we all had to take part in, all the family, you shared it. Then you'd stick new brown paper on the back of the pictures and hang them up on the wall where they came from.

Henry Corke

My mother used to smoke the rooms out with a sulphur candle, twice a year – before April, and when the summer had finished. But, Gawd love us, we had thousands of 'em! My mother was a clean woman, but you couldn't keep 'em away. They was in the walls – we had wallpaper, my mother had it papered every year – they was under the window sills, in the cracks in the walls. My mother used to smoke the place out, year in, year out. We used to cut strips of paper and she used to plaster it round the doors and windows. Used to sit outside, and she'd take all the food outside in a shopping bag, and we used to eat. Couldn't get in. When we went back, there was a pile like this! I always remember, I had a friend up there and they were crawling up the walls; I didn't know where to put my face. Not because we were dirty; we could not stop them. Everybody had them.

Miss H

I was involved in a day nursery. They used to take them to the nursery at about two weeks old, until they were four or five, and when they arrived, their things were put in the fumigating cupboard. The little girls were dressed in pink and the little boys in blue and their own clothes were put into tubs and washed, and they went home in their own things which had been fumigated. Because in the rooms of the places they came from there were bugs on the walls – vermin. They were difficult to get rid of because there were so many children living together.

Florrie Passman

I remember coming home and sleeping and during that night when I woke up there was bugs, and I mean dozens of them, on my pillow. They used to get on the ceiling and then they'd drop on to your bed and on to your pillow and they used to stream all across the walls and we would be up either with a candle or hitting them. This is the conditions we were in as children, and if you was up all night with this type of thing, you know, it became that you took it as a way of life as a child, and you didn't know no more.

Stan Rose

When the temperature rose a bit, you couldn't stay in because the bugs would come out and torment you so everybody took their chairs, ordinary kitchen chairs, outside and spent their leisure – their spare time in the evening when they weren't working – on the pavement outside, and that engendered a great community, because you walked past and there were all your neighbours sitting there, the people who lived in the same block as you, and you exchanged greetings and gossip and ruined each other's characters, of course.

Charles Poulson

Living downstairs in the basement of Rothschild Buildings, there was a family called Binstock. They had eleven children, including two sets of twins. When it was hot in the summer, the husband and wife used to sleep on chairs out in the playground, because they couldn't sleep inside with all that crowd of children. It was hot, and perhaps buggy, and so they slept in the playground during hot weather.

Mrs A

Wouldn't have wallpaper up anywhere because the bugs'd get behind it. Course Hitler got rid of the bugs, you know. Nobody had bugs. My dad's job on a Sunday was to paint all the woodwork all round the bottom of the wall, all round the doors, every bit of woodwork, with paraffin. That was to kill the bugs off, that was. Never did. You can smell them – they're a sweet smell. If you're used to them, you'll go in and you'll know what it is. I worked in the building trade for a little while and I went in one place, smelt them and I wouldn't hang me coat up. I actually opened a window and put it outside the window. But after the war there was very, very few bugs about.

Dennis Pike

The destructive moth was considered more of a nuisance than bugs, fleas or lice. These latter merely sucked your blood, but the moth destroyed invaluable, and almost irreplaceable, property. Bugs, fleas and lice were – well, they were commonplace. You couldn't get rid of them. You could rid yourself entirely of them, but as soon as you went to school, you picked up some more, and of course, having no change of clothing really, your clothing, even if you got rid of all the lice, your clothing was still full of nits – eggs – and within a day or two these were all hatching and it was just as lousy as ever.

Louis Dore

Nitty Norah, she used to come round the school and comb your hair, and if you had them, you got sent to the cleansing station. That was Nitty Norah. But my dad wouldn't have that – Dad used to do it always, sit you down, and he was horrible, 'cos them combs coming through your matted hair... He used to shake them out if he found them, and I detested it. Dad used to wash my head in paraffin – that was horrible. Horrible. You stunk with it as well, didn't you. Horrible, and everybody knew: 'Yeah, you've had your hair done.'

Dennis Pike

We used to go to bed with a candle. It used to be our job to have a good look round the room and round the base of the bed to make sure there were no bedbugs knocking around. If we did find them, we put the candles to them, they dropped in the saucer. A terrible smell, there was, too. I understand that they used to live off humans. I don't know – I only knew that they were there.

In our opinion, the only good job that Goering did – he got rid of all London's bugs. Think about it, they all went. We never saw them again after the war.

Some people used to have sulphur candles burning all night long, in one room. They shut the room up for the night and all the next morning, and then during the week, they could open the room again. And they would guarantee that there would be nothing living in that room.

Norman Grigg

It got warm in summer and the bugs came out – you couldn't prevent it. Every spring there was mass activity right down the street, stripping off wallpaper, repapering, taking down all the beds and disinfecting them. All the pictures on the wall went; everything was crusted, you see, with bugs' eggs. We used to have bug weeks in my family, all of us – the men standing on chairs, brushing away and tearing off the lino where it was loose. Repapering and disinfecting it. You could buy stuff that you burned to cleanse it and thoroughly kill all insect life. You put it in the middle of the floor on a large enamel plate and you set light to it and then you went off to the pictures, 'cos you couldn't live in there while it was burning, you see.

Charles Poulson

The main pest in the tugs at that time was bugs. The only cure known then was to get a five-gallon oil drum filled with coal, put about twenty-eight pounds of sulphur on top and you stored it in the aft cabin and shut all known orifices. I always recollect the deckhand who'd left his best shoes in the cabin, and we had to forcibly restrain him from opening the door to get his shoes back. But it never really got rid of the bugs. In fact, there is a tale told of one of the Wapping tugs being sunk in Gravesend Reach, and on being raised and got underway, the bugs were still there – so they must have been there with their diving helmets on.

John Henry Arnold

In the cheese department, there used to be this dust all over it. And I said to the chap there, 'Cor, there's dust on this cheese, is it dirt, or what?' 'No,' he said. 'Look at them.' And he got out of his waistcoat pocket a little magnifying glass. I looked through the magnifying glass and this dust was like little crabs, all live they were, all over these cheeses, and it was sort of part of the maturing of these things, you see, an accepted thing. But they was all live and they used to be blown about, you know, as light as that, they were.

William Abbott

I come home once from the West India Dock, we'd been doing a rice boat and there was millions of weevils on this rice, thousands, millions of them. Well, from working all day long, there's three of us on the train coming home from Poplar, from Mile End. We sat down and all of a sudden, everybody got up and moved away. So I said, 'We've got plenty of room now, Bill.' So he said, 'Yes, stretch out.' Everybody moved – they thought we was lousy. They was running all over us, but they don't hurt you, they're only weevils. But of course, they didn't know.

Alfred Green

On this occasion, on opening the hatches, a horde – I think that's the best word for it – of copra flies and bugs flew out and swamped the area. A great cloud of them swamped the area and the next thing, I had phone calls from two sources. One was from pubs – particularly the pub that was on the dock doorstep, complaining bitterly about the copra fly and bug, whatever it was called, getting into the beer, and I couldn't resist saying, 'Well, they don't drink very much, and what's more, for your information, they can't live on anything except copra, so,' I said, 'they'll quickly go away.' He said, 'Well, the quicker, the better – they want to get out of the premises much quicker than my customers have gone, because the whole pub is empty.'

The other point was they also got into the Peek Frean biscuit factory. And the manager, he got on, he said, 'What the hell's going on – they're getting into my biscuits.' So I said, 'You'll have to change the production over to Garibaldi – you've got everything made for it.'

I won't say what he said to me, but I had to put the phone down. I can stand abuse from publicans, but not from biscuit makers.

Dick Butler

CHAPTER 2

Growing Up in the East End

Mum and Dad

In a working-class marriage, the roles were clear and unambiguous. Fathers worked and mothers ran the house. This was not a matter of choice, it was the only possible system when men worked long hours and six-day weeks. When work was available, fathers would be absent for most of their children's waking hours because providing for your family was the priority, even if you barely saw them. So whether feared or revered, fathers were often a remote presence until the day their children joined them in the world of work.

About 60,000 London men were killed in the First World War. Recruits came from all areas of the East End, including the Jewish community where, under an agreement with the British government, men were given the option of returning to their home country to join up. For many years after the war there was an imbalance in the proportion of men in the population, with widows being left to bring up children alone and many young women having little hope of finding a husband.

When mothers went out to work, as many did, care of the youngest children was passed to a suitable female relative, often the maternal grandmother or an older female child. If both parents worked, it was still a woman's responsibility to organise the feeding, instruction, education and disciplining of her brood. The image of the East End mother – solid, aproned and indomitable – is hard to shake, probably because it is an accurate reflection. Mothers were omnipresent and omnipotent; the source of all good things and the absolute arbiter in all disputes.

My dad – and me brothers – worked in the dock. He was a quiet man and he always kept himself to himself. If you went out anywhere, he'd always be a loner. But he was a nice man – you know, he'd say good morning or goodnight – but he always sort of centred on hisself. But he was a good father, he worked hard for us, brought us all up.

Elizabeth Butler

Your father was not with you all the time. My father would go to work in the morning, to a hotel or restaurant in the West End, and come back late at night. He had to be there at ten o'clock, he'd leave at nine o'clock, he'd get up at eight o'clock – we'd gone to school – and he couldn't come home for the two hours that were given to him in the afternoon after lunch so he'd stay up there and meet his Chinese friends who were also hotel workers. He'd begin again at five after finishing at half-past two, and work until probably twelve o'clock at night.

When my father got home at night I didn't see him, you see. The only thing I remember is if my mother reported me for being cheeky, I would be got out of bed and given the cane. That was the thing in those days in most English families; you could go to the local shop which was called an oil shop and you'd buy a cane and you were able to cane children.

Leslie Hoe

Another time I remember when I was very young, I never saw my father, though he saw me, for about three weeks, because

Amateur photographer and missionary John Galt took this picture of a Bethnal Green family making shovels from scrap metal in their backyard. Galt was keen to document the hardworking poor to show they were deserving of help and salvation. John Galt, 1900–19

when they were busy they worked. And if you wanted time off, the foreman asked you what was wrong with you. Say you was tired, he'd say, 'Well, go and have a sleep for two weeks.' So men just literally worked until they dropped.

George Adams

I never used to see my father as a schoolboy; never saw him in the daytime. Well, I never saw him till the weekend. The only time I saw him was Saturday – because he went to work in the dark and came home in the dark.

Mr P

My father was not given to talking to me a great deal; when I think back, my father hadn't really got a role model for a father – he'd lost his father quite young. He was a good father, very kind and gentle. He was very strict about precepts like holding your shoulders back, sitting up straight at the table, always cleaning your shoes, undoing the laces of your shoes before you took them off, but he was very thoughtful.

Freda Hammerton

Even now, I'll get a smell of clothes, overcoats, drying... because when it was raining, Dad had to come home from work. Got to go back, he would put his coat over the guard, he'd shift the nappies and that, put it over the guard; you'd see the steam. And his cap would go over the door of the kitchen. And that was me dad in the winter. It's the smell. If I can smell that, I'm right back to being a kid again.

Our girls could do anything with Dad. Anything. When he was asleep, they'd tie his boot laces up – Mum being an invalid, I suppose. They used to make him up – Mum sitting in the other chair, watching them. They'd put powder on his face, jam round his lips, cherries in his earholes – all sorts of things. And he used to sit there asleep, as we thought. He was a good old stick, the old man.

Dennis Pike

Christmas, New Year's Eve, birthdays, you could never say, 'Oooh, we'll go out to dinner for a birthday, or have a party' – you never knew when they was coming home. Christmas Day, we've waited till five o'clock to have our lunch, our Christmas dinner. Keep thinking, Oh, Dad will be in in a minute; leave it a while longer and Dad might be home.

Anne Griffiths

My father at that time was a bosun at Plaistow Wharf. So he was one of five men who worked twenty-four hours on, twenty-four hours off. Those were the conditions. So every day of the year, he was either going to work at seven in the morning or coming home at nine. And he could predict months ahead whether he would be at work on Christmas Day or Boxing Day. No paid holidays, though we always had a week's holiday at Margate. And he would lose three shifts. So Mum would take us all on the *Golden Eagle* on Saturday and he would come back with us, so then he'd have Monday, Wednesday, Friday off, and come back with us and go back to work on Sunday.

I used to go to work with him on Saturdays when I was twelve, thirteen, fourteen – I used to take some food for him over the weekend and spend the night there with him working. A great adventure for me. The thing I remember about it was on the other side of the river, there was the South Metropolitan Gas Company's works. And they had tiny little locomotives shifting the trucks. And they had a delightful brass whistle which could sound across the river. You would hear this peep of the locomotive and then the crashing of all the trucks and the buffers, and to me it was adventure.

Edwin Hunt

One of my earliest memories is clinging to my mother's skirt – I can see my father, and I can only have been about four I suppose – and she was crying and we were all crying, and my father was in uniform, and he was going off to I don't know what. I don't even remember what regiment he was in.

Dorothy Shipp

My father had to go back to the Soviet Union because the Russian authorities of the time had an agreement with the British Government that Russian nationals living in England would either have to join the British army, or return to Russia to join the Russian army. And my father, along with quite a number of other Russian Jews, decided to go back. I presume they thought that by the time they got there, the war would be over. When my father left, I was about sixteen or seventeen months old. Anyway, he never came back.

Emanuel Litvinoff

I remember the way a lot of young fellers used to be on the corner of the street, because as me sisters come home from work, you know – the usual thing, whistling and all that. And then all of a sudden, it came to me – they're missing. They'd all been called up to join the army.

Charles Beck

I was born in the middle of the First World War, so I reckon I'm the result of the old man getting six weeks' leave from the Western Front.

John Cleary

My father didn't bring a lot of happiness into the home. He had a good trade – he was a bread baker, and everybody knew his bread – but he worked when he felt like working. My mother – I think probably her brothers made an arranged marriage. That's what happened, when you had a young sister, you made sure she was married. She protected us, she sheltered us. He was not interested in the children. No, it's not a good memory. But my mother supported us financially, and morally.

Vicki Green

My father would never accept swearing, he wouldn't even accept the word 'bloody' or 'bleeding' indoors. He was very strict on that. Never laid a finger on me. My mother did – she'd hit me with anything, my mum.

Len Faram

I always felt cheated that I had such lousy parents, you know, in so much of the hypocrisy. That's one thing nowadays – the young can say things that we couldn't say. It all had to go under the carpet. It was the age of men being the 'big man' kind of thing. It was the same with my friends – they all hated their fathers because of the domineering way that they were.

Florence Mugridge

It wasn't until I'd grown up and I had children of my own that I realised that my dad had never laid a hand on me. I always thought he had – I was always frightened that he would, you know. I always had the impression that Dad hit me. But I realised that it was our mum that used to do all the whackings, not Dad.

She used to say, 'Wait till your father comes home.' Father would never come up to our bedrooms to tell us off, so Mother used to say, 'Best thing for you is bed.' And we went to bed, not because it was a terrible place, but so Father wouldn't come up – but he never did.

Dennis Pike

My mother was very strict. Cheeking elders – you wouldn't dare cheek an older person, because if you did, you knew what would come. I mean it would either be the hand, the strap or even a cricket stump, and you just did not cheek anybody older than yourself. You weren't allowed to interrupt older people's conversation and you weren't allowed to be in a room while older people were having a conversation.

Mary Partlett

Let's allocate the functions; the mother looked after the children, the father worked. So my father went to work and my mother would shop, mainly down the lane, and when I came home for dinner there was always a nice cooked dinner, the beds were made – she was a superb cook in the Polish style. Everything from the repertoire of Polish cooking she could do.

Jack Miller

She was always the mainstay of the family – never mind about Dad, it was always Mum, because that's the one you looked toward for a bit of bread and jam.

Maurice Foley

She was lovely. I have a beautiful photograph of her. She was a typical Yiddisher mother. She cared for us, she would take the food off her own plate and put it on to our plates. In those days we had open coal fires, with an old-fashioned grate to protect us from the fire, and in the morning she would light the fire before we wakened and hang our vests and knickers on the top of the grate so that they would be warm ready for us to put on. She would bring in a little stool and a bowl of hot water where we could wash in front of the fire.

Vicki Green

Mother was a fish buyer in the fish market. I think Mother's family were well-to-do, but they never left her anything. She was a lovely person, small, short, but she looked after us and she was as brave as anything. I've seen her fight two fires, one in her own house. Well, we set the curtains alight – I think it was naughty old Walter – and we called down, 'Mother, he's set the curtains afire striking matches.' She was up on that table and had those curtains down in no time. My Sunday suit was on the table.

Charles Lisle

Mother was left a young widow. She was thirty-five when Father died, and two of the boys went to West Norwood orphanage, so she had four of them at home and us two girls. They left West Norwood when they were fourteen; they went in there when they were six years old and they were sent home when they were fourteen. One of them that came from West Norwood, he wouldn't stop at home; he went to Manchester and Mother didn't see him for years.

When they came out of West Norwood, they were like hooligans. They were kind of so caged in when they were in there, very strict, that when they got out, and Mother made a fuss of them, they were bad. They used to smoke in bed, many a time. Mother used to go up there and there was a fire in the room where they'd been smoking in bed. Oh, my mother had a handful, but she was mother and father – they were frightened of her.

Mother used to hit them. They were frightened of her. Hit the girls and all. She'd pull my sister round the room by her hair. She had a terrible life that poor sister – and yet she doted on my mother.

Mrs B

I was the youngest but one of twelve, and the first lot of family were then old enough to be my mother. So you see, my mother was always an old woman to me – but she had, as you did in those days, a terrible life. She got married at eighteen – she had stayed at home as she was the eldest of the family, so she went from one drudgery to the next. She used to say to me, 'Don't talk to me about the good old days, you don't know how lucky you are.'

My father, as most men were in those days, was not the best of husbands. He was still of the Victorian mould, and of course, I was of the generation coming up, which was the first of the rebels that came.

Florence Mugridge

My mother never played with us. I never had a lot of love when I was young. My mother didn't have the time. She was a very good mother, but she never had the time for all that. We never had a party, no birthday, no toys, nothing. No, my mother didn't even know when it was our birthdays.

Miss H

Once my grandfather was killed, my dad's father, I think perhaps my mum sort of gave me over to my gran as a sort of consolation at losing her husband, because I was with my gran on and off until I was about fourteen.

Lucy Collard

Please Don't Have Any More

Mrs Moore who lives next door is such a dear old soul,
Of children she has a score, and a husband on the dole.
I don't know how she manages to keep that lot, I'm sure,
I said to her today as she was standing at the door:
'Don't have any more Missus Moore;
Missus Moore, please don't have any more!'

– Don't Have Any More, Missus Moore,
HARRY CASTLING & JAMES WALSH, 1926

By the dawn of the twentieth century, the size of the average British family was shrinking. It was in the middle of a sixty-year period of contraction, during which it dropped from five or six children in the 1870s, to just two in the 1930s. Infant mortality was also falling, from about ten per cent in London in the 1890s to three per cent in the late 1940s. However children from Shoreditch were still twice as likely to die in childhood than those born in households in an affluent borough such as Hampstead.

Large families remained the norm in the East End during the early decades of the twentieth century, particularly in Catholic and Jewish areas. Apart from cultural or religious attitudes towards procreation, there was very little publicly available information or products that would help with birth control – a popular disinfectant called Lysol was widely used for this purpose.

I have three brothers and two sisters, but my mother brought three boys up as well, so there was six boys and three girls – there was nine of us. As a matter of fact, when I was twelve there was 'no room at the inn' for me. My aunt had adopted my eldest sister, and my mum only had two rooms, that was one upstairs and one downstairs, so she used to have to sling me out every night. I used to have to walk Victoria Dock Road every night to go round and sleep with me aunt.

Eileen Gibbons

Big families were the thing of the day then. There was me eldest brother, Ted, then next came Celia, next to that came Emily, then myself. Then there was Fred – Frederick – who died as a young baby. Florence, then Marie, another sister, then Henry, another baby who died. Now, the question of

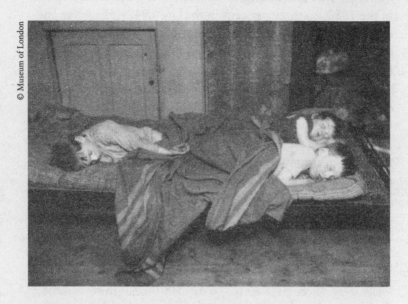

Having a room, or even a bed, to yourself was unknown in poor East End households. If the family were fortunate enough to have two rooms, the parents and the youngest children usually shared the bedroom, with older children sleeping in shared beds in the sitting room. c1910

babies dying, youngsters, this was common. The death rate of children was very, very common. Once they got over about the age of ten, say, they were past the post, but up till then, there was measles, whooping cough, chickenpox, scarlet fever. All those diseases of children that killed 'em off.

Jack Banfield

My mother was one of ten daughters and two brothers, whose father, having worn his first wife out siring twelve children, had another woman and had eight more with her – I mean, he must have been an expert in his day.

George Green

I remember Lysol because we always had Lysol when we had a new baby. That's the only time we ever had Lysol – all the other times it was iodine. I should imagine it had something to do with childbirth. If I ever smell Lysol, it all comes back – the baby, and everybody.

Dennis Pike

There's my second brother Terry, and the third brother, Frederick, who's six years younger than I, and then the daughter, my sister Iris, was born in more or less the week the war broke out. I don't think Fred and Iris were planned because, in families, you pass things on. Cots were passed on. My mother insists that when Fred was born and Iris, and I forget which was which but I remember one had an egg box and the other had an orange box as a crib, but by the time Dad had sandpapered it and mother had padded it out and lined it, you couldn't tell the difference between a real cot.

George Adams

'Cos we had some Catholic families along near us. And this woman was absolutely dragged down with children. She had all these kids. And she wasn't up to it. But I mean, that was what the Pope says. You take no precautions, you just, 'Every one has its own little pleasure. Every child brings its own little pleasure.' This poor woman, she was knackered.

Joanna Roberts

If the teacher said where was I, like, I'd say I was home looking after the baby. Because that was the biggest gap in my life, looking after babies – I mean, do you realise, fourteen of you in the same family? You can't sit down to a meal. Half at a time. Six in at one time, probably another four afterwards; 'Go out and play' while they have something to eat, then you come in.

Henry Corke

I had a blind brother, and he died a few years ago, and then I've got a crippled brother who's still alive. There was eight of us – Laurie, me, Charlie, Billy, Georgie, Esther, Harry and Frankie – five brothers, and three of those were dockers. My eldest brother was blind, then there was me, then there was my Charlie.

Elizabeth Butler

There was seven brothers and two sisters in my family – I don't remember either of the sisters, they both died young, unfortunately. The elder brother, Edward, he died young – I don't remember him. Then George was the eldest, then William – he got killed in France, in 1915 – that's why I wanted to go. Then there was Harry, he was a footballer. He died in 1913 from knocks on the football field. And then there was Walter, myself and Joseph. George went in the KRR, Will went in the Rifle Brigade, Walter went into the Royal Artillery, and I went in the infantry, Royal North Hampshire Regiment.

Charles Lisle

We went to live with my aunt, Mrs Hannah Mastin, at 42 Glasgow Road, Plaistow. She had been widowed earlier on and was left with a family of Walter, Wilfred, Winifred, Albert, Queenie, Avis and Beatrice and Alec. How she managed to raise the family on the pittance that she got, I just don't know.

John Henry Arnold

Of course, my mother didn't go to work, she had her hands full with us, doing the washing, scrubbing. I had two brothers and I've got two sisters – my two sisters came first, I think my mother had a miscarriage somewhere along the lines, then my two brothers, then there's a ten-year period with no children. And then my mother was about forty when she had the shock of her life to find out she was pregnant – with me.

Joe Morris

See, my parents weren't worldly – they never went out. All they thought of was, I think, really, having children. That's all.

Jane Smith

When abortions were illegal, of course you got it all over London; I've dealt with the Harley Street abortionist, the superior doctor charging God knows how much money, and the backstreet woman in King's Cross or anywhere you like, with her knitting needles – there was a lot of that going on. In south London, there was a famous or notorious doctor who was a well-known – almost international – abortionist, and he did it on principle. Couldn't help admiring him. If you were a washerwoman, he didn't charge you; if you were a wealthy woman, you had to pay. And he ran his own nursing homes. Time and time again, he'd been arrested and charged, but no woman would give evidence against him. He was a public benefactor.

Graham Rutherford

I'm one of twelve. The first three boys died and my mother promised anything if I lived – if somebody – lived, if the next one lived, anyway. Well, I lived, and she said, 'Look what I've got for a prayer.' And she said she'd never waste so much time on the rest of the family as she wasted on me, when she saw the product, the live product.

Sister Pat O'Sullivan

Childhood on the Streets

If you had just a room or two in which to sleep, wash, prepare food and often work, having a crowd of children hanging around was not an option. Most children slept at home, sometimes ate there, and that was the extent of their occupation; spare time was spent outside. Before the Second World War, there was little in the way of traffic once you turned off the East End's main thoroughfares, and it was expected that children would play out in all weathers, bigger children looking after the little ones, families and neighbours watching over each other. There were many seasonal and local forms of street games, and if you ran out of games, the streets had a lot to offer in the way of diversions. You could watch the characters who passed through with goods for sale, listen in to family feuds, start or witness a fight. The streets were the place where special occasions were celebrated – religious festivals, such as Passover, or the Catholic processions; or Empire Day, a celebration of Queen Victoria's birthday that began the year after her death. These were times when scattered families returned for joyous reunions.

The street was where everybody played and most of it was relatively safe because most of the traffic was horse-drawn, and if a motor car came down, all the kids crowded round it because it was something to look at and wonder about. We had an assembly place, it was a toy factory, and we used to sit in the doorway of the toy factory, and that's where I got most of my early education about life and sex and that sort of thing. From other kids who were more knowledgeable than I was. The oldest would have been about fourteen and then they moved into an adult world, because at fourteen, after all, you went out to work. You had to leave school, you started a job, and so they were already smoking and going round to the fish and chip shop and treating themselves, and occasionally even having a drink.

Emanuel Litvinoff

We used to play out in the street. You'd go up against a wooden fence and you would play with buttons; they would bounce off of wood and you'd bounce them against it and then the one who got nearest to the other would take it. Piggyback jumping over piggybacks, and a rope round a lamp post and swing on it. Hundred and one of our own games, we'd make.

Stan Rose

In the winter we'd make parcels and put them underneath the lamp posts, attached to a piece of cotton, and we'd be hiding somewhere and somebody would come along and think they'd found something very nice and go to pick it up and as they did, so we'd pull that away. And there was a bar sticking out of the street lamps and we used to throw a rope over that and swing on it.

And there was 'Knocking Down Ginger'. We used to knock at somebody's door and run away, or we would tie a piece of string from one knocker to the other and knock on one, and as the lady or gentleman of that house opened the door, so he'd knock at the other door. But we'd be well out of the way by then.

Lucy Collard

There was a game we used to call 'I Jimmy Knacko'. Why it was 'I Jimmy Knacko' I don't know. One would stand with his back to the wall, that was a cushion, then the others – you'd split yourself into two teams and probably there'd be three in each team – the others would bend down like the front and back of a horse, then the opposing team would jump on their backs and the three of them would have to be on there without the horse collapsing. And when you got on there, you'd call, 'I Jimmy Knacko, one, two, three. I bobbaree, I bobbaree, I bobbaree and away.'

Jack Banfield

Marbles came in three kinds: small ones made of plaster or cement and painted various colours, larger ones called bobsters, similarly made, and most prized of all, gallanis – these were made of glass with strands of coloured wire running through them. The manager would sit, legs outstretched against the wall, and place a marble or a bobster or a gallani a few inches in front of him. The punters would then bowl marbles at these targets and the pay out would be two or three marbles per hit – or he would take the bobster or the gallani as a prize.

Louis Dore

Gaisley Street had a number of Irish people living there, some Welsh people, people who'd come from Norfolk and Suffolk, and there was a Jewish family. The Irish families were related and they could never really see eye-to-eye with each other, with the result that day after day, the ladies of the house, which I suppose were about eight or ten houses apart, would come out and pick up the row which they had had the day before. The rows were carried on from their respective doorways, so everybody bent their ears from their windows and doorways to listen to what was going on – family matters, all the evil things that the other family did, religion was brought into it and so on.

Tom Stothard

Princes Court was a very narrow court and it widened out at one end and down one side was this family who lived on the top floor and they were famous for not bothering to put anything they wanted to get rid of in the dustbin, just throwing it directly out of the window. On the other side of this street was a few houses and there was a few steps running into a house which was used by a bookmaker. He didn't live in the house, but the people who lived in the house let him use the steps, and if the police came, he'd run into the house and out the back. This rather narrow court was ideal for this bookmaker because he had a lookout at both ends and there was a whistle that was the warning. All us kids knew this whistle – in fact, there was a blackbird that used to sing it.

On a big race day, like Derby Day, you'd get a queue of hundreds of chaps, regardless of the illegality, and when the whistle went, to see all these people scatter into houses, and walking along as if they had nothing to do with it, and all this rubbish coming out of the windows – it was hilarious.

Alfie Bass

Street fights – they were lovely. I was supposed to go to housewifery classes with my friend, and it was the turn of my friend and myself to go to Chrisp Street to get all the ingredients for the lunch that was going to be prepared for the day. On our way back, coming through Grundy Street, as we came past the pub, these two ladies were being thrown out of the pub and they started fighting. So instead of going to housewifery class, we stood and watched the fight until the police came – they didn't have a van in those days, they had a sort of barrow affair with just a hood over so that the top half would go into this contraption, but the legs would be sticking out. Just the head and top half would go in, but the rest, from the waist downwards, the legs would be sticking out. It was well past lunchtime when we got back to school and we got six of the best because no one got their lunch that day. We'd been too busy watching the fight.

Lucy Collard

A man used to hump a large basket on his arm around to all the pubs in the area, calling out 'Hold your leg, hold your leg'. And we used to go around, risking a clip round the ear, you know; we used to go round following this man, holding one leg and hopping on the other, calling out 'Hold your leg'. And he used to disappear into the pub and then come out, you know, and we found out in the end he was calling out 'All jellied'. The commodity he was selling was jellied pigs' trotters. People used to love 'em.

Norman Grigg

One particular lady, she was about six foot tall and used to wear army boots and that was the cats' meat lady, and we children used to call her the ogre lady. We were all frightened of her because she was so big; she used to wear an old hat and to walk down the street with a big basket which was full of skewered pieces of horse flesh. It was just like the Pied Piper, but instead of rats it was cats; she'd walk down the street and all the cats would follow her. If the people weren't in the house, she'd put this skewered cats' meat underneath the knocker of the door. Our cat always knew. It was absolutely

Cats' meat men – and women – were a common sight on East End streets, often followed, in Pied Piper fashion, by hopeful pets. They sold rotten meat that was unfit for human consumption, and sometimes even for cats and dogs. 1900–1910

amazing that the cat always knew the days she would be coming because he would never sit out on the front, especially in winter. But the days the cats' meat lady came, he'd always be waiting on the doorstep, and I think half the moggies in the street did the same – those that weren't following her down the street.

Lucy Collard

One fellow used to go round calling out 'Any urskin'. We used to wonder about it – what's an urskin? But when you followed him around, he used to knock on people's doors here and there: 'Any urskin, lady?' And then the lady would say, 'Yes, I've got one or two out the back,' and come forward with a couple of rabbit skins.

Norman Grigg

My brother, or it might have been my two brothers, and I were playing round the corner at a blank brick wall with the ball and along came two or three big Yoks as we called them, and they grabbed the ball and said 'You killed our Lord so we can keep your ball'. And they did. We were quite nervous about walking down the street, although apart from occasionally somebody would shout something after you, or maybe run after you for a bit, I can't remember that anybody came to any great harm.

Emanuel Litvinoff

We used to play on the street – the boys played football, and the ladies who had their windows broken used to come out and say 'Go and play outside your own house, break your own mother's windows'. In those days, cigarette packets contained pictures, and we used to collect these pictures and put them on the windowsill outside and blow them, and if you could blow one enough to turn it over, you won a picture.

Vicki Green

Sunday mornings, the girls always used to have their white pinafores on, they always had their best. Well, their best was always the white pinafore, it covered up everything else. And they used to get a skipping rope, and it would be about thirty foot long, from one side of the road to the other, over the different pavements, because there was no traffic to worry about, and they'd skip. And then one would go in skipping, and then the second one, there'd be two in and three in and then they'd be calling 'Four in', see. Until eventually they'd see how many they could get in without anybody tripping the rope. And then at the same time, they used to walk along so that they'd be passing along that street and going round into the next street. You know, and we'd watch them. Well, I mean, that cost nothing to do, and yet – there's the songs they used to sing. The circling round in a circle, the different songs they used to sing.

Jack Banfield

You used to have the water cart man come; he used to come round cleaning the streets. Especially in the summer, little girls used to tuck their knickers in their dresses and take their shoes and socks off and run behind the water cart. That was great fun. Of course, the boys used to do the same but I think the girls were the ones who always used to start it off. We always thought it was great running behind this water cart getting our feet wet.

Lucy Collard

For a real street fight, a declaration of war would have to be made and, armed with broom handles and sticks, not to mention a pocket full of cobbles, the invaders would slowly advance, chanting various insults – 'Go home, your father wants his boots' or 'Get your hair cut' or, if names were known, little jingles like 'John, John, put your trousers on'.

Battles seldom lasted long; parents would sometimes wade in and drag their offspring – still screaming imprecations – indoors, with threats of bashings, tannings and crumpings. Flatties [police], too, might interfere, but if the fight were allowed to continue, it would usually devolve into a kind of championship bout. A lot of sparring, and invitations to 'Come on' opened these encounters. The second phase was a sudden attack with wildly swinging fists. Again, one or two results would ensue. Either the combatants would clinch and roll over and over on the ground, punching and kicking as opportunity allowed, an all-in conflict which might go on for several minutes, eventually finishing when one, after gaining his feet, would back off, still uttering threats, whilst the winner held his ground, with fists still at the ready. A second result which might bring things to an end was if one, during the fight – the fist-swinging episode – happened to get snot-tered; that is, his nose made to bleed. In this case, the injured one could break off without losing too much face and be carried away in some triumph. Blood, after all, was a badge of glory. He didn't try to stem it for the more blood, the greater the glory.

Louis Dore

We'd get clog dancers – for a few paltry pence, you know, up and down the streets, sing a song and the people would come to the doors and throw a few coppers out. They was ever so grateful. But they did it because they had to do it. They had to live somehow and that was one way of getting money. Between the wars, there used to be a gang of four men who came around, er... they came round dressed up as women. They used to dance and sing to the music of a barrel-organ. One bloke used to play the barrel-organ, and the others would dance and sing, and supposedly make eyes at the men as they were going by. They used to collect money – they used to do fairly well. The faster the bloke played the barrel-organ, the faster they danced. They were very good though. Very cheeky, very cheeky men. And all the ladies used to go out the door and laugh their heads off at them.

Norman Grigg

When I lived in Hind Street, which is now Hind Grove, I think there was just about every nationality down that road, but everybody was friendly towards one another. We shared in their feast days – the Devali with the Indians, Chinese New Year, Pesach, the Jewish festival. It was just marvellous.

Lucy Collard

There were processions in all different parts of the East End. And the churches used to bring out their regalia and their statues of Mary with Jesus or Jesus on the cross. I mean, you would get men who were part of the church with their green braids across and hats too – they would play quite solemn music. The kids would all be dressed, white; boys used to wear black short trousers and a white shirt, white socks, black shoes. The girls used to wear a white dress like a confirmation dress. They would have blue ribbons round their hair. And this procession could be anything up to about half a mile long and it'd trail through the streets.

Joanna Roberts

A big event of the year was procession day – the Catholic procession. That would go from the Catholic church and round the streets of Wapping. Early that morning, you'd see the men out with the buckets of whitewash and a brush, whitewashing the kerbstones of the route that the procession's gonna go. The Catholic families, the majority of them, would endeavour to make a grotto. Downstairs, they'd take the window frame right out and a table outside and a table inside the window. If they didn't have white sheets, they'd borrow them, and drape these white sheets around, make it similar to an altar. The statue of the Virgin Mary, they all had one of them, and that would be there with brass candlesticks, and it used to be really decorative, you know. In the evening, the priest would go round and visit each grotto and probably bless the grotto and the people who'd built it. Anybody who'd left Wapping, that was the day when they all came back so it was a great get-together, you'd see people you hadn't seen since the last procession.

Jack Banfield

All the people, all the relations from everywhere came. They loved it, spent a lot of money on their dresses, a lot of money. White dresses mainly for the children, white long frocks, wreaths – and once or twice, a terrible catastrophe, they had red flowers, you know? The red ran down when the rain came, on the frocks and everything. Heartbreaking, you know, for people that had spent their last ha'penny on frocks, that were going to do for parties and that. And they all had banners, every saint under the sun. It finished up in church, generally, with Benediction.

Sister Pat O'Sullivan

Empire Day was absolutely wonderful. It was the highlight of our lives, simply because it was something to look forward to. Little girls would have red, white and blue ribbons in their hair, and red, white and blue round the tops of their socks – then if anyone was well off, of course, they'd also have red, white and blue dresses.

It was a marvellous day – the same as the Boat Race. Because all the shops used to sell the different ribbons and rosettes and whoever you supported, you'd either have a light blue or a dark blue, and it was just lovely. I suppose because we didn't have much, therefore all the things that came along was a way of taking your mind off of the poverty that you actually lived in.

Mary Partlett

Mother's Little Helper

Children learned to pull their weight from an early age; as well as looking after younger brothers and sisters, there were plenty of errands to do. They might be dispatched to take food to their father's place of work, or sent out with a barrow or pram to deliver or pick up piecework to be assembled at home. A popular song during the First World War was *Sister Susie's sewing shirts for soldiers*, and many mothers in the East End earned extra money sewing khaki uniforms and greatcoats.

There were many ways that children could help put food on the table: small groups of youngsters from the poorest families could always be found scavenging for scraps around market stalls, or seeing what food could be cadged around the docks. Gathering bits of wood from the markets and streets or searching the foreshore for driftwood and coal was another vital contribution as, for most of the year, the primary purpose of fuel was not heating, but cooking; without a fire, there could be no hot food, no cups of tea. Formal work was also something that might start young. In 1901, the Factory and Workshop Act raised the employment age to twelve, but part-time casual jobs were common and it was not unusual for children as young as ten to be in work rather than in school.

———◆———

© Ian Galt/Museum of London

Matchbox making involved pasting together strips of paper and wood called skillets, to make lids and trays. Workers were paid tuppence ha'penny per gross (144 boxes) and had to supply their own paste. Children often helped with this kind of work.
John Galt, 1900–1907

I had no schooling, or very little schooling. I didn't have a rough upbringing, I was just the eldest of the family and of course I was expected, if Mother worked, to help my mother. I started work at ten years of age – sweeping snow, scrubbing doorsteps, helping Mother out. I went out with the barrow, or helped out the winkle man on Sundays. My late husband was a costermonger at eight years of age – he didn't have a barrow, he had a little old-fashioned pram. He used to go and get his beetroots.

Gracie Smith

My mum, she used to go wood chopping when I was a kiddie. That's some years ago. And she used to work down Albion Street at a place called Padmores. She used to go down there wood chopping and do them up in bundles. And when my mum was wood chopping, 'cos they used to work till late, you know, of a night-time, I was a proper little skivvy. Well, I was only a little girl – a kid myself – but I used to have to look after the children, and perhaps wash and put them to bed or see to whatever they had to eat, what was left there – you know, you had to share it out between them.

Elizabeth Butler

I used to have to care for Joe because he was my younger brother and he'd only got one eye. He'd had an accident – a cinder fell out the fire into his eye when mother laid him on the mat, just in front of the fire, and a cinder popped out. That's why I always tried to protect him as much as I could – I was four years older than him, you see.

Charles Lisle

Me mother was a tailoress and she worked for herself. She worked at home and she had people working for her. She had a machine down in the basement and she made trousers. I used to have to take the bundles – I had a little handcart – and I would take the material round to people to machine, and when the trousers were made out she used to fetch 'em home and press 'em up and take 'em back to the warehouse in Tredegar Square. I used to have to go to the gas works to get her coal to make the fires to put the irons on. The gas works was in Bow Common Lane and I'd take the barrow round there and get four or five hundredweight each time.

Joseph Milchard

Even when I was at school, when I was thirteen or fourteen, I used to work in the sawmills attached next door to it. We used to turn those big legs on tables and sideboards, and I used to collect the work and take it there to be turned and then return it to the merchants again afterwards.

Harry Plum

In the First World War a lot of women used to take in tailoring – my mum sewed greatcoats. She always used to bring home piles of greatcoats and she'd sew the buttons on and we used to help her – and if it wasn't good enough, she had to cut them off. Oh, these coats was as hard and as stiff as anything, they were horrible.

Mrs P

The khaki, they got paid very well for that, they got good money. Everybody did. Everything was cut, came in bulk, and they'd machine it and it'd go out as greatcoats. The tailors used to sit on the table with their legs crossed and do all the sewing, because it was too heavy to sit with it on your lap. So you sat on the table, the table took the weight of it. Very heavy coats they were.

Mrs B

My father was forty-three when he died in 1926 – he'd been ill for eight years before that, so he hadn't been the breadwinner for a long time. He had what you would call cancer today – he had a tumour on the back of the spine. He had been a boot maker. My mother was left with five children and we all had to be breadwinners, you know. We all worked and produced something and kept the family going.

Alfred Alexander

We used to nick any food, keep going round. Especially fruit; used to get lots of fruit on market day. If I didn't nick it, nobody else'd give it to me. My father was out of work, like millions of others, and there was practically nothing, you know.

Henry Corke

They used to make money by dredging for coal off the gas works at Beckton. It was a noted thing, like, they'd tell you when you went up Bow Creek that every child, every youngster, would throw stones at you. No fool – well, you could throw one thing back and that was the coal you had in the barges. And so it was a real sort of tealeaf paradise. If barges were put there with coal, half of it would disappear overnight.

Len Faram

One of the routines was on the way home from school, you'd pick up what bits of wood you found along the wharves, so that when you got indoors Mum'd be able to light a fire. And then coal. We always had a coal sack for the kids so whoever went for the coal would take the sack. We'd go and get seven pound of coal, and that would be fire for that evening. Perhaps the next day. If Dad's not at work and there's no sixpence sub, there'd be no fire apart from the bits of wood that you brought home.

Jack Banfield

Me and my brother, the eldest brother, we used to go down alongside the river – we was called shore rakers then – and what we used to do was collect wood and anything like that that was floating in the dock, take it home, break it up and sell it in small bundles for a ha'penny or a farthing to people. Wapping Gas Works was on the shore – well, there was two ships used to come up there and fetch the coal up twice a week – one was called the *Stepney* and one was called the *Mile End* – and the grabs used to come fetch this coal out and put it in like a chute affair and load the barge to take into the gas works itself. Well, so much coal and dust used to fall over the side of the barge. So us being kids, as soon as the tide subsided, we'd take it out – of course, we had no boots and shoes at all. We used to go across up to our knees as the water fell away from the barge. We'd have a sack and we'd pick up all the coal dust and coal – we used to get a bag and we'd take it home and that used to be for our fire.

Sidney Bell

Seamus's job was to go down to Blackwall foreshore every evening to see if he could find any driftwood that had got thrown up on the foreshore or on to the causeway, and he would gather it all together, pull it up to the top of the causeway and carry it home. If any of us were about we'd help him take him home. On other occasions, we could get the skiff, go underneath West India Dock pier head and collect that great mass of wood that was always underneath there.

I think we used to come back to the causeway with about one inch of free board, such was the weight that we had on board. I know on one occasion we came out stern-first from the pier head jetty and a Sun tug run by, light, and of course throwing up a terrific bow wave, and we went stern first on to the wave which looked colossal from where we were, and little Seamus, he just dropped to his knees, put his hands together and started praying.

The danger passed, he got up and there wasn't a giggle or a smile from any of us within the skiff – because he knew his religion and he knew that when he prayed to Mary, he was all right. So he took that for granted. So we took all this timber back to the causeway, offloaded it, and went out for another lot. Now, the peculiar thing about this is that when that timber was put at the top of the causeway, nobody else ever took a piece. That was Seamus's wood.

Tom Stothard

My father's employer did not provide tea. My mother gave me as a duty to take a blue can, with a handle, and some brown bread and jam sandwiches, and as the governor was not going to open the door, I had to bang down on a grate and my father would come up and I'd give it to him.

Jack Miller

My mother used to send my brother and I with the can to take my father his tea. I remember him having a mouthful of nails, and it was very dim, and when we used to go in we would stand at the door, my brother and I, and somebody would say – it sounded like 'sadliemein'. And afterwards, when we asked my father what it meant, it meant 'Stop swearing', see, because children were there.

Mrs L

My father was an old-time railway employee basically working as a shunter in the docks around Blackwall Tunnel and the railway yards associating with the East India Docks. Didn't have a very rich life, in the late 1920s, early Thirties. It was very poor indeed, in one of those two-up, two-down sort of three-shillings-a-week-rent houses. Life, as you can imagine, was hard. Mum and Dad broke up, which left Mum and I. We used to have to fend for ourselves – I often used to scramble down the market as a child, under stalls for potatoes that had accidentally fallen off the stalls.

Albert Patten

A way of getting a few coppers was to go down to the local markets and get orange boxes and egg boxes, break them up and sell them as firewood for a penny a bag. Also, the disinfectant which is now known as bleach was given free by the local council in their various establishments over the area and we'd go up and ask people if they wanted a bottle of bleach and we'd get a few coppers for getting their bleach.

Dick Allington

I used to go in the slaughterhouse, spend the day in there, watching the cattle being slaughtered and all the meat being dressed up ready for market, Smithfield Market, in the morning. Used to go in there and get pigs' bladders, you know, to play football with. Used to go and collect those, and get a lot of offal, used to take that home: offal, like chitlins, stones, sweetbreads, throatbreads, all that kind of stuff, used to get that and take it home. But you had to climb nearly a twelve-foot wall to get out. You can walk in easy enough, but getting out was different – there was a copper on the gate in a box, and any parcel that you had, you weren't allowed out with it, you know. And if you was a bit slippery, used to get someone to sling something at him and while he's arguing, run out quick.

Henry Corke

Learning the Facts of Life

East Enders – and dockers in particular – are known for their forthright and direct speech, but this did not extend to all areas of life, and certainly not to what was said in front of the children. On the whole, children grew up entirely ignorant of what went on behind bedroom doors – which must have been particularly tricky at a time when few parents had a private bedroom, or even a bed to themselves. But when it came to sex and procreation, the family, church and state connived to keep children in a state of innocence. On the streets, young children played together, but as soon as they went to school, they were segregated – the separate entrances for boys and girls on many Victorian school buildings bear witness to this system. For boys, the transition to adulthood happened a lot earlier than it does now. The common term used for older boys was 'yob' or 'yobbo'; this was an example of costermongers' back slang, where they simply reversed a word – in this case, 'boy'. But most left school at fourteen and took a job, at which point they were privy to the jokes and conversations of men, which soon put an end to childhood innocence.

Girls, if they did not take it upon themselves to discover the facts of life, were more likely to remain unaware of what precisely it was that they were saving for a future husband. In many areas, such as the pubs frequented by sailors around the docks, and the notoriously disreputable Flower and Dean Street in Whitechapel, there were examples of the distinction between respectable and fallen women in the shape of prostitutes, whether glamorous-looking creatures in red shoes or sad destitutes looking for the price of the next drink.

In the docks, there seems to have been an awareness – even an acceptance – of homosexuality among some ship's crews. If this was something that did not remain hidden at a time when it was still illegal, it suggests a broadmindedness that one might not immediately associate with working-class dockers.

The term teenager was not by then coined. Up to the age of eight or nine, you were a kid, up to fourteen, a yobbo, and above that, until you acquired the status of a man, you were a hobbledy hoy or hooligan. It wasn't until you reached about fourteen or fifteen that boys used to talk to each other about these matters and, you know, whisper that this sort of thing happened – grown-ups do this. And, of course, I didn't believe my parents did. But of course, I realised that there were people that were filthy-minded and so on, and did these horrible things, and then, of course, when I began to think about these things – as one does in puberty – I just considered that I was an out-and-out filthy-minded scoundrel.

Louis Dore

On one occasion, we had a party and my brother's dare was to dress up as a woman and we had a very vinegary-type lady next door who was a very large lady who had a very tiny meek husband. She was about three times the size of this poor little man, Mr Prager – and my brother's forfeit was to dress up as a woman, put a pillow underneath the dress and go and knock and ask for Mr Prager and say what was he going to do about his forthcoming baby. So Arthur came and knocked and Mrs Prager came to the door and it must have been about eleven o'clock at night and she said 'What do you want?' and then there was something about 'we were in bed'. And Arthur put on a very high-pitched voice and said, 'I don't know about you being in bed – what's he going to do about the baby?' And they never had any children, and she said, 'What bloody baby?' He said, 'Well, what do you mean, can't you see that I'm expecting a baby, and it's your Ernie's, it's your Ernie's baby.' She said, 'Not my Ernie, he wouldn't do anything like that.' My mother was in the back bedroom, saying, 'No, he wouldn't dare!'

Of course, we were absolutely in hysterics, trying hard not to make any noise. And then she called, 'Ernie! Come down

The boy at the front – described by the photographer as a 'young hooligan' – appears to modern eyes a dead ringer for Dickens' Artful Dodger. Many of these boys will have left school and have jobs; working life began at fourteen, and often as early as the age of ten. 1900–1910

here!' And she set about poor Ernie. Of course, when that happened, my mother said, 'Oh no, we can't have that' and she came out and said, 'Oh, they're only playing forfeits' – and then, of course, Mrs Prager walloped Arthur. After that, I don't think she ever spoke to us again.

Lucy Collard

At thirteen, it's when a boy gets Bar Mitzvah-ed – that's when he becomes a man. So if anything happens to your father, then automatically, the older brother, he takes over the responsibilities of the house.

Joe Morris

The moment you are fourteen, you put on your first pair of long trousers and you buy your first packet of fags – if you've got a job – which was usually five Woodbines. You're standing on the street corner, talking to the other kids, flirting with the girls, very shyly.

I was very sweet on a girl called Hannah Jacobs and we used to walk around and occasionally have enough money to go into a milk bar and have a milkshake – a very sweet and innocent relationship and on one occasion she asked me 'Do you believe in platonic love?' and I was fifteen years old and I didn't know what it was, but I said of course I did, and she said, 'Well, you won't when you're older,' and off she went. She was the same age as me, but obviously a little more sophisticated.

Emanuel Litvinoff

Sex was dirty; it was indulged in only by the depraved. However, it happened. And the young man would boast secretively to his friends of his prowess whilst the girl would make an open secret of the matter. Thus it remained knowingly unknown to all concerned. At which point it was automatic that wedding bells would soon ring.

Infants was mixed, but as soon as you got to the big boys, at the age of about seven, then you were segregated, and if you were ever caught in the girls' playground, or any part where the girls were, then you got the cane. There was absolute complete division between boys and girls. They weren't allowed to mix in any circumstances. I think it was an old Victorian idea that men shouldn't see women, or boys shouldn't see girls.

I'll tell you this honestly, I didn't know there was any difference between boys and girls until the occasion arose when I actually saw the organ of a girl and it was my impression that she'd been operated on, that she'd lost something. It wasn't until I reached my teens that I realised there was a difference.

Louis Dore

My father never actually sat down and talked to me about these things, but instinctively I knew, if you know what I mean – I suppose from friends and things like that, and I'd hear my mother have conversations with my sisters, how to behave and all that, to be careful, shouldn't do things they shouldn't do and all that.

Joe Morris

In the winter, we'd play under the coats – boys and girls would play under the coats, that's how I first learnt about sex, playing under the coats. If you got a girl in those days, it would be round some dark back alley, and that's where you learnt your sex. Your parents wouldn't tell you because it wasn't proper decorum to talk to the children that age about sex, so you learnt it on the streets.

Jack Dash

We used to go to Poplar Park and used to go around by the bird aviary with the boys. It wasn't a mixed school. The boys were one side and the girls were the other. And we used to go around by the bird aviary and it was called Kiss in the Ring – a sort of Postman's Knock sort of thing, but out in the open air.

Lucy Collard

If I wanted to find out anything, I went to the library – I liked fact. When I was about sixteen, my mother tried to tell me the facts of life, and I ended up telling her. She said, 'How do you know this?' I said, 'I got a book out the library – I thought you were such a long while telling me these things, I'd better find out what's what.' I can remember getting this book and reading it, and thinking, 'Well, at least I know now.'

Jean Cunningham

Parents were very strict as regards their daughters – they didn't stop them going out or anything like that, but it used to be, don't get disgraced, because once you get disgraced, no boy is going to get married to you – a lot of that. The Jewish girls were very, very – well, I won't say every one, 'cos some of them did – but the majority were very careful not to have sex till they got married. And the boys were told to behave themselves – we shouldn't be villains or we'd end up in prison where none of them were Jewish.

Joe Morris

When I was young, I used to like dancing, and we never got up to anything bad, and that is the truth. Boys in those days did not go with girls for sex because they knew full well that nothing could go on because girls were brought up so strict. My mother was so strict, I had to be indoors by half-past ten – if it was a really special dance, I would tell my father and my father would say, 'All right, but don't you dare do anything wrong because I'm putting you on trust.' And my father would turn the clock back; him and my mother would go to bed and my father would turn the clock back and when my mother said to him, 'Time Mary was in,' he'd say, 'Oh, it's all right, it's only ten o'clock.' But it would probably be eleven o'clock.

Mary Partlett

My dad used to tell me that when he was younger, passenger trains used to run from the Brunswick Pier up to Stepney and Bow and Poplar and places like that. They were frequented by, he was telling me, the local ladies, um, with the seamen, as it cost about a penny from the one trip to another – as far as the fare's concerned, anyway.

Dick Allington

Some of the boats, they had women stewardesses. And, of course, the dock was full of French letters, and the dockies used to hook 'em out when these boats came in and put them all on the chains hanging. You used to see them there like a lot of flags. Course, the police removed all them. That's why they had them in rowing boats, riding round, see, 'cos the docks were full of them.

Walter Dunsford

I know my mother had what they call a Dutch cap – I asked her what it was one time and she was very uptight about it. After that, I never saw it no more. My mother didn't explain things – she didn't know much about sex herself, actually. When she had me, she didn't even know how I arrived – she had me under chloroform, and as far as she was concerned, I came down the back passage.

Jean Cunningham

I knew one of the stewards very well – Murray used to give me afternoon teas and everything, it was smashing. And I should say he was a man of about fifty, nice grey hair, very smart. And this day I walked in the Connaught – you know, the public house

81

near the Albert Dock entrance – and I walked in there and I'm sitting with my runner, Curly, and he says, 'See who's come in?' And I says, 'No, who is it?' And he says, 'A couple of lovely birds.' Cor; dear, oh dear. They had short fur coats on, black skirts, lovely dressed, oh really. And suddenly I said to him, ''Ere, one of them's Murray.' He said, 'It isn't.' I said, 'It is, you know.' Of course, all the dockers are all whistling and that, and we're just sitting there having our drinks, and one of the pair of them got up and they only want to use the Ladies toilet. Oh dear, oh dear, that was funny that day. I never got over that.

Harry Foss

It's surprising, when you look around, the different types of people that you meet in the docks. I mean like, there's all sorts, all trades – there was the dockies, the ship's crews – you had the Chinese and the Indians and what-have-you, all very interesting people. Even the queers, with their handbags, walking up and down the dock. The Castle boats was one of the worst ones of the lot – there was more on them than there was anywhere else. They was a big company that used to run into the docks, and the Castle boats that used to run to South Africa was notorious for this. And it's true, they used to walk along the dock, like they'd got a brass neck, because there's nothing like a dockie to take the mickey out of anybody.

They used to call them jerkers. Them days, ships never had toilets in every cabin, there was only a few that had toilets in cabins, so of course, everybody had a pot, and this is what they used to be called; the stewards was called 'pot jerkers'. They was all stewards – most of the bent ones were stewards.

Stan Bryan

I'd gone straight from school to have tea with May and I came out, was on my way home. There was this lady being brought out by the police, kicking and screaming. I didn't realise until later years that she was a prostitute. You know, where there's seamen, there's all these sort of places of ill repute, and she was being dragged out by the police to be put into one of these little carts, and she had red shoes on and red garters – and I went home and I said to my grandma about this lady, I said, 'I'm going to be like her one day,' and my grandma said, 'What do you mean, you're going to be like her?' I said, 'Oooh, Grandma, she had red shoes.'

I must have been about fifteen or sixteen, I'd been to this girl's father's restaurant again, and my grandma said, 'I'm gonna have a chat with you.' So I said, 'What about?' She said, 'About those red shoes.' And I couldn't think for the life of me – what red shoes? Then Grandma reminded me, she said, 'You know what she was, don't you?' I mean... but that time, I'd given up on the idea of red shoes anyway, because you could get them quite easily by that time. Coloured shoes were beginning to come in, so that was quite all right – I didn't have to go down to The Oporto to do the same job she did, to get the shoes.

Lucy Collard

Nearby was Christ Church, Spitalfields, which we used to call Itchy Park. These people – waifs and strays – used to sit in the park until the crypts were opened for the night. In those days, beer and intoxicants were tuppence a pint, and they used to get drunk, and these women were available – prostitutes; we used to call them 'fourpenny bits' or 'Woodbine Kates'. And they used to come along, drunk as a lord, walk down and meet a man, and sometimes used to do their business in the flats up and down the dark staircases. Sometimes you got up in the early morning, they'd be lying in a drunken stupor, both of them.

Mr U

I went into the kitchen and all I can remember is this big zinc bath with sheets and things in and a lot of blood. And when I saw all this blood, they said, 'Violet, you're not supposed to be in here – go out in the other room.' I went out and I thought, 'What's going on?' And then they said, 'Come and see your new sister,' and there was Mum sitting in bed with the new baby. She must have spent nine months going round with a bump, but I didn't know that was a baby or anything. I didn't know anything till I was quite old – no facts of life or anything. Babies just appeared.

Violet Kentsbeer

CHAPTER 3

Encountering the Wider World

School and the Uniform Problem

After the First World War, schooling became compulsory up to the age of fourteen, but as this coincided with a shortage of labour, it mostly meant that non-attendance rates became higher. For bright children, education was a potential route out to a better life, but in the cycle of poverty, family incomes are hardest stretched when there are lots of mouths to feed, and as young household members become contributors, conditions improve. This meant that future earnings often counted for little against the urgent need to earn money as early as possible.

Elementary schools were set up to educate the working classes from the age of five to fourteen, with an emphasis on basic literacy and arithmetic. Brighter children transferred to municipal or county secondary schools, or grammar schools. There were also church schools and the very successful Jews' Free School in Spitalfields. However, the major bar to continuing to a secondary school was usually the cost of uniform. This was well beyond the means of most working-class families, and only occasionally subsidised.

Committed head teachers took a genuine interest in the welfare of their charges, some going as far as to drum up money from local businesses to fund annual outings and treats. Despite the fact that discipline took the form of corporal punishment, many children enjoyed their school days.

Good teaching could inspire a lifelong passion for learning, and at a most basic level the classroom was a safe and predictable haven in an uncertain world – even if the same could not always be said for the playground.

<hr>

My first school, in York Road, it was a dull, depressing place, lit by candles and gas, gas mantles in the cloakroom, and heating was very small, you know, it just wasn't sufficient to keep you warm. All you had on was a little jersey, used to roll me hands inside it and if the teacher walked up the row and he saw you with your hands like that – wallop! 'Get your hands out!' You was sitting like that, your hands between your legs, trying to keep 'em warm, and all you had on was a little jersey, short little trousers, full of patches, clogs – wooden-soled shoes, you know, things like that.

We had to more or less do what we was told and we used to do it, but at the same time, I never seemed to learn anything. I was always hungry. I was cold. And in fear sort of all the time. So you were unable to concentrate – I mean, you wanted to read and write, with the gaslights popping up, throwing shadows over your desk and all like that. But all you used to look for is waiting to pack up so you could get out of school and if it was market day, go to the market, to nick food.

Henry Corke

The training ship, well, it was the *Exmouth*, and this thing was built in 1906 as a training ship for orphan boys, mainly London, from every district in London, and it was run by the Metropolitan Asylums Board. School started at nine o'clock – before that we all got up, bugle reveille, about half-past five or six o'clock, then we had to go and bathe in divisions, all under showers. Brrr, it's cold! And we all turned round and washed each other's backs and so forth, then you got your towels and had to pass through a drying room with an officer ticking off the boys – you went, you gave your number, and he ticked you off and he looked you up and down to see whether you were clean enough, you'd washed your ankles and stuff that boys don't do.

George Barnes

I went to school for just one year before the First World War and I was only in what we called the Infants, and it seemed to me to be a lovely place to be in, because coming from a home like I'd come from, into a nice warm room. The teacher was very nice, she was a sweet lady, and I felt, well, this is nice. But when the war started, all the men were taken into the army and most of the teachers, even in the boys', the big boys', were elderly Victorian female teachers, so we had female teachers almost until the war finished. Although they were good, they knew their stuff, they were pretty heavy with the ruler or the cane.

Louis Dore

We had a very long day as children. We were at an ordinary English school till about four-thirty, then at Hebrew classes from five-thirty till about eight o'clock. The trouble with Hebrew classes, which I hated, was that the teachers in them were totally untrained. They worked at a job during the day, and worked at the classes in the evening. They didn't know how to teach, they didn't know how to get on with children. They were brutal. They used canes, and caned you for nothing.

Victor Leigh

There was strong emphasis on discipline in these elementary schools in those days, not just New City Road but all over the borough, and corporal punishment with the cane was the accepted punishment for any misdemeanors. The learning was slightly mechanical by modern standards, but it did include poetry and music. I can remember learning *O, Young Lochinvar Is Come Out of the West* and *Daffodils* at the age of nine and ten, and every Friday afternoon we used to have twenty spellings for which we had to prepare during the week.

In 1935, I won a scholarship to Plaistow Municipal Secondary School. This, of course, was a great feat inasmuch that only two or three people went on from the elementary school, where education finished in those days at fourteen, to a secondary school, where one carried on to the age of sixteen. My mother received a bursary of £12 per annum to help to maintain me, and also for uniform because it was necessary to wear certain items of clothing: blazer, tie, socks and cap was mandatory.

Ken Gill

I was held up in front of the school because I wasn't very fond of writing letters and I hadn't written to my mother, and she had written to the headmistress, and I was up in front of the school. She said that Mother was the most sacred word in the English language, and I'd abused it by not writing to my mother. It did something to me, it completely shut me off, and I found it very difficult to be with people when I left.

Doris Salt

Once when I got knocked about by one of the teachers, me mother went up there and knocked her about, and every time I played up a bit after that, she used to say to me, 'I suppose you'll bring your mother up here again.'

Eileen Gibbons

I remember we had this master, Mr Parker, who was constantly going into a corner to smoke his cigarettes. He had a horrible cough, and kept spitting into his handkerchief. He used to distribute *Geographic* magazines, and these had pictures of African tribes, and I always remember him coming in and saying, 'Look at old Litvinoff, looking at all the naked ladies.' Which I might very well have been doing. I would have been eleven or twelve.

Emanuel Litvinoff

Mr Penfold, he was our biology and maths teacher. If you wished to be excused, he was rather sadistic – he would say 'Yes, you may go', and as you reached the classroom door, he would call you back by saying 'At three-thirty' or 'Four o'clock', whatever time you left school. So therefore you had to sit in the back of the class; hopefully your bladder was strong enough to hold out.

Albert Patten

There was one teacher, a very manly woman, everyone was terrified of her. Tall woman, like a man, great big feet. I don't think I remember her punishing the girls so much but if a boy got caught talking or anything, he'd have to go out in front, kneel down, and she kept a special big ledger and she just picked it up and bashed it down on the boy's head. And then, this boy, he screamed the place down. He said, 'I've just had an operation on my head.' And that really frightened her. She said, 'Why didn't you say so? Why didn't you tell me?' I don't think she did it again.

Hilda Bunyon

I was very unfortunate in that my form master was a Mr North, and he frightened me. He disliked me intensely. After a time it seemed to me that other boys in the class would make a witty remark and everyone would laugh, including Mr North. But if I made a witty remark it would be 'most uncalled for, Hunt', you know. And I was scared. Just could not wait for the day to come when I could leave school. I wondered at one time if I would live long enough to leave school, seriously. Terrible – I disliked it. And when I did start work, oh, I was so happy.

Edwin Hunt

Mind you, we used to get the stick at school, and every time I got the stick, I used to say to Dad, 'I got the stick, Dad.' 'What for?' 'Nothing.' He said, 'I think you get the stick more times for nothing than anybody else in the school. Never mind, it makes up for all the times that you don't get caught.'

Dennis Pike

One morning, I was going in the class and my friend said to me, 'Here you are, Liz, there's a seat here.' So I said, 'All right, Vi,' and the teacher came in, caught me and told me to get out. I was only saying I'd go and sit next to her because she was my friend, and he said, 'Go and get the cane.' So I had to get it – no man was allowed to cane you, but a woman teacher did. I wouldn't have minded if she'd give me a one-hander – I mean, that would have hurt me enough – but she give me two.

Elizabeth Butler

When I was at school, I remember in the 1914 war, we never had many teachers and what the girls used to do, we used to sit and knit socks for soldiers who were in the war. My father was in the war and my mother had to go to work. I liked it, school, very good; the only thing was during those crucial years we didn't have the teachers to learn us, so we lacked in our learning, but we made up with our hands. We was always knitting or sewing, which I still do today.

Annie Pope

In my family, my brother Ted, he won a scholarship to Raines Foundation School but it meant a uniform. Well, to buy a uniform's right out of the question so we couldn't do that, so he was transferred to Cable Street Central School, which was a secondary school but no uniform. Then the next one was my sister Emily; she won a scholarship. Mum managed to find her a uniform – I think someone gave her hand-me-downs – so Emily did go to Raines, but couldn't stop there long because of the same thing, this uniform business, the special ties and the shirts and things and the gym kits. So she had to leave it. I won a scholarship, I couldn't go. My sister Florrie, she won a scholarship, she couldn't go. Now, out of those, how far one of us would have gone, I don't know. Obviously, one of us would have made the grade.

Jack Banfield

I couldn't stay on at school – you had to buy the uniform and a straw hat and when you walked down the market all the boys who lived in the market would throw things at you. And everyone was supposed to have a violin to play in the choir and that was a shilling a week and, oh God, that's all we had to live on some days, so I left at fourteen.

Hilda Bunyon

I won a scholarship which would have taken me to probably a grammar school, or whatever, but my father said, 'Oh no, you've learned enough, you've done your education. You come to work.' So I had to go to work at eleven. I had a cousin, a female cousin, who won a Christ's Hospital scholarship and she won another scholarship to Cambridge from there and now she's very upper class – she got a job as a secretary and married the boss. She lives in a mansion now.

I had to attend school occasionally. After an absence of a week or two, the school board man would call on my mother to demand a reason for it. The answer was, of course, simple: I'd been took bad. The real joke that resulted from all this hole-in-a-corner business was that on two occasions I was sent away to a convalescent home. Imagine my father's chagrin when he found that he had to pay five shillings a week for this.

Louis Dore

The headmistress and some of the teachers used to stay behind after school and we used to go back for what was known as evening classes or night school, and we used to get a good two hours' further education as regards arithmetic and English to help us for when we took the Junior County Scholarship. I found this very helpful because there wasn't a lot of room at home and being in the classroom it gave you more incentive, you know.

I did very well. I got a special place at what was the local grammar school, Howrah House, that was in the East India Dock Road and was run by the Faithful Companions of Jesus. They had their convent there. I only attended there roughly for three years, till I was fourteen, because my mother found it difficult to get out, do the chores at home and to do the shopping, and I also seemed to be rather worried, taking on extra subjects at school, so eventually I had to leave school at fourteen.

Pat Thompson

We had a very nice, gentle headmaster, who was nevertheless quite a strong man. He had been a captain in the war and he was still known as Captain. He was a great big fine upstanding man, he walked like a guardsman, but he was very gentle under his strict discipline. And I shall never forget, he got all the leavers together – there was about twelve of us who were going to leave – and he stood us in a semi-circle round his desk, and there were only him and us, and he gave us a pep-talk. The main themes were, your schooldays are over, life is before you and the first thing you have to do is to fight the world for a living.

He didn't say act in cooperation with your fellow citizens. You had to fight the world, you see – that was the Tory philosophy, I suppose, which he enjoyed, and it affected all of us. It was always a puzzle to me how a chap can have reactionary political ideas based on violence and the idea of everybody in competition, everybody was everybody else's rival, like telling boys of fourteen that you've got to go and fight the world for a living, and yet be gentle, pleasant and humane people in themselves.

Charles Poulson

I went to a Church of England school – the church, St Luke's, was on Stratford Street and all the Empire Days and Armistice Days and that, we used to assemble in the church and pay our respects. The school was poor – you know, the people were poor, and some of them in bare feet. And the headmaster, he lived in Southend and he used to go round all the factories on the Isle of Dogs raising money to give us underprivileged children a day at Southend. We used to look forward to that day.

Robert Stapleton

We used to all fight in the playground, dragging one another about by our jerseys. Some of the kids had no shoes. When we passed up to the senior department of the school and the hall was given over to boxing, dry swimming on forms, choral music for those that had a voice. Some were making plaster models of the monuments they'd seen on a school journey. In the playground, there was all these bits of paper from the lunches being blown about because things were a little rougher in those days, people weren't as tidy – it used to all blow up one end and blow down the other end – but it used to strike me that everybody was quite orderly. They'd blow a whistle and everybody used to stand still, fall in your classes.

They were given military instructions: form twos, quick march, left wheel and so on.

Leslie Hoe

School fights used to take place between North Street and Queen's Road – the trouble with North Street was it had two entrances, one at the back and one at the front, and we used to get attacked from both sides by Queen's Road School. The only other thing that used to happen there, we used to go to Queen's Road because North Street hadn't got any facilities for carpentry, and all of the North Street boys were shut out in the playground in the depths of winter with snow on the ground, and you can imagine how we suffered at the hands of the Queen's Road School because we were pelted unmercifully with snowballs.

I eventually went to Cave Road School which was slightly upmarket compared with North Street, and there I met Mr Harvey who was my mentor, there's no doubt about it. He introduced me to Tom Clare, the nature poet, and I've never forgotten him.

John Henry Arnold

There was a Catholic school further along – the Isle of Dogs school – it was contained within bridges. They lived the other side of the bridge, that was another world. They used to have a cap badge with IDS on it, and we used to call them 'Idiots and Dunces'. And ours had SL on it – we was the 'Silly Lemons' according to them. There was a bit of a feud. The people living on the other side of the Millwall Bridge, they were like a different world; they were mainly Catholics and dock workers, when they were working.

Robert Stapleton

In 1924 when I was fourteen, things were so bad at home money-wise, we was actually starving and I used to go to school with no boots on or shoes. I can assure you that I ran to school with no shoes and socks on, in bare feet, in frost. Not snow, but in frost, and that is a fact. I don't tell nothing but facts, because I loved school and the atmosphere at home was very bad. I used to go to school with no shoes on, naturally in old trousers with holes in them. You were living a hell of a life – hell of a life, it was.

Stan Rose

The chap alongside of me, Stokes, his father was a costermonger. In the winter time, and in the mornings, he couldn't hold a pen, because his hands were that full of chilblains, where he used to have to go up with his father, you know, in the early morning, and sort all the celery and things like that out, and he had no boots. Boots were not available in that time for some of the kids – I would say, on average, about five in a class would have no boots, in North Street School.

John Henry Arnold

When they got to school, the teachers themselves had made up felt slippers and as the children got to school, they'd go into the hall entrance, feet would be dried and these slippers would be put on. The great pity was that during the morning, if the child wanted to go to the lavatory, they had to take the slippers off, walk through the snow across the playground, into the toilet, come back and have the whole thing repeated. Incidentally, of course, for them there was no overcoats. Might perhaps have an extra jersey, or something like that on, but there was no comforts for them.

Tom Stothard

We had a girl in my class called Nelly; she was a Christian girl and I liked her very much. She used to come to school without shoes on her feet – I couldn't understand it; no shoes and stockings, and it's raining, it's winter. She used to sit next to me. Her feet were so cold, and I said, 'Aren't you cold?' No, she didn't feel cold. I often used to go home to hers for tea, and one time I could smell a very nice welcoming smell – it was bacon. Although her mother offered it to me, I had an idea I mustn't eat it. I told my mother what had happened and I asked her, 'Why mustn't I eat it?' My mother said, 'Because it's not very healthy.' And I said, 'But Nelly Conlan walks about with bare feet and she's never had a cold in her life!'

Mrs A

About once a fortnight, the lady would come round from some cleansing department and you used to stand in a queue for one class at a time and she used to run a comb through your head looking for nits and all that. And if they found any, used to put you on one side till they'd finished and then they used to parcel us off in this old motor – I can see it now, old ambulance, a Talbot – and they used to take us to some place in Seven Sisters Road. And there we'd be stripped of our clothes what we had on – jerseys, trousers, pair of clogs, probably no socks – and they used to paint us from head to foot in sulphur. Slap it all over us, and we used to have to stand about and wait until it had its effect, and then they give us a wash down. When I get home and tell the old woman that I've been deloused, she used to do her nut. You can understand the mother's side of it, when she's got all those children, and sent them to school and done her best. If somebody picked you out at school, that was an attack on the dignity of the mother. It used to cause a lot of friction. So if we knew the lady was coming, we wouldn't go to school that day, we'd stay away.

Henry Corke

Kind Ladies and Philanthropists

Apart from parents, teachers and shopkeepers, the adults in most regular contact with East End children were those who helped run the clubs and youth groups that were open each day after school. Some clubs were organised by local religious institutions, others drew in volunteers from outside the area – some religious, some with a more socialist bent – but all keen to help relieve the hard lives of children in the East End. The clubs provided a warm place to go on winter evenings, with games for younger children, physical activities and occasionally dancing for the older ones. Toynbee Hall, set up in the 1880s by Samuel and Henrietta Barnett, a Church of England curate and his wife, was at the heart of Jewish and Irish Catholic communities in Whitechapel and brought in social reformers who wanted to live and work alongside the poorest in society. Oxford House, set up in Bethnal Green at around the same time, had a less radical and more overtly religious agenda for its philanthropic work, which was carried out by earnest young men from Oxford University; Mahatma Gandhi was a visitor when he came to England in 1931. The Dockland Settlements in Canning Town grew out of a school mission run by Malvern College in 1895, one of many set up by wealthy public schools. It provided lessons in carpentry and boxing, as well as free dental treatment.

At school, once a year, they'd send us up to Toynbee Hall in Aldgate, one of us, to get the old tennis balls, the discarded tennis balls. You'd get a dozen tennis balls – well, that would last us all through the year. And for cricket – you'd chalk your wicket, make a bat out of a piece of old wood.

Jack Banfield

This Grundy Street mission in Poplar advertises a gospel service, the poster asking, 'Where will you be spending eternity?' For many East Enders, the prospect of spending an evening somewhere warm was a sufficient incentive to hear God's word. John Galt, 1900–07

There was also in the 1930s, some young Methodists that went to a lecture on the China Inland Mission. And one of the Chinese at the lecture, he said that there were plenty of Chinese in England that could benefit from the China Inland Mission. So these young people from Peckham came down to Limehouse and took a survey of all the Chinese families and their children. And when they realised there were such a lot of children they knocked on every door and registered each family. When they realised there were so many children they opened up, once a week, a club for the Chinese children which became the Children's Club and that went on until the war broke out.

Connie Hoe

Most of the boys belonged to clubs which were a great asset. I belonged to the Jewish Lads' Brigade, which had a place in Aldgate. We never stayed home. Our life was this: we went to school, finished at half-past four; either we rushed home and had a good cup of tea or we went to Hebrew classes; and then from the Hebrew classes, at half-past seven, we rushed home again or to go to a club. Either the Jewish Lads' Brigade or the Brady Club or the Oxford & St George's Club. The whole of the East End was full of these boys clubs which were marvellous. You had the gym, you had a meal if you wanted it – the greatest meal I used to have was to go to the club and get a hot-dog roll and a hot drink. It only cost tuppenny ha'penny in those days, and it was marvellous. Either my mum was busy getting ready for the next day or too tired after doing the washing in the old copper in the scullery.

Mr U

They had a man over at Oxford House and all the Bethnal Green kiddies, he used to take us out – he would take us all out for the day, all expenses paid by him. And he fixed so many children up, those that wanted looking after, that sort of thing. And he'd go out and buy them skates, scooters, things to play with. But my sister, she only had one arm and he bought her a bike. And he had it built so that she rested the arm that she'd had off on the handlebars and the other one was free. It was a three-wheeled bike. It was a marvellous bike and it must have cost a lot of money. He lived in the Oxford House.

Dolly Cooper

When we came from school at four o'clock, we'd go to Ben's Chapel in Old River Lane, and that was run by social workers, and we'd have a mug of tea and bread and jam again. In later years, I used to think, I wonder how Mum and Dad went on? The only support they got was if there was a young baby, not going to school, Mother could go to the relieving office – Board of Guardians, that was called – and they'd get milk tickets or bread tickets which they had to exchange. It was looked upon as charity, so if they could avoid it, they did. It was looked on as a disgrace to have charity.

Jack Banfield

St Patrick's Church was obviously the Catholic church, and St Peter's was a Calvinistic type of church. St John's Church basically Church of England and orthodox. Then there was Ben's Chapel, which was non-conformist, the gospel mission. Now, that was a big asset to us as kids because, of an evening, they used to open up. The social workers used to come down. We didn't understand it at the time, but later I worked out that they were mainly shop workers and City workers, and they'd come down in the evening after they'd finished their job and help us, help out. They'd fetch table games and toys and things which they'd got from the big stores and that would be from about six to eight o'clock in the evening. Every evening, there'd be a queue of kiddies outside Ben's Chapel, waiting to go in there, and that would be warm, especially in the winter times. That was a place to be warm.

Jack Banfield

I will say this, people were marvellous in them days, and we were all in the same boat. I thanked God there was such a place as Dockland Settlements, because there it was a club and there was afternoons where you could go, and evenings, and they had all types of ages, from say about seven or eight upwards to fourteen or fifteen, and you went in different rooms and there was card playing, table tennis, dancing certain nights – but before you'd go dancing, you had to go to church – and they had football teams. Thank God there was a place like that for us when we were young, because there was something we could do.

Stan Rose

At the clubs, they very often did skipping. You wouldn't believe that – a long rope was very popular. There were girls from about six to sixteen, and then of course, the older ones would be telling you what fella they were out with, their latest romance. And they would think you know nothing of such a thing, you know. I said to the priest once or twice, 'I have heard more confessions than you'll ever hear'

Sister Pat O'Sullivan

On another occasion, Gandhi was in Poplar and a friend and I we just stood there – 'Look at this funny little man, you know, with the sheet around him' – and we were sort of giggling as he came past us and he patted us both on the head. Course, we went into fits of giggles, you know how stupid little girls can be. It wasn't until after years we thought, Oh, we've been patted on the head by this great man. He was a great man – but as a child, you would see somebody with a sort of sheet round them. He just looked strange, I suppose.

Lucy Collard

One night at the club, a girl said to me, 'Can I bring my doll?' It was Christmas – to show the other children. I said no at first, and they said, 'Oh Sister, do!' I said, 'Well, you bring a written note from your mother that if it's broke or anything, I won't be responsible.' So she did, she brought it. And after a bit when they'd seen it and everything, she said to me, 'Can I bring it home and bring the monkey to show you?' And I said, 'Yes, that would be nice, a change.'

And when she brought it, it was a live monkey. Her father had just got home from abroad and smuggled it in, you see. And of course the poor creature ran up and down the walls, frightened. It ran up and down the walls, and they were all screaming. Oh, we had a terrible time. It ran up and down everywhere and there was screaming and scratching. So anyway, they caught it, had to get the police to catch it. And the next day, it died. The husband was annoyed about the whole thing. He went to all the trouble to bring it home. Got pneumonia, I think, with fright.

Sister Pat O'Sullivan

Holidays Away from Home

Churches and charitable organisations also gave most East End children their first experience of the world outside the city. As well as Toynbee Hall, the Barnetts set up a Country Holiday Fund in 1884, and various churches and schools arranged special summer outings. Some excursions were a reward for good attendance, others required small regular contributions, or were restricted to the most deserving families, although it was not always easy for those in authority to discern which these were.

Families with a bit more money made their own arrange-ments to travel by train or Thames paddle steamer to places such as Margate or Southend; the less well off would settle for a day out in a local park with a picnic. The most popular way of affording a holiday, however, was to combine it with work. To this end, every autumn, about 250,000 East End families would travel by cart or truck or on special trains down to Kent to help bring in the hop harvest; this gave them a country holiday for free and several weeks out of doors, living in a big group and relaxing together at the end of each day. For the older children and adults, it seems to have been a time when they could loosen restrictions, and many an East End relationship had its beginnings over a stand of hops.

The only time I was religious was when I used to get sent to Sunday School and they used to give you a card and they'd stamp your card and if you had a full card – it's like lottery – if you had a full card you got to go on the outing, which was in the summer. And you went to Loughton – lousy Loughton, we used to call it.

Joanna Roberts

Southend was only half a crown from the station; used to go very often. There was no sand like there is now – they've only made a false beach, ain't they? It used to be cobbles and all that, but you had good times down there. Used to have donkey rides along the beach. There was a big funfair, called the Kursaal, then you had the train along the pier. Oh, you had to go to the Kursaal. And you could get a good meal there – your pie and mash.

Dolly Cooper

We used to all go on our holidays from school. We – the whole street – used to go to Victoria Park or village or else we used to go to Tunnel Gardens and that used to lead us down to Blackwall Pier, where we used to spend all day with just a bottle of lemonade and a few sandwiches. When we were really right tired out, we used to drag ourselves back, you know, the whole street, about twelve of us.

Saturday nights, various neighbours used to have drinks and my sister and I used to lie in bed and listen to all the songs. We learnt all the old songs like that, just used to lie there and pick up all the words. That was part of our Saturday enjoyment.

Anne Griffiths

Ben's Chapel outing was always walk up to the bottom of Dock Street, get on a tram, they'd hire a special tram, and that would take you to The Rising Sun in Epping Forest for the day. When you got there you'd get a jam jar to catch any tadpoles or frogs that you could get – 'cos that place, Epping Forest, was alive with wildlife – there was all natural ponds. Whatever the time of year, you could either get frogs, or tadpoles, or tiddlers. You'd always get something to take back home, although they finished up down the sink, I suppose.

Jack Banfield

We used to go away as kids through the Country Holiday Fund – that was through the scouts and the church. Dad used to pay so much a week, a penny or tuppence, whatever it was – it was a nominal sum. We'd be taken and we'd be put up out in the country. Best of all was up in Norfolk. We were sent to Norfolk and it was the doctor who picked us up from the station and took us to a place called St Peters, which is right on the banks of the Ouse – as far as I remember, that was the first car ride I ever had. We got new wellingtons, new macs and new hats. And it was smashing. And, when it did rain and they let us put it on, Auntie and

Uncle whoever they might have been, we wouldn't take them off. We'd never had the lot all together. And fresh eggs every day – big 'uns. 'Cos the ones we used to get, I think they was pigeon eggs – they wasn't a lot bigger. We used to have one every Sunday – that was proper breakfast, that was, with your soldiers, and that was lovely. All the rest of the week was bread and butter, or bread and jam – always plum, 'cos it was the cheapest.

Dennis Pike

The river, Limehouse Pier, was our outing. That was just all the mothers taking their children down the pier on a summer day. One time the tide was coming in and I couldn't have been more than three, and I'd made my way to the top of the steps to the river, not realising, and the next thing I know, I was being yanked up by the knickers by one of the trawler men that had seen me go in. But that was the highlight of our life, Limehouse Pier.

Mary Partlett

My father was a baker. I don't suppose he was earning more than fifty shillings a week but we always had a holiday at Great Yarmouth and we used to go down by boat – from Tower Bridge, I think. It was very cheap. Later, we used to go down on the *Golden Eagle* to Margate for three-and-six return. I remember once we were going to have our photographs taken and apparently they lost me – I was always dragging behind, apparently, but we were all dressed in sailor suits. And Father always had a straw hat and always marched on about two or three yards in front of the family.

Charlie Gubbins

When I was at school, there used to be the Country Holiday Fund. I didn't have a suitcase, we had a basket made of a sort of bamboo, a straw sort of basket. It was a long basket and you packed the clothes and then a top would go on it, a sort of lid, and you just put a couple of straps round. I went twice – once to Worthing and once to Colchester.

The local council would pay people at various country or seaside towns to take the children from the East End and we would go there for a fortnight. The place in Worthing was pretty horrible because we had a street light outside the room and there were bedbugs and me and the girl I was with, I think we spent most of the night trying to get rid of them. A man came to see us from the local council to see how we were, and we started crying – we said we didn't like it because there were bugs there and we didn't have bugs in our bedrooms at home. And he found another place for us.

Lucy Collard

My wife Olive's dad was a docker. And Grace, that's the oldest sister of Olive, she put down to go to Country Holiday Fund, and they wouldn't let her go, so old Daise, that's me mother-in-law, she's gone up the school to find out, and they said, 'Well, she doesn't need it.' 'Well, why not?' 'She always comes to school nice and clean, always got a clean hanky pinned on her.' But it wasn't – it was a piece of rag stitched up. But because she went to school like that, they thought, you know, she didn't need it. Anyway, they let her go.

Dennis Pike

St Peter's Church, one day a year, there used to be a coach outing. That was the old horse brakes, and that used to go to Petersham. In order to qualify for the day out, you went to church, the Sunday morning service, the children's service, and you got a card and a little indelible stamp put on it for your attendance. So if your attendance was right, you got a ticket to go on the day's outing. This little stamp, what used to happen is they used to do 'em on with ink themselves in order to get it. Eventually, you'd go, at nine o'clock, the coach would be outside St Peter's Church, and you'd get up there and away you'd go. Probably be pouring with rain, you'd get soaking wet. With those horse brakes, you used to have a canvas cover but if you sat on the outside, any rain that dripped off, your back'd get wet. So if it was raining, you'd be huddled into the centre. But they were good, these people, they gave us one day of excitement a year.

Jack Banfield

My dad's family all used to go hopping and when they went hopping, Grandfather used to pack up paying the rent of his house. They'd all go down hopping, he'd come back two days beforehand, and when he came back, he'd find them a place to stay. So when all the kids came home – and there was a lot of them – they used to go round to the new house.

Anyway, the story goes that one time they've all come home and Grandfather is Billy Monk [drunk] and couldn't remember where it was. So they all went round the arches and slept in the cart.

My mother's family never went hopping, my dad's family always did. Not me mum. I did hear that later on, that me dad took me mum to the hop fields for a visit, 'cos Uncle Harry and the rest of them was down there. They were courting. Well, Grandmother, me mum's mum, wasn't very happy about that at all. You know. You've heard the stories of what went on down the hop fields!

Dennis Pike

First of all, the old motor come round down the turning with Mike Hayslip of Silvertown; he was an old contractor, and he had an old motor. And all the locals used to get all the old stuff in trunks, baskets, bags, everything, and we all piled into the back of the motor. We'd all be sitting there, kids and the

A family enjoys a working holiday in Kent, stripping leaves and stalks from hop bines into a canvas bin. The work was tough on children's delicate hands but for poor East Enders, it was the only chance of a holiday, and an eagerly anticipated annual trip. Cyril Arapof, c1931

old women and odd bits of table – anything to make comfort in the old huts we used to go on the farm in. And away we'd go. Across the ferry sometimes, but mostly through the Blackwall Tunnel. Then he'd make his way towards Gibsons Farm in Chislehurst, in Kent. We used to get there, and we'd be allocated our huts – this farm had a good lot of army huts – and get a key to our place. We used to go out and get bales of straw and there used to be heaps of what we call faggots – they used to be cuttings of trees done up in bundles, so you'd lay them on the floor first, and we'd pile our bales of straw on top of that and then we'd make the beds. Then with the table and the old chairs that they'd brought with them, a few curtains, they'd try to make it look good. Outside the huts there used to be a sort of fireplace, like a barbecue idea. And they used to boil the pots – not kettles, pots in them days – and of course, they'd make tea, and we used to have our meals out on the lawns, sort of thing. Great big fields, everywhere.

Charles Beck

The worst holiday I ever had was with my mother. In common with lots of English ladies of the time, she went on holiday in the country on an excursion called hop picking, where you stayed for the season to pick the hops. We went by lorry, a local fruiter took us all, with zinc baths and mattresses and everything, and we went hop picking, we picked the hops, got up early in the morning and everything. It was terrible. If you're brought up in the city, the country's an abomination with all its rain and its cloddy earth and getting up at half-past six in the morning. My father came down to visit us from London Bridge and saw us living like that and he took my sister and I away. He said, 'This is only for peasants. If your mother wants to stop here, she can stop here, but you two are coming home.' And I thought, Thank God for that.

Leslie Hoe

Once we got settled in, over the weekend, we used to start work at seven o'clock and we used to go out in the fields, used to be masses of hops, and you'd gradually have a bin; some on their own, or two with half a bin each. And they'd be picking – no leaves, or nothing like that. You used to have to keep them clean – and we'd pick hops about three or four hours. All the kids would have their bins and all go on it. And after two or three hours, the farm people came with a basket and they used to measure up; so many baskets, and they'd put it on a card for you.

About five o'clock we used to finish. Then we'd go in to tea, and that used to be outside, and they'd boil the pots up again and make tea. Then as the evenings went on, all the kids used to make a bonfire, they used to be sitting outside there, chatting. The old people would be up the local pub, you know, the usual thing. We used to get tucked up, and start telling stories – we used to get the wind up because of telling all the ghost stories, and we used to be frightened to move.

It used to be harvest time, beginning of September – it's usually three weeks – but one year, it must have been a good year, it went all through September and we worked into the first week of October. And we used to come out of the fields in the dark – seven o'clock in the morning – and it used to be dark when we used to come home. The last night we was there, they had a bit of a party. All the kids had a treat outside the farmer's cottage – they put tables out, put out sandwiches and cakes.

Charles Beck

Danger from the Skies

Not all encounters with the outside world were beneficial. For children growing up in the second decade of the twentieth century, there was the shock of discovering that strangers could enter your country – indeed the airspace above your own street and house – and rain down death on you. During what was originally called the 1914 war, or the Great War, now known as the First World War, for the first time in history you didn't have to join the forces and travel to a distant battlefield to experience war's violence, explosions and sudden death.

The earliest raids were by Zeppelins, which were beautiful but sinister silver, cigar-shaped airships with a cruising speed of fifty-four miles per hour, which meant they could reach London in about six hours from their sheds in Cologne. In preparation for these expected raids, London underwent its first blackouts, and air raid warnings were given by policemen cycling round with sandwich boards, or by firing small fireworks, known as maroons, which were kept at police stations.

Presumably out of sentimentality, Kaiser Wilhelm, the grandson of Queen Victoria, would not permit bombing raids on London's historic buildings, government or museums – but the docks, and anywhere east of the Tower of London, was fair game. By the end of the war, Britain had suffered fifty-one raids, in which 5,806 bombs were dropped, killing 557 people and injuring 1,358. The raids were a terrifying invasion of London's skies, and morale was hugely boosted when one of the newer wooden airships – not a Zeppelin, but a Shutte-Lanz, although that name never really caught on in Britain – was shot down over Cuffley in Hertfordshire, by a British pilot called Lieutenant William Leefe Robinson, who earned a Victoria Cross for his daring.

From 1917 onwards, raids were also undertaken by Gotha aircraft, and the worst raid of the war involved seventeen Gothas flying over in broad daylight, on 13 June 1917, carrying thousand-pound bombs. Aiming for the docks, one of them scored a direct hit on Upper North Street School in Poplar, the bomb smashing through two storeys to explode in the infant class downstairs. Across London that day, there were 432 serious casualties, and 162 deaths. But what really horrified people was the loss of eighteen children, sixteen of them under the age of six.

———•———

In the First World War we had air raids, the first air raids that ever was. I was living in Mile End and we used to go and shelter in the Underground station, and the Zeppelins used to be coming over. The bombs, they used to practically chuck them out by hand – they were like fifty-pounders, not like the bombs that they give now.

Joseph Milchard

We had a blackout of sorts – nowhere near the blackouts they had in the Second World War. Street lights were on, but they were dimmed.

Cyril Demarne

My earliest recollections of the war were of seeing a boy scout on the street blowing a bugle for the all clear. My only other recollection is being under the kitchen table which, my father tells me, had mats piled on top to form a bomb-proof shelter. My mother and sisters and myself were under the table. My father, being rather stout, could only get his shoulders under the table, and he always said that if anything had ever happened, his nether end would have copped the lot.

My mother, unfortunately, didn't survive the war – she was of a very nervous disposition and the air raids put paid to her.

John Henry Arnold

IT IS FAR BETTER
TO FACE THE BULLETS
THAN TO BE KILLED
AT HOME BY A BOMB

JOIN THE ARMY AT ONCE
& HELP TO STOP AN AIR RAID

GOD SAVE THE KING

This First World War recruiting poster was issued by the publicity department of the Central Recruiting Depot in Whitehall. Its ghostly airship hovering over a familiar London skyline is clearly designed to stir up the patriotic urge to protect family and home. Recruiting Depot, 1916–18

We didn't have sirens in those days for an air raid warning – they used to fire flares called maroons. There'd be a loud bang, and police used to ride the streets on bicycles with a sandwich board. It used to have on one side 'Take Cover' and on the other side 'All Clear'. So they used to ride around and blow their police whistles as a warning, and you'd hear these maroons, very loud – they used to go 'boom!', like a gun going off.

Cyril Demarne

The river police station, I always looked upon that with affection, that river police station because, and this goes back to the First World War, when the Zeppelin raids used to be on, we used to go for shelter, and our place of shelter used to be the police station, in the drying rooms down below. Nice and warm down there. Some of them used to go to the church crypt, some would go to the wharves basements.

Jack Banfield

It had been the Great War and I was just a tiny child, and my sister too, and I had a feeling once of a kind of luminescence, and I said to my mother, 'Did you carry me somewhere, you know, where there was noise, and people?' And she said to me, 'Yes, when you were about three' – and by then my father was in the Russian naval corps, this was in about 1916 or 17, and I was about three or four – and she said, 'I took you once across to a *shul*, down in the basement, and once to the crypt down at Spitalfields.' And I said, 'That light!' I always recall that about my infancy.

Jack Miller

We used to go to shelter down the railway arches, and Mr Carson, who used to manage the dairy, afterwards he used to ride about on a bicycle with 'All Clear' – or 'Take Cover'. No sirens – he used to ride about with a bicycle and a whistle. Princes Square was where the first bomb dropped – they wanted to get the Tower Bridge, I think. It dropped by us and killed a couple of cows and a girl – a girl got killed there. And when the bomb fell, all the glass shattered, and my younger sister and I, we run upstairs to take the baby out of the cradle and carried her into the garden and we were shivering.

Mrs P

We used to be called up for when the air raids were on, because of my father being in the army. We had a person to knock on the door to let us know – that was a warning. And we used to take shelter down in the subway. I can still remember a bomb dropping in Strattondale Street, not far from where we lived, but it was only a small crater and it was nothing compared with the other war at all. Also, I can still remember the Zeppelin going over, what came down in Cuffley – I can see it now in my mind's eye, coming down in flames.

Annie Pope

They'd had a lot of trouble bringing down these Zeppelins because the conformation of the skin tended to deflect the machine-gun bullets. The Royal Flying Corps, as it was in those days, they used to go up and rake their gunfire along the length of the Zeppelin, but Flight Lieutenant Leefe Robinson thought about it and he had a theory that if instead of scattering the bullets, he went up and fired at one spot and kept on firing, he could break through it. And this coincided with the discovery of an explosive bullet. So with the combination of the explosive bullet and banging away at one spot, he was the first man to bring down a Zep. It fell at Cuffley. People were just going barmy. This was the first one, and after that, the fate of the Zeppelins were sealed.

Cyril Demarne

I remember when they had the Zeppelin come over that was all alight. I remember that because I was quite a kid, 'cos Nana took me out of bed, me mother said – well, I remember it – took me out of bed and said, 'Look at the so-and-sos – look at what they're doing.' And I lost me sight for a little while because it took all the nerves out of me. I had what Nana called the blight – they called it the blight years ago.

Dolly Cooper

We had a bomb in Flower and Dean Street, smashed into a flat in the basement there, and the superintendent went down to see the damage and it seems like there was a burst gas pipe, 'cos a couple of weeks later, he died.

Mrs P

There was a school during the First World War in Upper North Street and they had Zeppelins used to drop bombs, very rarely. I mean, you didn't get a lot like the Second World War. And apparently a bomb was dropped and it hit the school in North Street and about eighteen kids were killed and there's a memorial which is now in the recreation ground up in East India Dock Road.

Joanna Roberts

I was in school, ten o'clock or half-past, in the morning, and the maroons were going bang, bang outside. Our instructions were to go down to the laboratories in the basement for safety. Some of the boys got up and Miss Gunner was, 'Sit down, sit down.' She was the personification of calmness. She said, 'You know what these Germans are up to, don't you? They're trying to frighten us. But they're not going to frighten us, are they?' And we were more frightened of Miss Gunner. So she said, 'We'll go down in a moment. All right, boys, down we go.' And down we went. There were several loud explosions from bombs – one, in particular – it was the bomb that hit the school at North Street in the East End and killed seventeen toddlers. That was a terrible day in the East End of London.

Cyril Demarne

The First World War, it was terrible – there was no end of people killed around us. There was a bomb dropped at the back of us and there was a row of houses – there was ever so many people killed there. Another bomb killed about twenty in our road. There was a shop that sold grain and they had a cellar, and lots of people went there because they reckoned it was safe. And they all got drowned. A bomb dropped and burst a water pipe, and they all got drowned. It was when I was working at the docks in London, and they dropped a bomb on a school in Poplar, and thirty children were killed there.

Alice Humm

In the First World War, when we were living in Bowman Street, which is opposite Stepney Green station, I remember the warnings when a man used to come knocking at all the doors and tell us to take cover because there's going to be a raid. And I remember one morning the sky being full of aeroplanes – the Germans had managed to come over. It was the famous Saturday morning and they brought a few down.

Philip Bernstein

The biggest shambles that I ever saw was after that Zeppelin raid – dear, oh dear, there was six inches of fat and sugar all along that factory road, along the side of Tate & Lyles. September seventh, at two minutes to five. I always remember it because I was working that day till five o'clock, and the siren went at five to five, so we all dashed down to the office but the time keeper wouldn't let us out. I always thank him now because if he had let us out, I'd a been down at the shelter at the police station at Pier Road, or the one up the tunnel. I'd have been dead and buried by now. There was five killed at Harland's at the time. And when we got down to the police station, there was all them shops there, next door to the Standard pub, opposite the police station, and there was all them shops there, and there was a cow shed. But from the Standard to the cow shed, they'd all gone. There was a bloke there, trying to dig his people out, and he called us everything 'cos we wouldn't go over there to help him try to dig them out, but it was really ridiculous even to try and attempt it. I was only sixteen or seventeen.

Stan Bryan

CHAPTER 4

East End Communities

Four out of every hundred Londoners in 1911 had been born overseas, and the East End docks offered a major route into the country for people from all over the world, with most immigrants disembarking at Tower Bridge. Before the First World War, one of the East End's largest foreign communities was of German origin. From the early eighteenth century, immigrants from Hanover dominated the vast sugar-refining trade which took place in sweltering 'bakeries' in streets around the West India Dock, into which the raw sugar cane was imported; they could be glimpsed, often working topless, in the intense heat of the refineries. German residents numbered about 30,000 in 1911, and in Leman Street, Poplar, there were dozens of German shops, with German bands a familiar and noisy street entertainment. This all changed during the war, when shops with German names were attacked and looted. The bands disappeared and thousands of 'enemy aliens' were interred and many deported.

The German community never returned, but others took its place. New arrivals, whether they stepped off the boat with a contact's name scribbled on a piece of paper, or just seized on the first friendly-looking face, often settled near their point of entry. The poor and the rootless will always be drawn to places that offer the possibility of work and affordable lodgings and London's East End held out the promise of both. The availability of work fluctuated according to economic slumps, strikes and the effects of war, but with so many industries and avenues of employment, there was always the chance of picking up a job. And in the hundreds of densely packed streets and subdivided houses, there were rooms – if you were not too fussy and didn't mind sharing – for even the poorest of tenants.

A Little Bit of Tsarist Russia

By the beginning of the twentieth century, Spitalfields and Whitechapel were predominantly Jewish, with whole streets occupied by Russian and Eastern European immigrants who had fled from pogroms – the mob riots encouraged and approved by the Russian authorities – during the 1880s. They had their own synagogues, shops, newspapers, theatres, coffee houses and pubs, and there were Jewish trade unions for the clothing, shoe and boot, bakery and cigar industries. By 1900, the Jews' Free School in Spitalfields, which was founded as far back as 1817, was the largest in the country with some 4,300 pupils.

Spitalfields had earlier been colonised by Huguenot silk weavers who began the area's long association with the cloth industry by bringing over their weaving expertise, mulberry trees and wooden handlooms from France from 1685 onwards. The remnants of this community were still hanging on by a thread 250 years later, with four weavers operating out of Fournier Street as late as 1930.

Bagels and flatbread are stacked up in the window of Levy Brothers Jewish bakery, which opened in Middlesex Street, Whitechapel, in 1710. By 1900, about 135,000 Jewish emigrants from eastern Europe lived in London, mostly in the East End. John Galt, 1900–1907

My mother's father's people had come over to this country with the Huguenots and they had been silk weavers in Spitalfields. My grandfather, I vaguely remember, was the absolute caricature of what one expects a Frenchman to be, what one at the time thought. He was a small man, quite short, with black curly hair, very blue eyes, very small hands and feet, and on Sundays when he went out, he always had pearl-grey gloves and spats and carried a walking stick. My father's parents had always been in Poplar. My mother, her parents had always lived in Wapping, except I think my grandfather at one time lived in Spitalfields. But I think by that time the silk weaving had gone bust, so they were moving into other circles, rather than being in that sort of trade.

Lucy Collard

We employed these two brothers who were Huguenots. I'm talking pre-war, so this would be 1937-38, I suppose, and they were about forty-five, fifty, then. I can remember them when they first came to Norriton and Adams, coming with what appeared to be two lorry-loads of old wood. These pieces of old wood, in actual fact, turned out to be their two looms, which they started to assemble. I suppose it took them about a fortnight to three weeks to rebuild their looms. The majority of their work was in making braids, fringes, ropes and cords to match antique ones. It might take them anything up to a day or two days to set the loom up to weave a piece of braid possibly about eighteen inches long.

Gordon Beecham

They came through the docks. In Leman Street, there was a shelter for those who didn't have anywhere here to go to – the shelter took them in and looked after them. They were specially for if you didn't have anyone. Usually perhaps one family came over here, and that one family brought all the relatives, all the cousins, and all the relations – they all came to someone. And they all clung together – they all used to meet in the synagogue. There were so many synagogues, there was one in every turning, all down Commercial Road.

Jane Smith

Most of our contemporaries came from parents who were immigrants from either Russia or Poland; they left home in their youth to get away from pogroms and the Cossacks who would ride through their villages pillaging and destroying people's humble homes. They left their parents, fully realising they might never see them again.

Vicki Green

I remember coming over. Mother was with three children – there were two boys and myself. The agent would meet you at every port or station or whatever. We went by train as far as Bremen from a little village between Brody and Lvov. Mother got lost in Bremen – my youngest brother wasn't very strong and she carried him over her arm – she was twenty-six or twenty-seven – and everybody ran to meet this agent and mother couldn't run with the children. And she was lost.

My brother was older than I, he was like my mother's husband; she always used to say Sam was her husband, he looked after her on the journey – a boy of seven. And she said to my brother, 'I've lost the people we're supposed to meet. What am I to do?' My brother said, 'Well, let's go into that shop.'

I remember the girl was jerking some lemonade into a glass, and my mother could speak German, and she went in and she began to cry and she was very agitated, and this girl said, 'Just sit here for a while, and perhaps they'll come and look for you.' Which they did. The agent was just as anxious to find us as we were to find him. She was so overjoyed at meeting this man that she took his hands and kissed him. Then we went on this cattle boat – that's all I can describe it as – and there were a lot of girls from Hungary going to America and they took me under their wing.

Mrs A

My mother came to London about 1905, from Bialystok in Poland. She came to some relatives who lived in the West End and used to relate to me that she was treated just like a servant. However, she got to know some friends and eventually went to live in Folgate Street. My father came from Latvia; he had really intended going to America, but could only afford to come to London. Of course, it was near Tower Bridge that he disembarked. He spent a couple of nights in a shelter and then found employment with a bootmaker.

We lived in that part of Brick Lane that was primarily Jewish – there were non-Jewish families in the street, but very few of them. There was a Georgie Vincent who lived in the most terrible poverty that one could really depict, with his sister Katy and his mother, who had one eye. I happened to go up his place one day and saw that they slept virtually on the boards, with a rickety table and just one gas ring. He used to put on the lights at the synagogue and put them off at the onset of Saturday, on a Friday night, and come up to my mother who would often give him tea and cake. I would sometimes speak, and even go for a walk with Georgie Vincent – I was not exclusive.

Jack Miller

There's a lot of deception that went on around immigration. The people who moved them said, 'Where do you want to emigrate to?' and they said, 'To America.' So they got them aboard this ship and it stopped at London docks, and they thought they were in New York.

Victor Leigh

My parents, I suppose you could call them refugees from Tsarist Russia. My mother was born in Riga and my father in Grodno, which were both parts of the Russian Empire, and they came here in the 1890s. The first thing that my father did when he got here was to wait all night in Ludgate Circus so that he could see Queen Victoria when she drove to St Paul's on her Jubilee – that was 1887. He became a great patriot; he realised the privileges that Englishmen enjoy which he didn't enjoy. He was a studio photographer. He started in Russia and then he came to the East End – as so many people did from there – and he had relations here, and they had a shop, and they let him use part of it as a studio.

My parents were foreigners and remained foreigners, although they spoke broken English as well as they could. My father used to read a lot, but he didn't speak like he read. None of them were citizens of twentieth-century London, so to speak, none of them knew what it had to offer. They lived a completely isolated, ghetto existence, like a bit of Holy Russia of the 1890s plonked down in Whitechapel.

Charles Poulson

I can remember a Rabbi telling me, 'Do you know, when I first came to England, I fell on my knees and I was kissing the earth. Where I came from in Russia, I was frightened to walk through a street in case I was going to be arrested for doing nothing. But here you can walk about, you can laugh and talk, and no one's going to touch you here. What better place can you be in than in England?'

Florrie Passman

It was all Jewish people in our area, all immigrant families, and most of them couldn't speak English. Our parents spoke to us in Yiddish until they got a bit older – and my mother was a very forward-thinking lady, but she never got the opportunity to go to school either in Russia or here. She learnt quite nice English, of course, with an accent, but she never had the opportunity to learn to read or write, so she couldn't read a paper.

Vicki Green

Broomhead Street, off Commercial Road, gave us the impression of a little village town somewhere in eastern Europe, because it was mainly populated by Jews. There was a synagogue in the street, there was a kosher butcher, a greengrocer and fruiterer and a newsagent and tobacconist; there was a cobbler in the street, and they were all Jews. There were tailor workshops at the bottom – it was a dead-end street, and it was very, very cosy. They all spoke Yiddish among themselves.

Anna Tzelniker

I lived in Hoxton, and my mother was born in a place called the Jago. My father was born a bit farther east, he was of Huguenot descent, but my mother was Irish and Jewish, my grandfather was a Jew, my grandmother was Irish. On my father's side, they were French and German, so I'm a bit of a cocktail, you know. But I didn't know my grandmother was a Jew until just before my mother died, and it was a dark secret, a dark skeleton in the cupboard, never spoken about.

Louis Dore

The Perils of Puk a Poo

London's first Chinese district grew up in Shadwell but later became better known as a distinctive part of Limehouse, along a street called Pennyfields. This was the forerunner of today's Chinatown in Soho. Chinese seamen arrived in England from the eighteenth century when they worked for the East India Company in a lucrative trade that took opium

© Museum of London

'In Soho one can eat Indian or Japanese, but for Chinese food, you most go to Limehouse' says this Illustrated London News report – which describes the district as 'law abiding' and the eating houses as 'very clean, frequented largely by sailors and stokers ... the better-dressed ones would be stewards.' Samuel Begg, 1920

from India to China, where it was sold to buy tea, which was then shipped to England. In the nineteenth century, fast tea clippers such as the *Cutty Sark* raced home with the tea, and sailors who were paid off at the end of their voyages often chose to remain near the docks, ready to take a new ship.

In Pennyfields, they created their own community, with shops and cafes selling Chinese food, as well as cinemas, barbers shops and famously, gambling houses where puk a poo was played. The name means 'white pigeon ticket'; the story behind the name is that as gambling was illegal in China, winning numbers were delivered on tickets carried by pigeons. Because most of the immigrants arrived through work there were few Chinese women, although occasionally one could be spotted, recognisable by her hobbling gait, the result of the old Chinese tradition of foot-binding. Many Chinese men married local women, particularly from the Irish community, and became to a large extent assimilated into the East End.

In the 1920s, when the ships used to dock in the West India or East India docks with the Chinese crews, and the ship had to be unloaded and have things done to it, they crews were victualled in the local boarding houses. My father used to be in charge of all the crews while they were in London and give them their pay on behalf of the shipping agency. My father went to college in Hong Kong, the same one as Sun Yat-sen, and he spoke English fluently and wrote English.

Connie Hoe

Chinatown was in Limehouse in those days – it's now in Soho. I had quite a lot of Chinese girlfriends, well, half-caste Chinese girlfriends. Mostly the fathers were Chinese and the mother was either English or Irish; the girls came to the same school as myself.

Pennyfields was all little shops and restaurants – well, not restaurants, cafes, I suppose you'd call them. I vaguely remember seeing a very old Chinaman with the queue – the pigtail – with a round hat and pigtail. There were Chinese laundries down there; there were puk a poo gaming houses.

In Pennyfields there was a Chinese barber who was called Tipperary Tim and he was wonderful because he looked just like Buddha, he seemed to have about six chins and was very short and very, very wide, and he spoke a sort of sing-song Chinese with a very pronounced Irish accent. Apparently he had jumped ship, sometime before he came to Pennyfields, he had jumped ship in Dublin and, of course, learnt his English with a very pronounced Irish accent. He was the barber that my brother used to go to. I think he used to charge threepence.

Lucy Collard

The thing that was Chinese that my father introduced me to was his tong, which was his club. It had a billiard room in it, and I could go in there and play billiards with my father, and I would then meet all his friends. But they had a secret prayer room, and it being a secret society, there was things going on there that I didn't know about – although I remember a great big painted god on the wall, and the usual sand with the joss sticks in, in a brass urn, and some fruit piled up in little pyramids.

I used to take some of my friends home sometimes and they'd come out of curiosity expecting to see my Chinese father. They'd see him – if he couldn't get work – he would do a gambling game for the general public, like bingo, called puk a poo, and they'd see him there with his brush, taking in these bills and doing gambling for the general public. They wouldn't see us eating with chopsticks or eating Chinese food. To our own minds, we were English.

Leslie Hoe

In about 1939, getting towards before the Blitz itself started, I had a Chinese friend, and with one of two of my other friends, we used to jump on the back of the horse and carts going up the High Street, Poplar, towards Limehouse. Peter, the Chinese chap, he used to go and see his auntie in Pennyfields, in the Chinese Seamen's Union, and there was a picture there, I always remember it, of Sun Yat-sen on the wall. Us three or four lads would wait outside the door, a very dingy place, and Peter would go in. He'd get half a crown from his auntie and we'd buy a pineapple.

We'd go next to the old Limehouse Police Station; there was a big Chinese seamen's restaurant called the Treble Seven. Peter would go down the cookhouse, one of us trailing behind him, and he would buy a couple of *han bail*, which is a form of Chinese meat pudding and *chang wing* – these were filled with chicken and all good meats and succulent juices. From there, we'd go to Sam's soda bar in the West India Dock Road and we'd get an American soda between us, and from there we'd go into the Ideal Cinema which was completely bombed during the war. It was a Nissen-hut type of thing, galvanised roof, and one used to sit on wooden seats. With your ticket, you'd buy some sweets, a lucky number, with Chinamen all around you and all the local riff-raff. And this is all on half a crown. The four of us would have a whale of a time.

Dick Allington

In the Chinese quarter, Pennyfields, it was nothing to see the taxis would draw up at a house, police would all pile out, go into a house and drag out some Chinese – English chaps as well – playing a game called puk a poo, it was called. It was like a bingo card, I'd say, with all Chinese letters. And the idea was that you'd get a brush and you'd mark off these things. And you could win quite a sum of money – I'm talking about £25 to £30, see, which in those days was a lot of money. Our week's wages as a messenger boy was 14s 5d a week; a labourer, he got about £3 at that time, in 1926.

William Abbott

The information my father got from China was through his countrymen and local people coming in to England on the very boats that drew in alongside his town. They used to come ashore and come to our house and tell him what's happening; he used to go and visit them on board their ship, and I can remember my father bringing bolts of silk as gifts from his native town, and chairs, woven chairs. And he'd hear information about his family and he would know the personalities there. Because, as a child going aboard a ship with him once or twice, I can remember them all being very friendly with each other and him saying, 'This is my friend.'

Leslie Hoe

We used to go up Charlie Brown's, to the Chinese places to play puk a poo, that was a gambling game. I don't know whether it still goes on now or not. They used to go to 47 Pennyfields, that was the puk a poo place. You'd go in and you'd get a disc, a little piece of paper about six inches square, and there'd be forty characters in the top, forty characters in the bottom, Chinese characters, you can't read them. And you'd dabble ten of them. Ten at the top, ten at the bottom. They used to cost you sixpence at the top, sixpence at the bottom, and if you got five right, when the results came up, every hour they used to get the results through, and when it came, it had ten marked off out of that top forty. If you had five that corresponded, you got your money back. If you got six, you got ten bob, and I think it was £4 if you got eight, and it went up to £80 if you got ten. I don't know anybody ever got the ten. Five and six, I've had many times. I've taken Mum back there of an evening to get the results, see, 'cos they used to call them banks, starts at twelve o'clock and there'd be results at one, two, three, right up till ten o'clock. So you could put your characters on for one race, or one bet, or write ten bets, right till ten o'clock at night, every hour.

And the Chinese, when they was writing, doing these characters, they never used a pen, they used a brush. Oh, they was clever, and when they used to do the writing, although it was a fat little brush it had a very thin tip and they write just as neat as you.

Walter Dunsford

Chinatown, they had knuckledusters hanging up for sale, you know, four rings – and they had the tongs down there, Chinese lot. Chinatown, yes, all the prostitutes; they had a big police station there, and they needed it.

William Mather

My mother died in 1930 and my father went back to Hong Kong because his father was dying and, as he was the eldest son, after his father died he was asked to stay in Hong Kong to run the business. When his sister asked him about bringing me from England to Hong Kong he said that I wouldn't like the life there as I was at school so I was brought up by my mother's friend who was almost Victorian in her attitude.

Connie Hoe

When they had a Chinese funeral, the kids used to line the road and the Chinese always threw money to the children; they used to scramble for the money.

The cinema – there was a cinema there called the Ideal,

next to the Blue Post outside. I took Mum there one night to see a film. We was up in the gallery. And when the lights went up, we were the only whites in there, they was all Chinese. Frightened her.

Walter Dunsford

There was very little name-calling – I think people with ginger hair were called more names than I was. If you're different, children will pick on this but by and large I think we fitted in almost unnoticed.

They only time we got a few remarks is if we were misbehaving ourselves. At a certain time of the year, at the back of one of the newsagents, there was a mulberry tree and we used to climb over the wall and pick his mulberries from the edge of the wall, and I remember his wife saying something like, 'Get away, you Chinese so-and-sos – and especially that one on the end.' And that was my poor friend who looked more Chinese than anybody.

Leslie Hoe

Processions and Pugilist Priests

There were substantial Irish communities in Whitechapel and scattered throughout the East End, especially on the Isle of Dogs. The Irish immigrants were not connected with the shipping trade but had first come to London many years earlier, the first colony, known as 'Little Dublin', being established around St Giles, near Charing Cross Road, before 1800. During the nineteenth century, there was plenty of labouring work, especially on dock and canal construction – navigation projects that gave Irish labourers the nickname 'navvies', which has stuck to this day. By far the biggest influx of poor Irish families came after the failure of Ireland's potato crop and the great famine of 1840–50.

The Irish were part of the East End's large Roman Catholic community, and their religious celebrations and processions contributed what seems to have been a universally popular free form of entertainment. Their tough, community-minded priests and extended and often excitable family networks offered another form of street entertainment.

Within the dock industry, at least two-thirds of those employed in it were mainly of Irish extraction. They were mainly sons, or some were born here, of those who came over either to construct the docks, or were driven here by virtue of the bad conditions that existed in Ireland arising from the famines of the 1840s.

Maurice Foley

My mother's grandparents came over from Ireland. Her parents lived in the borough, as well as my father's, and they all worked on the river. When the river was being built for the docks and all that, a lot of Irish labour came over because of the various problems in Ireland. It was a very large Irish community in this borough, but it's not so much now because a lot of them have gone.

Bernard Alger

My mother's family were stevedores and like a lot of the stevedores, their roots were in Ireland. The family came over in the famine in the 1840s and settled in Poplar. They had three rooms; it was an upstairs, house in Lochnagar Street, which cost seven shillings a week at the time.

George Adams

Because the bridges were built over to the docks, it made Wapping more or less an island, and the population was shanty Irishmen, because they were the people who more or less built London docks. No Jews was allowed over Old Gravel Lane Bridge – if they were ever caught over this side, on the Wapping, they were chased back again.

John Henry Arnold

The processions – generally they had one in May, Our Lady's Procession, they called it, and one in June for the Blessed Sacrament – they had them through the streets and they generally collected from the pubs and all round, and they did the houses up in great style. The night before, nobody went to bed, the pavements were all whitewashed for the edges, Sophia Street and Wood Street – they're all gone now. Every Catholic home had a little altar with Our Lady, and there's a great patriot, Robert Emmet, and he was nearly always on it – I think he was executed for high treason or something. The bands were a great thing, they played Irish airs.

Sister Pat O'Sullivan

There was a Catholic priest there. I always remember his name was Father Didi, and he used to turn the corner and the dockers who hadn't got a day's work, well, they'd be tossing up halfpennies and pennies, tossing up coins round by Charlie Brown's. He'd chase them with his umbrella. I suppose most of the dockers were Irish. You'd see them run and this old father bloke chasing after them.

Walter Dunsford

I remember watching a family who lived a little bit up to the north of us, and the family next door to them having a row. These two families were Roman Catholics and they were having a fight and throwing things over the backyard fence and things were really getting going and the fence collapsed and so somebody decided to send for the priest. Well, the priests were always sent for on these occasions and their coming was coincidental with the arrival of the police. Into the backyard came the priests and the police and then after a halt in the proceedings, when peace seemed to be established, everything started again with the result that not only were the two families having a fight, but the police and the priests were having a battle among themselves.

Tom Stothard

The Men in Pyjamas

The London Metropolitan Archives has a painting of The Strangers' Home in Stepney. It shows a large red-brick building which opened in 1857 to provide 120 temporary rooms for 'the natives of India, Arabia, Africa, China, Straits of Malacca, the Mosambique and the Islands of the South Pacific'. The picture shows a number of strangers, including Indian seamen known as Lascars – the word coming from Persia via Portugal, and originally meant a guard or soldier, later a sailor – wearing their distinctive white tunic and trousers. These sailors had been coming to the Port of London since they were first employed by the British East India Company in the 1600s and their pyjama-style clothing was a familiar feature of the East End. At the beginning of the First World War, there were more than 51,000 Lascars in the ports around Britain. Also familiar to the average East Ender were Sikh pedlars with their tins of toffee, and African and West Indian doctors of whom there were a number working in the East End.

Lascar sailors had been arriving in the East End from the Indian subcontinent since the seventeenth century, but never formed a clearly identified community. Rather than marry into East End families, most returned home at the end of their working life.
John Penry-Jones, c1920–50

We were accustomed to seeing sailormen generally, and Lascars, who were employed on the ships, they was a common sight walking about the East End streets. The thing that sticks in my mind was that they seemed to have a penchant for soap. You've heard of Sunlight soap? They used to make great long bars of that soap, packed in a cardboard carton, and they would be going along in their droves, dressed in their Indian costume, with flimsy cotton *dhoti* wrapped round them, and sandals, and they'd be over here in the middle of an English winter and their skin used to take on the same hue as a well-dressed East End man in his Sunday blue suit. I was always amazed at the fortitude of them. Some of them could speak pretty good English and they were pretty good at bargaining. I used to go round the local markets and they'd offer a man who was selling goods, he'd say, 'That's sixpence ha'penny,' and they'd offer him fourpence. And he'd say, 'No, no,' but they'd keep pushing it and sometimes he'd give way. They were expert bargainers.

Cyril Demarne

I first became aware of the docks when I was about six or seven, I suppose, in that my father took me to Petticoat Lane Market, a Sunday market, and I noticed a lot of, to my mind, people dressed in pyjamas. They were, as I later found out, Lascars, and due to their religion, they were dressed in white trousers with a white smock. I asked my father who they were and he said, oh, they were Lascars and they came off ships in the docks, and he said he would take me down one of these days and show me the ships.

Especially in the East India Docks, you could see all the Lascars on the ships. What I thought was strange was that all these Lascars at Petticoat Lane were buying live chickens and just carrying them by their legs upside down and they were taking them, and I asked my father what they were doing with these chickens and he said, 'Oh, they're taking them down to the docks and they're gonna have a meal.' So they used to come up to the Sunday market to get their chickens for their meals. I remember seeing on quite a number of these ships, you could see chicken coops and goats actually on deck.

Gordon Beecham

I remember being in the Albert thirty-three shed, just this side of the bridge, and it was a big day, a lot of Indians going back to Bombay somewhere. And up come one crowd with their hats on, and while the chief was there, all the others behaved themselves, but it got so many tribes that I couldn't follow – I was the only one there in uniform, 'cos I wasn't very busy and I was watching the boat go. There was one policeman keeping them in charge.

Anyhow, the trouble was, they all had their chief Sabis, you know, and they were behaving themselves while he's telling 'em. But all the time, they was drinking whisky. And this was all right. Then all of a sudden, all the old coaches come up, and all the trains come up, they loaded the ship away and started pulling out, and once the ship starts to pull out – this chap with this crowd, he's keeping them in order, but this crowd over the other side, they was insulting the old chief, and that was going on all the time. Anyway, once the boat pulled away, it was like a punch-up there, like the Bombay riots, and I'm in the middle of 'em. All up the dock. There were fights everywhere, all up and down the Albert Dock itself.

Charles Beck

It was when I was in the general office as superintendent's typist that I had the typing to do with the Lascar who murdered the other one as a vendetta. Apparently it's a vendetta that had gone on for generations and he thought he was doing the right thing in murdering this chap, and then of course he was taken to court over it, and there was one person in the general office who could speak his language, so he represented him, and I had the typing to do with it. And he couldn't write when he was first charged, and he just put a cross where his signature should have been, but later on, by the time he was hanged, by the time that happened, he could write his name. Which seemed to me to be rather a waste, teaching him to write.

Doris Salt

These people were very poorly paid. Down the High Street, Poplar, these Asiatics – Indians, they was, like Pakistani type of people – they'd go in to buy something to take back to India. What they used to like to take back was sewing machines. You'd see 'em always walking back with a sewing machine under their arm. When they used to pay for them, they used to undo their handkerchiefs, and it was all knotted in the corner, the few shillings that they had. They'd like argue and argue, they like bartering, and you'd see them always walking back with overmantels, sewing machines, regular, back to the ships. And you'd see them on the decks; they couldn't get them below sometimes. You'd see big overmantels, big old-fashioned things, they used to take back to India.

Walter Dunsford

Lascars, obviously, were the lower life of the ship, to do all the work, and you saw them all walking about. It always struck me that they were terrified of the white man – they were a half-starved sort of people. But they never ever even looked at you.

Florence Mugridge

At Tilbury, my dad was based at number thirty-two shed, which was an enormous shed – the P&O boats were all lined up at thirty-two, thirty-three, thirty-four berths, and before you approached the quay, one came across what looked to be a huge Nissen hut, and that housed the Lascar crew from the P&O liner, because they employed not English stewards, but Lascars. The were very good people, and my father used to place me in the hands of the sarang – he was the chief, sort of the captain of the Lascars, and his word was law. He would cut a man down with a knife – it was very primitive, you know, and death didn't mean a lot to them. They were very tough people. But they were rather lonely men too – they were away for many months and they all had families in India – and to see a little girl of three, with bright red hair, approaching in a summer dress, it was perhaps reminiscent of their own children, and they used to beg to be allowed to have me. So I would be taken off, and my father knew I would be quite safe, and he would leave me for an hour, go aboard a vessel and then come back and find me festooned possibly with cherries, you know, around me ears, in pairs, and it really was a nice introduction to the docklands, a very happy recollection.

Elizabeth Garrett

CHAPTER 5

The World of Work

The Work My Father Did

Many East End industries have ancient origins. Since medieval times, any process that produced unpleasant fumes was forced out to the east of the city, and the smells of tanning and brewing were still perfuming the East End in the twentieth century. Costermongers are mentioned by Shakespeare, and remained ubiquitous in the East End; they transported food from the huge central markets – fruit and vegetables from Spitalfields, meat from Smithfield and fish from Billingsgate – to sell off barrows and carts in the street.

In 1614, the East India Company started work on a shipyard at Blackwall in Poplar – this meant that boats did not have to navigate the great loop of the Thames round the Isle of Dogs – and the Blackwall Yard was still repairing ships 350 years later. The Blackwall wet dock became part of the West India Dock when it opened in 1802, and after the proliferation of docks throughout the nineteenth century, the Port of London Authority became the East End's biggest employer, providing work for about twenty thousand people a day, including porters, dockers, stevedores, lightermen, divers, coopers, clerks, rat-catchers, and even cats.

Many other London businesses grew up because of the docks, the gateway through which raw materials arrived – coal, timber, animal skins, food, spirits and 97 per cent of the nation's tea. Finished goods, proudly stamped 'Made in London', were shipped out to the rest of the world.

In 1801, there was just one furniture maker in Shoreditch, but by the end of the nineteenth century there were hundreds of small workshops around the area. Whitechapel's garment-making industry, often referred to as the rag trade, began with Huguenot weavers and later gave work to thousands of Jewish tailors. All these jobs, and many more, contributed to the life of the East End.

———•———

I was bound apprentice to my father as a waterman/lighterman in 1935. My father's father was born in 1861 and started work at the age of nine as a call boy on the citizen steamboats. When I came afloat, the old boys that I worked with – and some were eighty years of age – they remembered my grandfather and when they knew that I was from his stock, quite a number of them would say 'Twickenham Ferry'. Because in those days, before gramophones and radio, a man was known by the song he sang when the men got together. And it seemed that my grandfather's song was *Twickenham Ferry*. And so I was the grandson of Twickenham Ferry.

Edwin Hunt

My father was a labourer; he used to work on a farm at one time. He had all manner of jobs. He came from Devonshire, with his brother, they came to London. They were both strong drinkers, but William said, 'I'm getting married, I'm packing in the drink.' And he did. He got a job with the Post Office and was pensioned from the Post Office. Father had any job that was going. He was a devil-may-care sort of chap. He was a good father, and he finished up with the Port of London, working on the maintenance, building and any job that was going there.

Charles Lisle

Bananas being unloaded at West India Dock by porters, overseen by a foreman, identifiable by his bowler hat, and watched by what looks like a newspaper reporter – perhaps preparing an article on the work of the docks. Bananas arrived green, and were ripened in warehouses. PLA, c1935

My father was a self-educated man. He was quite good. He could even write Spanish, and that only started because he worked Middleton's Wharf and the Canary Islands' boats – their manifest was in Spanish. He used to mark out the ground for the stuff, so there were parcels of different foodstuffs. Might be tomato season, and he'd know where the ship was and who was receiving them, so when they had enough, he'd let them know – Smithfield Market, Covent Garden. He'd get on the phone and tell them whether they'd got enough for a load, to get it on the market early. He made it his business to know what every word said and he got a book from the library on Spanish and he got quite fluent with reading and writing Spanish. Lovely handwriting he had, so he was one of the scholars of Wapping. If there was a list going round, they'd say, 'George, make out a subscription list for me.' Or if they had a form to fill in, they'd come round. He was an apprentice bookbinder, and he went from bookbinding to cutting out overcoats, to gold beading, and he finished up as a dock labourer.

Jack Banfield

My father was a meat porter at the Smithfield Meat Market. They used to work all night and used to drink a lot of rum – as a matter of fact, it was over that that he had a coughing fit and broke a blood vessel in his throat when he was about forty-eight, and I was only ten years old.

Harry Plum

My father was a stevedore; before that he was a strapper, which is vernacular for a deal porter. Before that he was in the army, and the only thing I can describe him as before that was a racing cyclist. He used to ride a fixed-wheel bicycle in a team called Crystal Palace.

Norman Grigg

My father's father was a tanner at a place called Temple Mills and he used to do the hides. Fellmongers they was known as in those days, and my father obviously followed his father into the business. He had six sons and a daughter; everybody went into the fur trade. It was just done natural.

Terry Loveday

My father was employed at John Stewart & Sons, the ship repairers, and also for a time in Green's Blackwall Yard. He would often take me at the weekend to John Stewart's yard where, if the machinery was stopped, I could go up into the travelling gantry and manoeuvre myself along the rails up there, much to the alarm of my father when he caught me doing it. You'd see the great lathes being turned with a complete crankshaft in it, and one little man carefully tending all the work and the cutting. One thing about him was that nobody interfered with him at all – he would set up his own work, he would grind his own tools to his own satisfaction, and there you saw this little man with this great ponderous crank going around and around, glasses on the end of his nose, stopping every now and again with his micrometer, measuring up to see how he was going.

Tom Stothard

My father would go out in the morning carrying a big pack on his back. I think at one time he had a horse and cart, then I think he had a tricycle, and after that, I think he just carried them on his back. He went by train – workmen's train, he used to go by – just to places like High Wycombe, perhaps a thirty-mile radius of London. He'd go by the early morning train and come back at night. He sold linen, tablecloths, towels, socks, sheets; haberdashery. He got on very well with the people he went to, this foreign, Jewish man – he liked them and they liked him.

Miss M

My father was a French polisher. He used to work at Brick Lane, all round the Shoreditch area, different places. My father used to work very late at night – my mother left us when we was younger, left my father and me, my brother and sister, and he used to work late at night. I used to take him sandwiches and a bottle of tea in a sterilised bottle round about eight, nine o'clock at night.

Arthur Nouvall

I used to take my father his dinner when I was about eleven, straight from school, and when I was fourteen, in 1917, I started working for him as a turner. In those days you worked from eight o'clock in the morning till seven o'clock at night, and Saturdays till about two o'clock.

George Wood

When it was in season, my father could stay in the workshop all night. And he didn't tell us, and I had to go and find out where he was working. He sent us a postcard, but he got home before the postcard was delivered. He was working somewhere in a side turning in Leman Street. I had to go there and find out whether he was all right, and take him some food.

Mrs G

My father had a particular trade – the walking stick trade – which was diminishing, so he went and got a stall in Petticoat Lane. When he died, my mother and my eldest sister took over the stall. We had to live near there because it wasn't like the stalls of today, where you have stables and stabling – you had to pack everything up completely and bring it back. Part of my job was to come out of school and wheel it, stacked up, on a home-made trolley on old bicycle wheels, back to the house in baskets; old fish baskets which we used to clean. She used to sell hosiery: stockings, socks, handkerchiefs – all drapery of those days, and I used to carry that back.

Mr U

My father was an old-time railway employee basically working as a shunter in the docks around Blackwall Tunnel and the railway yards associated with the East India Docks. Didn't have a very rich life, in the late Twenties, early Thirties; it was very poor indeed in one of those two-up, two-down sort of three-shillings-a-week-rent houses.

Albert Patten

All my family were publicans – every man in the family was a publican; they knew nothing else. It was just: when you leave school, you're behind the bar. We had no thoughts of doing anything else. You wasn't allowed to do anything else, really.

Mary Ridgeon

My father owned an off-licence and grocer shop which was open from 8 am till 10 pm, so it was a long day. My mother helped in the shop and they really did enjoy the shop and being in contact with the public. But it had quite a severe effect on our upbringing because we didn't see too much of our parents.

Eileen Brome

My father was a Hebrew scholar of some great ability; he could quote you the Hebrew Bible by the mile. After his business failed, instead of an employer, he became an employee; he worked as a photographer in someone else's studio, instead of running his own. He earned £2.10s a week, never got more than that. Even when he transferred to a studio in Knightsbridge, a fashionable one, he still got £2.10s, which was the going rate for developing and printing.

Charles Poulson

It used to be an outing – my father would take us to Spitalfields, used to put us on his barrow. He used to push us, you know – oh, I can picture it now. There was certain turnings that knew him. He used to call out, you know, 'Cucumbers', if it was cucumbers that day, and they knew his voice. He was a very old man, you know. At that time, the people were very old looking; they were very, very old – they all came from Russia.

Jane Smith

My father was a no-good man, and he was a master painter, hanger, decorator and he could have took us to work because I have known him take work doing a pub out, the whole of a pub, and being paid in drink all the time so at the end of the job, he had no money again. Everybody said yes, a lovely fella, yeah, course he was, outside, in drink, but at home, no. He was a bad man and therefore we were starving.

Stan Rose

I slept in the same room as he worked. He had one long table where all his tools were, placed in a special order. And he would come home, and he would be drunk and he would clamber up the stairs. He would light his three paraffin lamps – he would trim 'em first, then light 'em – put his work in the vice and commence work. And perhaps an hour afterwards, you would hear a gentle whistle, and then he would be singing to himself. He was really happy when he was working. Invariably, if he had the money, one of us, every hour or so, would be sent out to get a pot of Burton – this was a strong, dark beer. We'd fetch it home, hot up the poker, and put the poker in the beer. This gave it strength. That pot would probably last an hour or so, then the next pot would be got. So he would continue. There were times when he worked nearly all night. The happiest times was when he was working; this was really the happy times because the workshop became a community centre. If I went to bed, invariably Mother and the kids would come in, all sat down somehow and with Dad singing or talking, it would be a very close association. The trouble was when he wasn't working; not when he was.

Bill Crook

A Boy as Big as a Man

Wanted: a boy as big as a man to pull a barrow as big as a van.

– EAST END ADVERTISEMENT

After leaving school, officially at either eleven or fourteen, boys started work as soon as they could find a job. If your father couldn't sort you out at his place of work or with a family member, the usual policy was to walk around looking for a sign in a shop window advertising for a 'strong boy'. The 'strong' was not just a turn of phrase; these jobs meant long hours and often back-breaking manual labour. They were often short term because it was cheaper for employers to dispense with your services and take on someone younger when you grew out of an errand boy's wages. For this reason, the ideal first job was an apprenticeship where you could learn a skilled trade: coopers trained up barrel-makers, shipwrights instructed platers, and furriers started as fur-nailers. The drawback to an apprenticeship was that you needed to pay money up front to be taken on and, for the seven years that it took to complete your apprenticeship, you were on the lowest wages, so it was not an option for the poorest families. If you did secure an apprenticeship, as the new boy, your role would include all the worst jobs, plenty of tea-making, and a few practical jokes to help you settle in.

It was a father and son industry, particularly in Stepney. You was either a son of a stevedore, a son of a clerk, or a son of a docker, so therefore you had cousins, and there was this salutation when you saw one another: 'Wotcher, me old coz.' Just like the breweries, the daughters always followed their mothers into the brewery industry, or their fathers and their sons. This is what the family industries do.

Jack Dash

I had to go to work at eleven. They had need of an errand boy who, besides running errands buying nails, screws, glue, varnish et cetera, could also put his hand to a bit of sandpapering. Who else but me? As my father, with perfect rationality, pointed out, I was already in the top class and couldn't be taught any more. I was working class and should be proud of it. How did I think my family was going to manage with me at school until I was sixteen or even eighteen, with no income from me?

Louis Dore

When I left school, I tried for several jobs – it was the Thirties and the Depression was just slackening off but everywhere I went there were no jobs. So my father took a hand then; he knew that people came out at half-past two out the side of the Criterion, the Savoy, Claridge's, and he'd go to each hotel in turn with me and wait for the head chef to come out and say, 'Chef, have you got a job for my boy?' And it worked; I got a job with the Bristol Grill Ltd, which was quite a big organisation – unfortunately, it went bankrupt.

Leslie Hoe

I was advised to go to the Jewish Board of Guardians and ask them if they could find me a job. They were very, very good. They found you a job. I could either be an optician, cabinet-maker, or a furrier. I choose to be a cabinetmaker because I had some experience of it and didn't find it altogether objectionable. They gave me a job in Chadwell Street, off Bethnal Green, and they gave me an envelope to take to this employer. When I saw him, I got a bit frightened; he had red eyes and looked fierce, but he turned out to be a kindly man. He signed me up for four years as an apprentice. I could read English and write English and he couldn't, so I was useful to him. He had a bank account which made me think he was a worldly man, till I went to his home. He had hardly any furniture there, he had a houseful of kids. He looked fierce and spoke in a gruff voice, but when he saw I had no father, he was very kind. Every Jewish holiday, he'd buy me something to wear – a pullover or something like that – outside of what he had to pay me.

Alfred Alexander

When I left school at fourteen, I just took a job that my parents found for me – I think my mother found it. They had no particular ambitions for me, I don't think – I simply started as an errand boy in a shop, at 109 Lower Clapton Road. It was a booksellers and a stationers, a fancy goods shop, and I was the shop boy there and I had to open up the shop and clean the windows and sweep out the shop, deliver goods to the customers and generally make myself useful in the shop. I started eight o'clock in the morning and used to finish at eight o'clock in the evening, and on Fridays it was half-past nine and on Saturdays it was half-past ten. I used to have an hour to go home for the midday meal, but otherwise I was there the whole time.

John Sleap

This was a period when the suburbs were developing. People were moving out. There was a firm called Drage who had a big shop in Holborn. Now, Drage's were the first to start selling furniture in a plain van, a shilling a week. It always had to be in a plain van so nobody knew where you came from. I used to take some of the furniture down to Drage's on a barrow, which we used to hire for sixpence an hour. I'd get in the front of the barrow between the shafts, like a horse, a rope around my middle, and pull it all the way from Shoreditch Church straight down Old Street to Holborn.

Alfred Alexander

My first job was what they call bottling and it was raw lime juice and rum. There was two separate vats and we had to mix the rum with the lime juice in a tank and draw it off into bottles. It was for sailors in the Royal Navy.

Sidney Bell

My father came home one Saturday morning and said to me, 'I've got you a job, it's at the top of the street at Harland and Wolff's.' There didn't seem to be any messing around with careers in those days – they were times of Depression and you just took the first job that came along and were really glad of it. Anyway, I reported there on Monday and was sent to South Dock, West India Dock, where the hoppers and dredgers of the Port of London were laid up for repair. I went to work as the chargehand fitter's boy – the shipwright fixed me up a little desk in the wheelhouse of hopper number fourteen and I was more or less in charge of writing out the work, writing labels to put on machinery, giving out and collecting time cards and running messages down to the Port of London wharf.

Another boy was taken on at the same time to dish out the tools and the gear, and at lunch time we used to take the ship's boat and row up West India Dock, and I remember that

Scott's ship *Discovery* was moored in the centre then and we used to bump alongside and peer up to try to look through the portholes.

Laurie Landick

I left school in 1924, and I used to go through the streets, in the way we all did, till I saw a notice in a shop window saying 'Boy wanted'. It's not very progressive, but that was all we could do. They used to use you for shop cleaning and messages and things like that, until you were about seventeen or eighteen and needed more wages, and then they sacked you and replaced you. That was the usual type of job... If you wanted to learn a skilled trade you had to become an apprentice which was still a seven-year business, and you had to pay a premium for that.

Charles Poulson

I got a job at Mann Crossman Brewery through one of their travellers speaking for me. I used to start at six in the morning till five, for twelve shillings a week. They started us boys in the box-knocking shop – the old boxes would come back from the pubs and we would have to pull the old wire off and put new boards in, and it was exceptionally hard work for us boys, with our soft hands gripping on pincers and bars.

I was sent to the brewery in Whitechapel Road down in the vaults where for some reason they wanted to count the barrels as they were filled and stowed away in the vaults. My job was to sit outside this door from the racking room and tick them off as they came. Well, the men resented it because now and again they'd roll a barrel round to their canteen and they thought I was there as a spy. So what they would do was to mix barrels up with firkins and throw a few pins – that's smaller ones – in between so as to get me moggadored [confused]. At the end of the day, the foreman of the vault would count them all that had been stowed away and he'd come up and check them with me. But rarely was I wrong. I was pretty smart, actually, at catching them.

Alexander Gander

When I was fourteen, I was forced from home to go as a pageboy in the Thatched House Club in St James's Street, in Piccadilly. So you can imagine how I felt at fourteen being sent away from home and into that type of life. My wages was seven and six a week so I used to be able to send me mother home a few bob a week.

You were up early in the morning and you would clean all the tables with Brasso – they were brass table tops – and go to do all the cleaning round the club. Members came in roughly ten o'clock onwards all day, and you would assist them with their coat, you would run messages for them. Sir Steve Donoghue, the famous jockey, he lived in the Pall Mall which was off of St James's Street. He lived over a gunsmiths, and he actually came in one day and I got him a taxi and he give me sixpence as a tip. Naturally, me going in that place, among gentlemen, so much of it rubbed off on me, because remember, I was fourteen when I went in there, and then I worked in a hotel, and naturally, the hotel was gentlemen and high-class type of people. When I came from there back to this environment in the East End of London, I'm going from one extreme to another. I wouldn't swear and so forth – and naturally, I had many, many a fight, but I am a determined type of fella and I can honestly say that I think I won more than I lost.

Stan Rose

When I was fourteen, fifteen, I used to run papers for the old *Star* in them days. We used to get paid ninepence a quire – we had to sell twenty-seven papers to get ninepence. I used to run from Bouvedeer Street, that's in the City, up Queen Victoria

Street, to Mark Lane, to sell eight quire of paper, and I'd have to run back. It was a penny a paper, in those days, selling. Them days, it was every race the *Star* used to put a paper out, see. I'd take the first race, miss the second, and get the third race and run another quire of papers up, see. But you had to run backwards and forwards all the time to nearly four o'clock. At four o'clock, we'd stop at Tower Hill for a break until about quarter to five, and a bloke used to fetch our papers up on a bike – seventy-four lots of papers on a bike, and we'd get two quire of papers each.

One day I remember when I was running from Bouverie Street with a quire of papers, a City policeman grabbed hold of me and he said, 'You're arrested.' I said, 'What's that for?' He said, 'Shouting in the City,' which was forbidden. So he took me up Snow Hill police station and I got a summons. I had to appear at the Mansion House to see the Lord Mayor of the time. He was sitting there and he fined me two and sixpence.

Sidney Bell

My father was in the coopering trade, his father was in it, and I followed suit. My father, he just asked me if I wanted to follow the trade, and I said yes and it started from there. For the first year you just help cleaning up in the shops, sweeping the shavings and different things like that. I started the apprenticeship at sixteen, but I started at the shop at fifteen so I had one year just learning little odds and ends, you know.

John Ardley

I left school at fourteen, that was the age we used to leave school at, and I always knew that I wanted to go into tailoring. Might have been because my brothers were in it, I don't know, but I had a sort of a flair for clothes, you see.

My brother was a cutter; I wasn't. My mother made him go and learn cutting and I wanted to learn cutting – years ago, just before the war, there used to be a school called the Parisian school of cutting in Whitechapel – it was a good profession at the time. That was one of my ambitions, to learn cutting and to be able to do a complete garment on my own. When I went to learn, they told me I'd have to have £10, to pay, but I never had no money. So I thought to myself, if I'm working and I put away something every week, when I have the £10 I can go and start learning cutting. I nearly had that money, then unfortunately, the war broke out, and of course they closed up, and that was it.

Joe Morris

When I was fourteen I went into the fur trade and became what they call a tubber. The name originated because to get the grease into the pelt – there was no mechanical kickers, as they are now called – a man would have to get in a barrel and trample the grease in with his bare feet. He would keep turning them over with his feet and jumping and pushing them and grinding them until he pushed the grease into the pelt, and he was called a tubber because he never came out of the tub from seven to seven. They always put me in with the pine marten, and pine marten have got a lot of claws which are very painful. Apparently this is what you do with all the apprentices – you learn the hard way.

Terry Loveday

So my father said to me, 'What do you want to do?', so I said, 'Well, I want to become a lighterman.' In the end, he came home one Saturday afternoon a little bit 'wine-ey', because they finished early and he said, 'Right, you want to be apprenticed, I'll apprentice you.' So in December of 1939 he apprenticed me to lighterage and I started. I was fifteen then, and so I was apprenticed for six years. If you started at fourteen, it was a seven-year apprenticeship, six years at fifteen, and five years if you were sixteen. The first day was a Saturday, and we was up at half-past four. My father was on a shift boat, a sixteen-hour boat; we walked down to Blackwall Pier, which was about fifteen minutes' walk, and started work at six o'clock. The first day's work was fourteen hours, till eight o'clock at night I did, and I was so proud I wouldn't wash me face, wanted me mother to see me dirty.

George Adams

The office of Locke, Lancaster and WW & R Johnson in Millwall was really a Dickensian place with huge sloping desks with high chairs. I was sitting next to a Mr Green – he was a brilliant pianist and he was always muttering to himself that his wife was trying to murder him. My first job was in the assay room – we used to have to take a sort of brazier along to one of the furnaces to get it filled up with hot coal and light our own coke fire where we used to do fire assays. That first day I had in the laboratory, when I went out to get this coke, I was hit in the eye with a lump of coke. It came over from another office boy – they used to get behind this big mountain of coke so that when we went in to get ours, you'd be assailed with lumps of coke flying in all directions. So there I was, with a big black eye, trying to read these scales on a fine balance.

Charlie Gubbins

You started at eight o'clock. When I say you started at eight, you were standing by – you didn't have a bench, you had a jig – with your apron on and your hammer and they used to come out of the office, which was on stilts so they could see all round the workshop, and they'd bang a whacking great circular saw. Crash! it used to go, and you started your machines up.

Ten o'clock, a boy used to go out with jam jars; you'd buy a ticket for cocoa or tea or coffee, jam jars and a big tray. Ten o'clock, you'd sit down on your jig where you was, and have

– you might have bread and ham, bread and cheese, whatever you had. Ten past ten, bang went that saw and you started work again. And this applied at twelve to one, and whatever our tea break was, and at five o'clock the old governor used to come round, well, he was the foreman – manager, like – and he'd say, 'Working late tonight, Jimmy?' He'd call everybody Jimmy; he was a Scotsman. Say, 'Yes, all right; what, eight or nine o'clock?' – but you couldn't refuse the overtime, 'cos they'd sack you.

Walter Dunsford

I walked out of school. I was the only Jewish boy in the school. I wasn't quite fourteen and I went straight out and got myself a job in the fur trade – the same day. I saw this board saying 'Strong boy wanted' – this was in the City, I think it was St John's Road, and I walked in, and I was quite a strong boy, and they gave me the job.

My job was to learn fur nailing. They used to make a lot of fur collars and fur capes, and it was my job, when the skins were sewn together, I was supposed to wet the garment, put it down on a chalk base and knock nails round it. So I became an apprentice fur nailer, from nine in the morning till six in the evening. I got a pound a week. I gave it to my mother and she used to give me a shilling.

I was given the usual treatment of a newcomer – they sent me out for pigeons' milk, rubber nails – I think I never went for the rubber nails but I did go for the pigeons' milk; they sent me to a cafe. The women working on the machines were always very coarse towards you, because you were a kid, but on the whole, I quite liked the atmosphere.

Emanuel Litvinoff

I joined the Port of London as a messenger in August 1923, aged fifteen. After a few weeks I was drafted into what they called the City gang. Here, you reported at eight-thirty in the morning, made up your turn, as it was called, and at nine o'clock you would deliver letters to one quarter of the City, be back at ten minutes to twelve to have your lunch and be straight out at twelve to do another part till three, and then you would work until you were finished which was generally something around about five o'clock. Another gang, four boys, would go out at ten o'clock, and the third gang would go out at eleven o'clock, so a gang of boys was going out every hour to do one part of the City.

This was absolutely a wonderful express service for the PLA to get letters written in the morning and delivered the same day. Unfortunately, the PLA's trade was expanding at a tremendous rate and nobody thought that they needed any extra messenger boys. Parents wrote in; one parent I remember writing and saying that their lad was a growing lad, he was losing weight; and I myself was an absolute bag of bones. It took about, I should say, six months to get used to this endless walking.

Laurie Landick

One of the things they used to send you for as the youngest apprentice, you'd be sent round to the fitters shop, the platers shop, the blacksmiths shop, for a bucket of A holes, and you'd go round, you'd go to the fitters shop and he'd say, 'Oh no, we've run out, you go down the stores.' You'd go down the stores, he says, 'No, we haven't got any, try the platers shop.'

In the stores, they had a big old diver's suit. Not the modern diver, the old big brass helmet and a great big weight. And the foreman – that's what made it so bad – our foreman came into me. 'You're the next one to do the diving,' he says. 'You go in there and try that suit on'. Cor, it turned me up. Upset me. I goes in there and they tried this blooming suit on, they done the helmet up, done face plate up, put – when they put the weights on, of course, I went over – with the boots, I couldn't walk.

I come home that night and I tell my Dad, 'I'm not going to have no apprenticeship, Dad, I'm packing up.' 'Don't be a bloody fool,' he said, 'they're only pulling your leg.' But they were so true, and the foreman sending me in, I believed it and I really made myself ill. I wanted to get out of that place.

Walter Dunsford

Another time in the West India Dock, I was getting all the punishments. So I go up the wood wharf, and I caught a pigeon, a little rook, and I've got it in my satchel, ain't I. Well, as I've come back, I had to go past the typists' room. So I've got this wood pigeon, and I've opened the girls' door and I've slipped it in and then shut the door quietly and I've come back and sorted out messages.

All of a sudden, ding, ding! I go down there, 'cos I know what's happening. And they say, 'There's a pigeon flying about in here, he's flying all over the place,' see. I said, 'All right, all right, don't worry, I'll catch it.' So I've gone round and after a lot of struggle and that, I've caught this pigeon.

So the head bloke, he used to sit in the middle on this big dais, he's got all us boys lined up, ain't he. 'Who put the pigeon in the typists' room?' No one knew anything about it, see, I didn't tell them nothing. So he said, 'Right, someone's done it – now you're all going to suffer for it if you don't own up.' So I didn't take no notice.

He said, 'Who was the boy who caught it?' So I said, 'I was, sir.' 'Right, go to the messenger's place.' So I was eliminated. Now none of those left knew who'd done it. They've all got punishments; buckets of coal to take up, late nights, early mornings. I ain't got none – I've got rid of all mine, ain't I?

Alfred Green

Young Girls and Single Ladies

Unless they stayed home to care for young brothers and sisters, girls were also expected to get a job when they left school. If they left at fourteen, the main jobs were cleaning or domestic work, working in a shop or factory, or in one of the many East End sweatshops. Many women left work to raise children after marriage, but most returned to some form of paid employment at some point – to supplement an irregular income, to replace their husband's lost earnings during strikes, or because they'd became sole breadwinner after being widowed or abandoned.

At the end of the nineteenth century, nearly half of women who worked were employed in domestic services, but the First World War opened up new opportunities. Women drafted in to fill posts vacated by men serving at the front showed themselves capable in all kinds of positions. The creation of the School Certificate in 1918, and the expansion of office work meant that if girls stayed on at school and gained a certificate at sixteen, they were eligible for a more comfortable type of employment. Large organisations such as the Port of London employed numerous female secretaries, as long as they were unmarried; in many businesses, marriage meant the automatic termination of employment (this was legal in England until the 1970s). However, it was not uncommon for women to simply remove their wedding ring and tell no one.

———•———

At about ten to eight, you'd see a stream of girls running as fast as their legs could carry them down Worship Street to get there in time, because if you didn't get there on the dot of eight o'clock, the door would be shut in your face. And more than once I got shut out. Only for the morning – in the afternoon you could go in.

Mrs L

Factory girls outside a 'hot joint' shop where they could get cheap midday meals. The initials in the left-hand window refer to a couple of friendly societies, and LCTU, on the right, is the London's Carmen Trade Union, a forerunner of the TGWU. c1910

You would go up Leman Street into Whitechapel, get the bus down to the Commercial Road. Now, you'd sit on the top of a bus and all the sweatshops you saw. Girls sitting at their machines, crowded like that, just able to move their material. You could buy a good dress for three and eleven, so you can imagine, can't you, what their wages were. Terrible conditions, absolutely dreadful, the sweatshops. All along Commercial Road.

Florence Mugridge

Suddenly there was a boom in cigarette making, and all around the mothers were saying 'Oh, it's a good trade, and they can earn lots of money.' A lot of the English Jewish girls went in for this trade because there was money to be made. Actually, it was slave labour, it was all piecework and you had to work like a devil to make two thousand cigarettes by hand. The quickest girls could do three thousand a day – £3 a week. I earned about £2 roughly, 'cos I could only do two thousand a day, sometimes not even that. I liked to have a chat with my next-door neighbour, and I liked to laugh and joke about. It's very monotonous, terribly monotonous work. I mean, you think of nothing while you're rolling these cigarettes because you do it automatically. You do get backache, and the smell of the tobacco gets up your nose, and you get terrible catarrh. It's horrible work.

Mrs L

I liked working at Tate & Lyle's because I could look over the docks from my window where my machine is. I used to look into the docks and see the ships coming in and going and the dockers all coming out at various times. We used to have little social evenings, dancing. We used to be two till ten, and at ten o'clock then we all used to rush up and have a little last hour in the dance. And when we was six till two, we could go early.

Anne Griffiths

We'd get fed up with a job – two or three girls would all get together, like they used to, and we'd walk down the lane and see an advert – say, blousemakers – and we'd go in there, 'cos there was no employment cards in those days, and we'd go in and get a job in there. All in Petticoat Lane that was. And we do it perhaps three or four months and we'd say, 'Oh, we'll have a change,' you know.

Alice Humm

It was a small place: there was a presser, machiner, two tailors. There was a governor, there was me, there was a buttoner. They weren't shops – they just took a room to work in. We used to get the work from the City. You go to the shop and bring the work back in bundles, cut up – they were cut in the shop, you see. The shop had a cutter and you used to bring it back in pieces, and those pieces had to be put together. We worked from eight till eight, and if there was no work, we didn't work. When you sat down to work there was no time off – you sat down, you had a cup of tea, and one hand you sewed, the other hand you had a cup of tea – you didn't have time off.

Jane Smith

I had to leave school when I was fourteen because my guardian said – well, her attitude was that education was wasted on girls. I wanted to learn shorthand typing and bookkeeping and work in an office, that was my ambition at the time. But if you left at fourteen, you had to do menial jobs in offices or work in shops.

My friend also left school at fourteen and we got a job in a press cutting agency in Fleet Street – I think it must have been through an advert and my friend's mother took us up there. My friend didn't like it so she left and took a job in a menswear shop but I stuck it out for some time. This agency had clients – say it was a film star – and you had to read the papers and everything pertaining to their clients had to be cut out the newspaper and collated, and all these cuttings were sent to these famous people.

Connie Hoe

When I first went to Lebus's I was a sort of sweeper-upper; I'd clear up in the spray booths. But then I got a job on the new runway – a runway is a moving belt where the furniture comes to you, you spray it, then it went away from you. I was fifteen when I first started to spray. Somebody showed me how to do it, and the very first bed I was put on, Mr Solly Lebus came and stood behind me – I was scared and I couldn't pull the trigger. There were no men sprayers at that time – all women, and very friendly. We began at eight in the morning, till six at night, with ten minutes for tea. We had a canteen upstairs, one side for staff and one side for the workers. There were no holidays, other than one day in August, Good Friday and Easter Monday. If you were ill, you were ill.

Sissy Lewis

I was under a worrying time because I'd left school without the character that was given to you by your headmistress or headmaster, so the upshot of it was I had to work in several places until I was sixteen. I then wrote after a job, which was office work. When the gentleman at Brown Brothers, in Shoreditch, read the letter, he sent for me and asked me if I wrote it myself and I said yes and he said, 'We're going to give you a chance to start in our office.'

Pat Thompson

If you had a Jewish name you couldn't get a job easily, except in the East End, so they had to start altering their names. Anybody who was Sara became Sally; if your name was Becky, you were Betty or Beatty. One of my friends was Esther Cohen, or something – lovely name – and she changed it to Stella Collins. She was in an office and if you were in an office and you lived in the East End, you were really somebody.

Miss M

Then I went to work at the Royal Mint. We had a tray and there's a long table with about eight girls sitting around, and we had a basin with gold in it, and the pieces of gold were about the size of pieces of rice, some smaller or maybe a bit larger. We had a tray and several lids that reminded me of cocoa tin lids, and we had to put a certain amount of gold in them. We had a balance, and it had to be exact, in fives – five, ten, fifteen, twenty. A very important civil servant was in charge of us. He never ever spoke, all day long. He just used to be getting on with things. We were each given a tray and our little lids, there was about thirty-five of them, and the balance had to be dead on; we had tweezers to take little bits on and off.

This girl next to me went to hand her tray to this big civil servant, this very, very posh bloke, and she dropped it. As he went to take it and she gave it to him the whole lot went right over me, showers of it, it never stopped coming. And I had loads of hair – it was the fashion then – great big hair all done up, and it was all in my hair. I was all afternoon, they was taking gold all out of everywhere. But as I say, I've been literally showered with gold – there's not many people can say that, is there?

Anne Griffiths

Mr Rowlatt, the managing director, he was a bit of a perfectionist. He wrote the most beautiful English, so that you couldn't make a mistake, and he used Latin and Greek phrases in his letters. I don't know who understood them when they got them, but the Latin phrases I was able to look up, but the

Greek symbols I had to leave a space and he'd put them in by hand. He was a Greek scholar so I suppose it wasn't done in any flamboyant way, but it really gave him pleasure to be able to do it. I've often thought back to our little homely firm, with these letters going out with Greek and Latin phrases in them.

It really took you quite a long time to type it back – we only did two or three letters an hour – three an hour, I think, we used to time ourselves, and that was really going hard, hand typewriters and you were working all the time. You might have a minute or two just to chat but very little here and there. We clocked on with a card that you put in the time machine – I don't think we clocked off though.

Dorothy Shipp

My first job was at Burrell's, I was on the enamels, filling tins – small tins, half-pint tins, pint tins, quart tins, then they used to have so many gallons. My job was to do the tins – fill them, paint the tops and label them, pack them in cardboard boxes and then we had a man come take them away and they were packed in caskets. Where I lived there was no bathroom at home and every Saturday after I finished work, I used to have a bath at work – they had a big bathroom with about two or three baths in there, so you always used to say, well, I'm having a bath after I leave off work, and that was it. We wasn't in the firm's time, we had it in our own time.

Burrell's itself was very nice to work in. It was run by three brothers – they were very nice and you'd come through the floor and they always just nodded their head, they did acknowledge you. We worked eight o'clock in the morning till six o'clock at night, lunch break from one to two. We used to take our dinner with us and we had a lady to heat it up for us when we came down at one o'clock. We had a proper dining room and we used to have a break in the morning for a cup of tea. My mum always used to have our dinner all ready for us before eight o'clock in the morning in the old-fashioned car – it was a red handkerchief with dots on it. Just imagine us walking along the street with our dinner. Thought nothing of it – way of life in those days.

Annie Pope

I got a boyfriend at that time, who was coming to London to be a policeman. So what did I do? I borrowed my sister's *Nursing Mirror* and started looking for jobs – I was a very forward young woman for that period of history. I thought, Right, I'll go to London as well, and I'll be a nurse. I saw 'St Mary's Hospital for Women and Children' – and I thought, That sounds a lovely name. I think I'll write there. So I wrote and was accepted.

In 1938, I went to St Mary's Plaistow, which was a hospital for women and children only. At that time, there was an epidemic of dysentery, or d&v, in the East End, and new nurses, at eighteen, always started on the baby's ward, so I and another girl from Wales started together on that ward. And in the first week, ten children died – babies, only tiny. Of course, we were devastated – all day, we used to have tears running down. In those days, nurses used to take the babies – porters used to take the grown-ups, but the nurses used to take the babies – to the mortuary downstairs in the basement. And we used to have to carry these babies down to the mortuary and join them with all the others that were lined up. We used to be weeping and weeping.

Elsie Edwards

I worked in what was the wool department. We had an office – the wool department was great open warehouses stacked up with bales of wool which came from all over the world, and our office was above that. See, it was coal-fired, so we had a man who saw to the fire bringing up coals for us, and he was very nice indeed to us. It was a very cosy atmosphere. When you look back, no wonder you had all these pea-soupers that you come across. All the offices, well, everybody all had coal fires going all the time – there was no other heat, was there?

Florence Mugridge

The outside work was done in the offices by all these men; they all sat at long desks, one row in front of another, about six to a desk. And each desk dealt with a specific item of the work that was done in their docks. I became friendly with the pay clerk – who better, of course? – who was very kind to me, because one or two of the men did take silly advantage of us and tried to catch us out with their talk, which I didn't understand in those days. However, he was often about to protect me and when I left we got married, which was rather nice.

I left the PLA at the age of twenty-two to get married to George Brome. I had to leave because the PLA, as most other big companies, didn't employ married women. So I had to stay home. But as my husband had a little girl, who was my stepdaughter, I had plenty to do. We'd only been married about eight weeks when the war broke out.

Eileen Brome

The worst thing that could happen to you in those days, and it did happen, was that you were given the sack. In those days, a lot of companies were not allowed to employ married women. There was unemployment and they wanted the men to have work. There was I, getting married in May 1940, and not allowed to let them know that I was married. I married on the Sunday and it was a bank holiday and so we had two days' honeymoon, Sunday and Monday, and then I had to remember to take my wedding ring off on the bus going to work.

Vicki Green

One of the girls that was there, unfortunately, she committed suicide. She married, and of course, you weren't allowed to marry in the PLA. But actually, it turned out that three of them did marry. Because you weren't supposed to get married, I wrote to the PLA and said I was getting married and could I keep my job on, and they said, no, they were very sorry, when you married, that was it. But these three were married and one was the typist for the general office and she lost her husband and was losing her sight and she couldn't take it – she took an overdose. When she'd taken the tablets, she realised that she didn't want to do it, and she rang her son, but by the time they got her to the hospital, of course, it was too late. She couldn't face up to the fact of losing her husband and then losing her sight – it was very sad, really. We didn't know she was married.

Doris Salt

The Hazards of Working Life

> *'In those days it was Wooden Ships and Iron Men.'*
> – WALTER DUNSFORD

Industrial accidents resulting in permanent disability or death seem to have been accepted as an inescapable fact of working life, particularly in the London docks. Here, heavy goods were constantly being moved through great heights: from the deck of a ship to the bottom – known as the ceiling – of an empty hold was several storeys high. Add to that sharp hooks, noxious cargoes, unstable platforms over water and even escaped animals, and the possibility of injury was ever-present.

Both in the docks and elsewhere, such were the physical effects of many labouring jobs that workers could be identified by specific work-related disabilities. These included the

This part of North Quay in the West India Docks was nick-named 'Blood Alley' because the coarse, sticky sugar being transported between transit sheds and warehouse caused the porters' skin to crack and bleed. Above the porters, the washed sugar sacks are hung out to dry. 1930

fatty humps that timber porters developed on their shoulders, the sugar-loaders' permanently clenched fingers, and the dyed skin of paint workers. Other conditions were less noticeable, particularly the internal damage caused by breathing in air-borne particles and chemicals.

Other industrial hazards were the jobs that affected your home life by rendering you unpopular back home – because of dirt, the way you smelled, or even the after-effects of working long hours in 'cold pot' – the refrigerated areas of the docks.

My father had an accident on one of the wharves – my mother thinks it was up Wapping Way – he was laying the gratings in the barge ready to receive the cargo, and he was lying outside a barge that was being loaded and the crane driver made a mistake and he went and loaded a set of cargo on top of my father and his back was damaged.

I remember, as a child, after he'd got better, seeing this compressed fabric jacket, like a tailor's dummy, in the cupboard, which Mother used to strap him into. And so she had two young children to look after and me father to dress and he was out of work for about eighteen months.

George Adams

My mother's father was a lighterman and he was drowned, just before one Christmas, I suppose it must be sixty years ago. They think he must have been walking along or running along the gunwale of the barge and it was icy and he slipped and fell into the water. Lightermen in those days used to wear Melton overcoats which were very, very heavy, and although he had been a champion of Wapping, he was drowned.

Lucy Collard

About this time I managed to fulfil my life's ambition and married my wife Esther. She'd had a very interesting war – her father had been an 'old contemptible' and had been all through the Great War, and he was employed in Tate & Lyle's as a fitter, and he was in the vat one Saturday afternoon when somebody turned on the live steam, and then that was the end of my wife's father.

John Henry Arnold

Chris Cobb was a boilermaker and he also did plate riveting on the ships in the graving dock, and his brother-in-law, Sid Howe, he was also in the trade. The remarkable thing is that just about the same time each lost an eye as a result of riveting – Chris was a left-hander and he lost his left eye, and Sid Howe was a right-hander and he lost his right eye. But I believe that afterwards they formed up a pair when doing the repair work.

Tom Stothard

It was all hard manual work, pushing, pulling – and many men of course had bad backs and ruptures, and it was caused through pulling on heavy weights. They used to wear wide flannel belts round their waist, thinking it was the cold that was causing it, but it wasn't – it was this heavy pulling and lifting the wrong way, which we found out in later years.

Alexander Gander

On the timber wharf, the deal porters, they'd get hummies – that's what they called them, hummies. Those chaps that continually do that job, there's a big lump of fat on their shoulder. You could feel it, big as your fist almost, over their shoulder there. It was a sort of corn really, I suppose, from continually humping these planks around, great big stacks. It's higher as you go up – used to be about forty feet off the ground.

William Abbott

When we worked in the Portuguese boats, and they had 'em a lot, we used to have a mile of asbestos sheets, rock asbestos, as they called it. After each ship came in, you had to sweep up the hold, you know, and bag it all up, all the dust. Used to do that. We never thought of it being horrible. But I was courting a girl once, Lou Brown, and she worked at the Cape Asbestos, Barking – smart girl she was. She died with asbestosis. Now that was in an enclosed space, a workshop. It killed a lot of people.

Alfred Green

I was a boat boy down at Spencer Chapman's at Silvertown where the sulphur barges were discharged and the cargo was used for making sulphuric acid. The most strange thing about it was all your money first of all would turn black. Secondly, if it was blowing a bit fresh, the dust got in your eyes, it made them very sore. And it was generally a sort of uncomfortable feeling bodywise, like an irritant more than anything else.

Jim Penn

The men who worked regularly on sugar, through lifting the two hooks, their fingers would be bent and crooked and you could tell if he was what we called 'a sugar eater' by his hands when he went in the pub and picked up a glass of beer with two hands, you see.

Long iron used to come from the north-east coast and men who worked on the ships all had fingers missing. The iron would be picked up by the winches and the iron chains, taking five or six ton, would be thrown underneath, and men would have a long piece of strip iron with a hook on the end to pull the chain through to save putting a hand under. Well, many men sometimes chanced it, and a piece dropped and several as I knew had their fingers chopped off.

Alexander Gander

On three occasions I've been down a ship's hold where chaps have got killed. One occasion, a chap just got engaged, a ginger-headed chap he was, and he was telling us about it. We finished work in this ship's hold at about two o'clock in the afternoon; we're all climbing up the ladder to come out, get a breath of air. As I was climbing up, suddenly I felt behind me, something patted me on the bottom – you know, like, who's that? Looked round, there was this ginger chap across the tunnel, where the screw goes through the propeller shaft, lying across there, dead. He'd fallen off. Climbing up, he must have slipped, his hands slipped off the ladder and as he went by me, he just touched me on the back, like that, you know.

William Abbott

One day, about sixty hives of bees were placed in number five shed waiting to be shipped to Spain. These created a lot of interest and many people came to see them. One bright spark wasn't satisfied with seeing a few stray bees flying around and crawling about. He prized the opening off one hive with his hook. 'They're dopey,' he said, 'they won't sting.' Then the insects began to crawl out. It was a lovely sunny day and when the bees felt the warmth and stretched their wings, they began to fly around everywhere. The first to get stung was the chap who opened the hive – he had very long hair and it was soon full of bees. He panicked and ran around trying with his hands to get the bees away – it served him right when a few got down his neck and gave him a few more jabs. Many more people got stung as the bees flew around the sheds and the quays. There were bees everywhere – I never imagined that a hive could contain so many.

Alexander Gander

Over in Silvertown, I worked for a paint firm, and I was very scared of the lead content in the paint 'cos so many blokes used to get this lead poisoning, and their hands used to go like this. Oh, you had to be careful with it, industrial disease. Another job I had just before I got married, I was there for about two years and we used to do hundreds of tar barrels over there, and we had to be very, very clean there, because we used to get what we called 'pitch warts', which were a cancerous growth, and these pitch warts had to be treated with radium. If you wasn't very clean, you were bound to get one. We used to be smothered up in blessed tar, repairing these casks, and we used to have to wash our hands in creosote and then scrub them afterwards with soapy water. You daren't go to the toilet. You had to wash your hands and scrub 'em before you even went to the toilet – it was laid down rules. Ones who got them, I don't think there was any cure – I know one or two blokes, one bloke had 'em on his nose – of course, working, he'd been picking his nose sort of thing. Another one had 'em in his ears. I know one had 'em all down in his privates. Oh, you had to be careful and clean.

Henry Harington

My father worked as a photographer... It had an effect on his health, for his fifty bob a week, because he had to spend ten hours a day in a dark room, surrounded by stinking baths of chemicals, illuminated only by a dim red glow, and it more or less killed him in the long run. He was an invalid for the last eight, ten years of his life and to be an invalid in Old Montague Street is not very pleasant, especially if you live on the second floor – it is very hard to get down the wooden stairs.

Charles Poulson

The company must have made a profit with the colour pigments because they opened the Barnfield Works in Millwall. When they changed from paints over to colour, they wanted the men to come from the paints into the colour, and they wouldn't – they left – they didn't like the colour getting into their system. It's a stain – just imagine you're looking at me and I'm like a Red Indian – eyelashes, eyebrows, your face, everywhere is colour. You can never wash it off. It was a colour stain that stained you. On your body, if it penetrates through the clothes, what must your insides be like? When they was mixing all that colour together as it was going into the vats, the men used to wear masks, same as the women below, but then it penetrates. And there was a silver which they used to use and while they were blending and mixing it the men used to wear the mask and we were supplied milk because of the danger. When I was filling out into tins, I used to have milk that particular day. It was supposed to cure you, if there was anything gone down into the inside.

Annie Pope

When I first left school when I was fourteen, I went round the tobacco factory, Rothmans. And I hated it. The smell. And I said to my mum, 'I can't stand that round there; the smell's terrible.' So she said, 'I'll go round and see them.' So she went round and saw the bloke and he said, 'If you give her a glass of milk every morning, she'll be all right.'

Eileen Gibbons

I was in the fur trade here and there, until 1935, and I was heartily fed up with it – it was having a very bad effect on my health, it made me very hoarse all the time. Doctors advised me to leave it because the air in these small, unventilated backstreet workshops was always full of floating hair and dust, and the skins were dyed and treated with poisonous substances and things like that.

Charles Poulson

Lampblack was a curse, it was a processed powder which was taken from the smoke of burning oil. It was brought to us in paper bags and the bags used to weight about thirty-five pounds. You can be sure you used to be very, very careful when you handled this. If you trod on a bag, it burst, and it only needed one bag to burst for everybody to be black as Newgate's knocker. It spoiled your clothes, it got in your underclothes, it got in your socks and your shoes and, it doesn't matter how many times you polished your shoes after that, you'd never get rid of the black. If you bathed, it never got rid of it. And the sheets and blankets where you slept were always fetching out the black that you put there. One man, his wife wouldn't let him in. She said, 'I'm not going to let you in till you clean yourself up.' So he said, 'All right, I'll sleep in the fowls' house.' And he did, he slept in the hen coop. He threw all the chickens in the run and pulled the shutter down and he slept there all night. That was a really bad episode in a man's life, when he had to go and work on lampblack.

Norman Grigg

In making tellurium alloy, the thing was to put metallic tellurium into the lead which was then fused at a high temperature to form tellurite, and you had to be very careful with the fumes of this. Men used to come to me and I used to tell them to wear a respirator, but if they didn't, the effect was to inhale this fume and it was a hundred times worse than garlic – so much so, that their wives refused to sleep with them. I remember I told one of our research people, I warned him about it and he didn't take any notice and he came up to my office one day and stood in the doorway and I could smell his breath. When he went home that night in the Underground, everyone gave him a very, very wide berth – and it takes about a week to get rid of it. I tell you, the wives would not sleep with their men because it was so terrible.

Charlie Gubbins

Working in a 'cold pot', a lot of men avoided it. It was a hard job and it was freezing cold. One of my mates was sent there and he was a good worker. He'd work on cement for ten days he never gybed the job – on sugar, he'd work – but one day he was sent there three times running and he gybed. So the dock board wanted to know why he'd left the job, you see. He didn't show up. So the welfare officer had a chat with him. He said, 'Now, look, you've done all these jobs you've never gybed, and everybody regards you as a good worker. Why don't you like going to the cold pot?' 'Well,' he said, 'it's the old woman.' 'What do you mean, the old woman?' He said, 'Well, when I get home at night,' he said, 'after being in the cold pot,' he said, 'I can't raise a gallop.' So he was excused. But the welfare officer said to him, 'That's all very well, but how do you think the Eskimos get on?'

Alexander Gander

You had a lot of accidents in the docks, you got men falling down the holds, you see. My husband had to go and see a wife one day, whose husband had fallen down a dock hold and been killed. And she said, 'Oh, miserable bugger – and we were going out tonight.'

Florence Mugridge

The Silvertown Explosion

During the First World War, there was a great push to convert factories to the manufacture of armaments. In the East End, the Green & Silley Weir shipyard at Blackwall was taken over for the repair of naval vessels and the Lusty factory in Limehouse was used to turn out ammunition boxes. In the face of objections from its owners, part of the Brunner Mond factory in Silvertown, which had produced caustic soda until

1912, was hurriedly converted to the manufacture of TNT which it churned out a rate of nine tons a day. The girls who worked there were easily recognisable due to their yellow hands and faces; these were caused by the picric acid used in the manufacture of TNT. Apparently, the effect was not harmful – it lasted for about a month – and it earned them slightly higher wages in compensation.

In January 1919, there was a massive blast at the factory, razing to the ground every property within four hundred yards. Flying molten metal set alight two flour mills and a ship in the dock. The fact that it occurred in the evening accounts for the comparatively low death rate of seventy-three, along with four hundred casualties, but nearly nine hundred properties were destroyed and about seventy thousand damaged. It is said that the explosive force nearly blew over a taxi in Pall Mall and the noise of the blast could be heard in Sheringham on the Norfolk coast, more than a hundred miles away. Among the deaths was the factory's chief chemist, Professor Andrea Angel; the youngest victim was Ethel Elmer Betts, aged four months. Compensation for damages ran to nearly £1.5 million.

———— • ————

The Silvertown explosion – the chap that was in charge, Professor Angel, he was in charge of a new thing that'd come out, TNT, they called it, I think, that was the new thing they was working on. And that afternoon, there was a big train load that was along the siding, and Silvertown right down, waiting for the train to be took away. And as luck happened, it was taken away that afternoon, before the thing blew up at about ten to seven.

Charles Beck

Flour mills on the edge of Royal Victoria Dock. Owned by Britain's three largest milling companies, the mills processed imported grain. They were among the 70,000 buildings damaged by the Silvertown explosion caused by the wartime manufacture of TNT. John H Avery, 1917

Man in charge, that was Dr Angel. In fact there was loads of rumours afterwards that he had something to do with it, because it was during the Great War – World War I – but that's only ever been rumoured, there's no proof of that.

Stan Bryan

No Londoner of those days will ever forget the dreadful consequences of the Silvertown explosion, the glare and thunder of which was seen and heard as far away as the outer suburbs.

Louis Dore

I remember sitting on the floor, undoing my shoes, ready for her to come in, clock had just turned ten to seven, and undoing me shoes, looking at me mother – 'cos the blackout wasn't all that stringent, like it was the next time – had a big, black shawl across the window, because we only had candles and all that. All of a sudden, she's looking up – she can hear rumbling upstairs, like somebody pulling the beds around, you know? I remember her saying this. And it turned out the blast was already affecting up the top, and the next minute all the soot started coming down the chimney, everything went black, and before we knew where we was, we was all blown up the passageway, in front of the front door. And I'm looking back, and I looked right through into the scullery, and you could see the red glow of the fire. We were opposite there – we were practically opposite Brunner Mond, where we lived at Hill Street, on the other side of the dock.

Charles Beck

My first year at the PLA in the Albert Dock, we were working till seven and one evening, there was a jolly loud bang and it was the Silvertown explosion and we lost three of our staff who were working. As far as I know, there was quite a number of casualties in the civilian population. We were lucky really because between us and the explosion, there was a large ship on the north side of the Albert Dock, and also on the south side, and they were both loaded, which stopped the blast. Even so, our tank in the office burst, and there was quite a flood. We all packed up work, caught the tram to East Ham, and home. It was quite exciting.

Herbert Hollingsbee

I remember looking up the passageway and seeing the back door hanging off its hinge, and the glow of the fire. Then my mother was saying, 'Well, go and see how Jim is.' My brother Jim's laying in his coffin in the front room. And, course, the house is blown to bits, near enough – when we go in, the windows are all out, the curtains, such as they were, was flapping on the ceiling, and Jim's laying there all serene – I remember that. The funny part about it was, of course, being Catholics, there was two candles at the end of his coffin, and even though everything of glass had gone, all the lights, all the windows, the flame was still like that – it didn't even flicker. And I remember my mother saying, 'It must be his faith.'

Charles Beck

My father was on that Silvertown explosion, clearing that up, all the mess there. Saw that blaze from a distance, from our back garden that was about five or six miles away, and all. We was living in Chad Street, Plaistow and had a very long garden, all open – I learned to ride a bike in this garden – and when we saw this blaze going up, he said, 'Crikey, that's where I work,' 'cos he knew the distance. He said it was, oh, a horrible experience he had, finding the bodies and all that, clearing up the debris. He wasn't a man who talked much, my father – got on with the job, you know.

Charles Lisle

Brunner Mond was one of the factories on the riverside, but where the actual explosion was was right close to the roadway. My sister worked just the other side of the roadway, inside the dock, in a sort of shed affair, where her and the girls used to be stitching up the sandbags. And they'd made a collection for my brother, for a wreath and they had it in a tin, in the office. The heat of the fire was so bad that what was in the tin – this here's some pieces of it, a two-bob bit, a florin – you can see that the heat melted all the stuff together. The office had escaped the full blast, being little, but the heat of the fire melted it all like that.

Charles Beck

CHAPTER 6

A World of Struggle

The Demon Drink

'Work is the curse of the drinking classes.'

– ATTRIBUTED TO OSCAR WILDE

Given the precarious finances of most families in the East End, it was easy to be tipped over the edge into poverty, and one of the key tipping points was drink. When Lloyd George was appointed Minister of Munitions in the First World War, he said, 'We are fighting Germany, Austria and drink, and as far as I am concerned, the greatest of these foes is drink.' His main concern was the effects of drunkenness on production in munitions factories – many of which were in the East End – and one of his first acts was to reduce the previously unrestricted opening times of pubs to noon to 2.30 pm, and 6.30 to 9.30 pm. He also introduced a 'No treating' order, forbidding drinkers to buy rounds. This was easily circum-navigated; men would simply offer friends a matchbox containing the price of a drink, saying 'D'you want a light?' After the war, the restricted hours stayed in place, but pubs within a certain distance of a market could stay open twenty-four hours a day for market traders.

Pubs were not just places for convivial drinking, they also operated as unofficial recruiting offices for trades connected with the port and river. Many pubs, known as six o'clock houses, continued to have special dispensation to open early for men waiting for a day's work, and easily the most famous in the East End was Charlie Brown's, on the corner of Garford Street in Limehouse. It had a legendary collection of strange souvenirs: a two-headed calf, a mummy that was half-fish and half-baby, poisoned arrows, African masks and odd things in bottles. Charlie Brown died aged seventy-three in June 1932, having been the landlord since 1893. His body lay in state in the pub, the Railway Tavern, surrounded by more than 140 wreaths, and 16,000 people were said to have lined the streets to see his cortège arrive at Bow Cemetery.

———————

Charlie Brown was quite a character. I never went in his pub because I was too young, but apparently he had bits and pieces from all over the world. You know, the sailors perhaps didn't have enough money, by the end of their being in London, and so they would give up something – some of the things they gave up were quite valuable in there. He had quite a lot of clocks in the pub as well. You used to see him riding round on his horse in the morning and as he went past the people used to sing together, 'Here comes the galloping major.' And he used to doff his hat. I think he thoroughly enjoyed that.

Lucy Collard

He had watches of every description, his fingers in rings and that sort of thing, tie pins, and curios all over which he'd got from seamen coming home. There was a brown bear outside there, been there for donkey's years, and of course, all the dogs in the neighbourhood used to come and pee against it. But he still took that bear to Ilford, when he moved there.

William Abbott

You see the men come in of a morning; they call them on the stones. They used to stay out on the stones, you see, outside Charlie Brown's, and the gangers or foremen used to give tallies to the mates who bought him a pint of beer the night before.

Walter Dunsford

I can remember the funeral procession and the hearse, his funeral cortège being pulled along by the horses. They had plumes – you know, feathers – black horses sort of prancing along with black plumes on their heads.

Lucy Collard

There was a lot of pubs: The Connaught, The Dug Out, which was the Tidal Basin tavern, a pub called The Steps which I believe was a Truman's house, next to the Seaman's Mission; another one alongside it called Cartridges, which is a Charrington's house on the corner of Freemason's Road. They was all well-known pubs, a lot of them frequented by – I won't say ladies of the night, because it was invariably ladies of the day then, especially when the seamen paid off. Some of the performances around there were quite hilarious and some of them were quite sad actually, seeing them lose their pay-offs and money. But invariably, those chaps who did get rolled were quite stoic about it, they'd say, 'Oh, never mind, there's another ship, another pay day.' And so, sort of, life went on.

All the pubs that I've mentioned used to be early-morning houses, open at six o'clock in the morning, that is. Invariably they was gang-packed with dockers and the chap that used to employ a particular gang would be called the ship worker. If you didn't give him a little drop of neck oil in the morning – whatever he liked to drink – you wouldn't be likely to be called on. This obviously didn't apply in every case, but it went on a great deal.

Albert Patten

In the bar, at one end there was a large red-faced fellow, and my chum pointed him out to me and he said, 'That's Barge Billy. Now, he's the bloke who, you want to go on a barge, you go to Barge Billy. And all the barge skippers go to him, and any men who want a job in a barge, they go and see Barge Billy, and he brings the two together.' And at the other end was rather a little man who was sitting there, and he said, 'Well, he's Schooner Charlie.' So anybody who wanted a sailing coaster, other than a barge, a sailing coaster or a steam coaster, the crews were all handled by Schooner Charlie. Well, I found this all very interesting. And outside there were chaps pacing up and down, all these coasting sailors waiting for a job, and all registered with either Schooner Charlie or Barge Billy.

Captain A R Williamson

I've often had people who don't understand how a family that was very poor, the father would invariably land in the pub. But to us it was understandable – invariably you were a family of three, four or more, living in two rooms, the mother having to do the ironing and everything else in two rooms, with the children. So that the husband would invariably find himself surrounded by washing hanging all over the rooms, children – and he would say 'My God, let me get away from this'. Perhaps you'd say the father was a selfish individual, but he wasn't – my father would work from morning till night when the work was there.

Bill Crook

Englishmen in those days, especially working-class Englishmen, treated their wives in a way that now would be abominable. They could beat their wives or throw them downstairs. And this is precisely what my grandfather used to do, if I can believe the stories. Shipping in those days was all wood, and his family business made the wooden nails that held them together. And he lost his business when ships started to be made of iron, and they didn't need the wooden nails. The proceeds of the business was shared between my grandfather and his brother, and from what I hear there was a drawer in my grandfather's house filled with sovereigns, which was the coinage of the day. He'd come home every day, take one, go down to the pub, do a little clog dancing to entertain the rest of the clientele, come back inebriated, throw the grandmother down the stairs, and the dresser top – with all the cups and saucers on – downstairs after her. This was why some of the local ladies wanted to marry Chinese. Apart from them being exotic, they were certainly more civilised in that sense.

Leslie Hoe

We used to court in a little pub down Plaistow Broadway, called the Coach and Horses, on the corner of Balaam Street. I remember the missus of the pub had just had it refurbished in a maroon Rexine, or leatherette, stuff and I had a little grass monkey that I'd brought home from a Castle boat with me. The rascal got a little bit excited in the pub and he, for want of a better word, shit all over the new Rexine, as the missus was serving a drink. I asked my girlfriend, who became my wife, if she would mind clearing it up, which she did – do such a thing now and she'd be highly annoyed.

Albert Patten

Some of the houses were very clean, the doorstep was always beautiful, and then you get the lower strata, those families, the unfortunate ones whose parents used to drink like anything – they weren't capable of managing.

Alfred Alexander

At the top of Flower and Dean Street, there was, I know now, a kind of brothel. All the Jewish people felt very superior to the families living down there – I think there was a pub at the corner – to think that people spent their money on beer! You know, when money was so hard to come by.

Miss M

Another thing that worried her, both sides of the family had alcoholic deaths, you know, we had a reputation for it – like me father, he had DTs now and again. I remember him seeing things up the wall, that sort of thing. Caught up with all this poverty, but he always seemed to manage to get a drink. And my mother was always dead scared in case I followed, and I made a promise that I'd never touch it. Well, I drink more now than I've ever done, but it's for medicinal purposes now.

Charles Beck

My father did like his beer, so that much of what he earned... – and it was perhaps unfortunate that he never received a weekly wage; when he done a job, he took it back to the firm and received the money for the job. This meant that on his way home, he would probably stop at the pub – and you must remember that the pubs were open all day – and he would invariably stop at the pub, meet his friends and have a real delightful booze-up. The result was, that the money that my mother got was inclined to be a pittance doled out after most of the money had been spent in other means. She managed the best way she could.

Bill Crook

My father, he drank, he drank – he loved his pint of beer. I'd come home from school midday, and he'd say, 'Go and get me a pot,' that's fourpence, a quart of beer. I'd go down to the off-licence – we were living then opposite West Ham Park. I used to have to come up the cul-de-sac, round into East Road, through the alleyway – it was a good ten minutes' run. I'd come back, have me dinner, just before I was going he wanted another pot. I said, 'I can't, Dad, I'll be late for school.' 'Go and get me a…' That was all, but he'd never strike. His voice was enough to – well, you know what fathers were in those days.

Charles Lisle

My father was a no-good man and I've never regretted his death. He was a busker. He used to go out drinking and playing the banjo and as he'd get money, so he would spend it in the next pub as he worked. He came home drunk all the time. There were fights – this is typical of the 1930s, specially weekends – there were fights with my mother, and my mother used to sell beetroots outside Bow to get some money to give us some food.

Stan Rose

We had a neighbour, Littman, always looking for 'an effing Jew'. My mother used to say to her, 'Your husband always wants to fight.' 'Ah, not you,' she says. 'You're a different Jew.' Oh, he was a drunken swine. They was drunk every night and they used to fight like cat and dog. I once fell down through all the stairs through him – he had a knife in his hand, and I thought he was gonna knife me, but he was looking for his old woman. But she used to like my mother.

Miss H

We was evicted many time because my father had become a drunkard after being a teetotaller for many, many years – through unemployment, he gradually became a drunkard. I was told by my brothers my mother walked the streets singing and selling bootlaces, with me in her arms suckling at the breast, then she died of tuberculosis and I went into many poor homes.

Jack Dash

We used chariots to take the inebriates to the police station. These chariots, I was thinking about them the other day, they had two large wheels and a stretcher-like top and when you could subdue some drunken woman who was trying to scratch your eyes out, you had to put her on the trolley, needing the help, sometimes, of as many as four or five men to do it. Then you had leather straps with which you shackled their arms and their legs and around their waist to keep them down. Then you pushed this wretched chariot through the streets with this screaming foul-mouthed woman to the police station, where sometimes she'd be charged, or else left to sober up.

Graham Rutherford

Father Thomas, he was a real character, a great character and loved by children especially. He was respected by every man and woman in the district and we would come round and talk to people. Anybody lost anybody, anybody was deceased, he would come round and talk them through, you know, give them counsel. It was said of him that if a man wandered into a pub without first going home to share his day's wages with his wife, Father Thomas would go into the pub and drag him out by the collar and threaten him with a thrashing if he didn't take his wages home. I heard this many a time when I was a kid – Mr So-and-so was pulled out of the pub by Father Thomas and sent home. He was a big man.

Norman Grigg

There used to be a woman in Green Bank, she was a marvellous Catholic, always cleaning – I can see her now with a straw hat and a white apron. And every now and again, she'd break out on the gin. There used to be a pub almost right next door to her – Moore's pub. And when she had the gin in her she was strong as a lion, she'd beat everyone up. I think it was her husband she'd usually have a go round. And the only one

Now known as The Star of Bethnal Green, *this pub still stands on the Bethnal Green Road. It was not considered respectable for women to go into pubs, but drinking while standing outside was acceptable, even in the company of babies and children.* c1900

who could do anything with this Mary, was the station sergeant at the river police. They'd dash up Black Boy Alley to
get him and he'd come down and everything would be all
right – 'cos he was a strong Catholic, see?

Jack Banfield

Fighting for a Living

With bodily strength a requirement in most manual labouring
jobs, and physical toughness necessary simply to survive, it is
not surprising that a number of East Enders found their way
into the ring as boxers. Charlie Brown, like many publicans
before and since, began life in the ring and was said to be very
handy when it came to chucking out. Clubs such as the Repton
Boys' Boxing Club encouraged boxing as a manly form of
exercise and York Hall, Shoreditch Town Hall and the Mile
End Arena were all popular venues. There were also plenty of
low-key shows in fairgrounds and small-scale venues. The
earliest rules for boxing were set out by a lighterman working
for the Port of London, called Jack Broughton, now interred
at Westminster Abbey. For two hundred years, his gravestone
lacked an epitaph as his choice was considered inappropriate,
but in 1988 it was engraved with his chosen words: Champion
of England.

There were many great Jewish boxers, including Daniel
Mendoza. Born in 1764, he was small for a boxer, only 5ft 7in,
but overcame much heavier opponents by developing a defensive style of ducking, blocking and side-stepping, and is the
only middleweight to ever win the Heavyweight Championship
of the World. He later wrote a book called *The Art of Boxing*
and retired to run the Admiral Nelson pub on the Whitechapel
Road. Much later, the notorious criminals the Kray twins both
started out in the boxing arena, and the East End produced

Olympic boxing champions Ted Spinks, Harry Mallin 'the Shoreditch Copper', and Ted 'Kid' Berg.

———————

Physical violence was the way of life, and you were taught that, and it was the currency. One of my younger brothers used to complain that one of my older brothers fetched him one round the ear, and it sent him deaf. This one who'd been made deaf, he was a boxer, he went through the clubs and became a professional boxer. His conversation and his attitude to life, the whole mode of life, was the boxing stance. So if you argued with anyone, you'll get a right-hander. See, the principle in boxing is, the left hand is used to probe and the right hand is the killer. That's the punch. So it's part of the vernacular – if he does that, you know what he's gonna get: a right-hander.

Alfie Bass

My father used to be a fist fighter for the fairgrounds and for charity. You know, they only got about a pound and they fought until they fell down. I know Dad had some fights, I think on the day he got married, and he was concussed.

Gracie Smith

After my father died, my mother had six children to bring up – my sister was still alive then – and she used to take in washing for neighbours, to do the sheets and things like that, and I took up boxing to give her a few shillings. That was when I was about twelve. I was always athletic and they had a boxing booth in Bethnal Green – they used to run boxing shows on Thursday nights and Sunday mornings, and I used to go there and I used to get the large amount of five shillings for six rounds, or ten shillings for ten rounds. I used to write to all the ones who used to run the shows, the Ring, Blackfriars, and I was used as a go-between; if a boxer didn't turn up, they used to put me on with them. Do you know, if they made a good show with me, they was very good – see, I was what they called a good second-rater – not a top man.

Harry Plum

I started to box in those days – I went to a youth club called the Charterhouse Youth Club, that was over in Bermondsey, started to learn a bit of boxing. In the hungry Thirties, I'd just got married, and I was unemployed, and my wife's uncle, his father was the chief second of the Blackfriars Boxing Ring for professionals, and he said, 'Tell him to come and appear as a substitute.' In those days, they had a little cubicle called the substitutes box, so you went there and sat as a substitute in case a fighter never turned up. So I went in there and the first fight I had was six rounds, got a good hiding and all that. In those days, you got twenty-five shillings for a win and a pound for a draw or a lose, and if it was a good fight, the audience was throwing money – nobbings – and of course the money was picked up and it was given on top of your pound as you went to your dressing room.

Jack Dash

I used to box at eight stone and I only weighed just above seven when I was a kid. I had to give all that weight away. I've had five fights in one day to get as far as a semi-final. So it shows you what boys we had. And we had good football teams, and you had your inter-docks football championships and all that. Joe Parker, West Ham was after him, but he wouldn't leave the docks – but they was well after him. Billy Skills, he used to play for Walthamstow, Danny Lynch, golden gloves, middleweight champion. That's all we used to do when we was kids out there, belong to the boxing. I belonged to the

PLA boxing club and also North West Ham at Plaistow, back of the Black Lion at Plaistow. So with all them clubs, whenever you met anybody, he was a bit handy, he wasn't a mug.

Alfred Green

In the 1930s, things were so bad that you either had to be a thief or try and get some money some other ways if you could, and I could never be a good thief, I'm no good, I'm not that way, so I went in for professional boxing. I had roughly about 250 fights and I think I've won, we'll say 180. One thing I can assure you, I was never knocked out. It was just determination, as far as I was concerned; I was fighting for a living. I got eventually to the top of the tree, twelve rounds, and I was up for five pounds – I started off with half a crown, three rounds. I was not interested in the game, it was only a means of existing, and I went on to box for about eight years. Eventually I got a job at Woolwich Arsenal, making ammunition ready for the 1939 war. I promptly gave up boxing, which I always detested. It did have a permanent effect on me which I didn't know about then, in that I suffered so much injury to my head that in 1941 I was graded grade four for the armed forces. My eldest brother is at present in Goodmayes [asylum], because of the boxing.

Stan Rose

She'd say, 'Where you going?' I'd say, 'There's a big fight on, Mum, there's a fight on, tonight – it's the slaughtermen having a fight.' They used to stand up, knuckles, you know, down at the front of the road there, outside the Lamb pub. Terrific fights there used to be there – that's what we used to look forward to, that.

Henry Corke

Working on the boats, they were rife with knuckle – we had some really good boxers amongst them. Just because they were hard. Not always the skilful ones, although we did have some skilful boys there, but hard as iron. You had to be hard – you had to be to live in that world

Norman Grigg

Fighting the Police

The East End was an area where some of the country's poorest people lived and worked alongside the greatest abundance Britain's vast empire could produce, and much of the impetus for building enclosed docks came from the need to protect valuable cargo. When ships were moored in the open waters of the Thames, thefts took place regularly, often with the connivance of watchmen and crew members. Before the West India Dock was built, sugar was carried off under cover of darkness in special black bags known as 'black strap', and a large ship was reckoned to lose about ten to fifteen tons this way. So right from the beginning, the new docks were closely guarded, with high walls around them. The Metropolitan Police reached the East End in 1841 when a dockyard division was formed. Apart from crime around the docks, the police were kept busy by the high numbers of prostitutes always found around any port. The East End was also home to a lot of illegal gambling, including Limehouse's puk a poo houses and the bookies who operated in doorways and on street corners.

As East Enders were a tough bunch, so the police had to be tougher still. They had to keep order among those queuing for work in the worst years of Depression, wade in to break up street fights, and combat gangs of thieves or pickpockets known as push-up mobs. The truncheon, a rolled-up cape, or a glove loaded with pebbles were all regarded as suitable tools for law enforcement. People talk fondly of a time when they

The docks offered plenty of desirable commodities for pilfering, which is why they had their own police force. Here, an officer searches a timber cart leaving the Surrey Docks in the 1930s, although it is hard to imagine what could be secreted under such a heavy load. A G Linney, c1930

could leave their doors unlocked, but it seems that the average East End household had very little in it that was worth stealing so the unlocked door may not be quite such an accurate sign of a law-abiding society.

———•———

I wanted the East End – all my colleagues in the police wanted the West End because it was far more glamorous, but I still had this awful do-gooder attitude, and I wanted the East End, where they were poverty-stricken. I knew of it, of course – I'd walked there and I'd driven through it, but I didn't know it. I went first of all to Hackney, which was a most cosmopolitan place then, but really poor, dreadfully poor. But I was impressed with the closeness to one another. They were individualists, all of them, really, and would fight like fury against an invader but generally were kind to one another.

Graham Rutherford

Laws were considered to be made for other people. You were, almost invariably, the victims of law. If you couldn't pay the rent, the policemen were the scavengers who'd put you out; if there was a dispute in a shop, the policeman would invariably support the shopkeeper; if a policeman wanted to drink in a pub, then he went in the back and drank to his content, on the house. There was the feeling, automatically, that laws were made for the other person, and we were the people who got the kicks.

Bill Crook

There was always a policeman on at the gate, and of course, they've got to watch who went in and out of the docks, and if they thought anybody had got anything, they'd naturally stop and search. One chap had got thirty oranges on him, and as the policeman was on his own, he went to the general office to fetch somebody else, and by the time he'd gone back, the man had eaten everything – skin, pips, the lot – so there was no proof and he couldn't charge him.

Doris Salt

Mrs Dumbrill was a large lady, and when she went to work, she had a man's cap which was kept on her head by two large hat pins. She always wore a long coat, and she went out with her bucket with a floor cloth stretched over the top and the brushes inside. Then of a night-time, she would come home and she would have the brushes in a separate bag on this occasion, with the wet floor cloth stretched over the top. But no policeman at the gate would ever stop her, or any of the other cleaners, to see what was actually inside the bucket – they wouldn't have dared.

Tom Stothard

The PLA police used to have nights when you could go out with some stuff, like. If you got a little pass, like especially on the banana boats – if you got some ripe bananas, they'd allow you out with an amount of bananas – but if they thought you had too many, they'd make you put 'em down. If you was going out with some bundles of firewood and they thought you had an excess, they would make you put some around the back of their police hut, or wherever they were. Or if they was having what they called a hospital night, if the seaman's hospital was running short of firewood – they always used firewood to light the fires in those days – you'd have to put your bundles behind the shed. So you knew when it was hospital night – you'd see bundles of firewood behind the policeman's place.

Albert Patten

I remember on one occasion, I think every window in our street had the same curtains. So obviously a few bales of the curtaining material had fallen off a lorry or the carter's van that he pulled along.

Lucy Collard

Gambling in any shape or form was indictable then, and the playing of pigeon toss ranked high in the list. Pigeon toss was played with halfpennies or pennies – these were thrown up into the air, and as they fell, the participants called heads or tails according to choice. When they reached the ground, you only picked up the ones that fell to your calling. In this sport, however, certain precautions were always taken. It usually took place on street corners with small boys as lookouts, and on the cry of 'flatties' there would be a general scramble for open doorways. At least a third of those who lived in our part of the street existed on their wits and the nimbleness of their fingers and demanded that escape routes be provided for others in difficulties. Anyone not leaving his door open was considered anti-social. They did not, of course, stay in the houses but went straight through the back into the yards, over a few fences and then into their own homes through the back door.

Louis Dore

On one occasion, Dad was working in West India Dock which wasn't very far from where we lived, and he thought he'd come home at lunchtime and coming through Dodd Street, he saw my mother being put in the back of a Black Maria. Apparently, she'd been to put a bet on a horse race on that day, and 'cos gambling on horse racing was illegal – there was no betting shops, so they used to have bookie's runners – and apparently this particular house that my mum had been to to place her bet had been under surveillance by the police. They'd been working, digging up roads or something, and the house was raided and Dad had the great pleasure of seeing Mum being led out of the house and being put into the police van. So he had to go home and get the rent book and bail her out. So after that I don't think my mum could say much about my dad playing puk a poo.

Lucy Collard

Sometimes you'd see the police appear – it was all silence and suddenly you'd be looking at the top of the street, waiting for the appearance of the police, and you'd see a great, enormous woman, walking unsteadily on high-heeled shoes. It wasn't a woman – it was a policeman dressed up as a woman. They used to adopt different disguises – and all the people there used to hoot with laughter and the poor chap would be so embarrassed.

Alfie Bass

The East End had razor gangs and racehorse gangs and that sort of thing – they were typical tough people in the East End but they were the type of people who never took on their own. Mugging was a rare thing – a very, very unusual thing. The average person, if he was a gangster type, he'd rather give an old lady or an old man a few bob rather than take it from them. They were very, very respectful of the ordinary family.

The push-up mob, in those days, as they were called – they were the light-fingered type, the pickpockets, and one Sunday morning, there was a hell of a do. It was a market stall that sold petrol and lighters and that, and one of the chaps started something and the stall went over and the whole lot went up in flames and everybody stampeded – they just run for their lives. We found a chicken in the backyard – there used to be a chicken market there as well.

Harry Silverston

I've seen, as a kid, many fights, gang fights, black-hand gang and all sorts of things going on. Today, we hear about the mugging and all that – it was just as bad then. You could say that it was a roughish kind of area. You would hear, at night, the pubs closing and terrible fights breaking out, doors being smashed, and windows. This was really part of the atmosphere. You very rarely went to bed as a kid and didn't expect to hear fights going on, especially in summer.

Alfie Bass

Policemen were disliked; it was a natural instinct that is still in the East End today. It was perhaps a bit unfair, but policemen could never be trusted. They would gain your confidence, perhaps, and then you'd find that your confidence had been betrayed. It was anger. Also there was more fights between policemen and the citizens of East London than there are today. When they took you to a police station, they gave you exactly what you tried to give them outside – except more so. Being assaulted in the police station was also a fact of life.

Bill Crook

If you looked at the *Police Gazette* – which was almost on a par with the *News of the World* at that period – you'd find stories of murder, of rape – the most terrible things. And it was traditional that the sewers – those lids you would see in the streets – at times of any trouble, usually on a Friday and Saturday night, there were cases when the police were actually attacked by gangs and murdered and the bodies were put down these sewer things, these drains. They'd take the lid off and put them down there, and cover 'em up, and later they'd discover these policemen's bodies. And there were many witnesses.

Alfie Bass

Though it's true that policemen seldom walked through our areas singly – two or three at a time was customary – nevertheless, if we strayed outside our usual haunts, the heavy hands or rolled-up waterproof capes would be applied to the sides of your head with considerable force. They were past masters at inflicting pain and degradation on their victims. The half-Nelson was the commonest form of restraint. This was painful in any case, but it you struggled, your arms would be twisted higher and higher, and the pain was excruciating. Frogmarching came next. You were branded a very amusing spectacle being carried face downwards with a flattie attached to each of your four limbs, but if you proved really obstreperous, a two-wheel stretcher-like vehicle was produced, and on this you were strapped down, from head to foot, and wheeled through the streets.

Louis Dore

All the police in those days, they used to go round the arches in the East India Dock. They used to all carry their poncho or cape under their arm and their gloves, and there used to be courting couples round there of a night, where they'd not right to be, and the police used to have these long gloves and they had a few pebbles in the end of the fingers and they'd just flip them round as they walked along. And every now and again, they'd catch somebody. Yeah.

Walter Dunsford

During that time, the women police wore the big bowler hats and the jackboots or gaiters. They were as big as men, naturally, and we feared and respected them.

Dick Allington

If a man was caught stealing they used to frogmarch him to the Old Street police station, four of them, you know; they were facing the ground, and held by two arms and two legs. Course, all us children, we used to shout and scream and run after the policemen, you know, and throw things at them, things we'd picked up.

Hilda Bunyon

When he wasn't at work, me grandfather used to sell flowers off a cart. He'd gone up with his barrow to the market to get some flowers, coming back, there's me grandmother on the pavement. Grandfather was pushing the barrow along and there was a horse tram behind him and it kept going 'ding, ding, ding, ding, ding' but Grandfather wouldn't get out of the way. In the finish – and he was only a little man, so they tell me – the driver flicked his whip, missed him, and hit Mother. So of course, Grandfather pulled the tram driver off this blinking thing and give him a basinful. He got six weeks for that. When he came out the kids wouldn't let him in because they didn't recognise him – Mother had said, 'Don't let anyone in.'

Dennis Pike

The kind of sentence meted out for minor offences was seven to fourteen days in the local nick. This may seem to have been a trivial sentence, but most men would prefer a lagging. A lagging meant from, say, a month to six months upwards in a recognised prison, Pentonville, for instance. Here you were overseen by warders, received enough food to keep you alive and when you came out you were temporarily free of vermin. You were bathed, your hair cropped to the skull, you wore broad arrow suits, and your own clothes were baked – sterilised. You could always tell a lag when he came home by his lack of hair, yellow complexion and scarred fingers from picking oakum or sewing mailbags.

In the local nick, your custodians were the very flatties you may have roughed up on your arrest, and you were made to pay dearly for this.

Louis Dore

The only crime that I ever heard of was there were a few villains in Limehouse, but they always went away – they never ever robbed poor people, always the higher classes, but never ever ever robbed down in Limehouse. The police all knew the villains, they knew the villains by name and they knew where they could put their hands on them if anything happened.

Mary Partlett

The East Enders, they weren't great criminals, you know. The Jews, of course, did a fair amount of fraud and blackmarketing, but they're not violent criminals. The Indian population is generally very law-abiding; you get very little violence or property crime, but you get fraud.

Graham Rutherford

I can always remember wandering out of what seemed to me to be the East End into the other side of Bethnal Green Road. I think I was five years old and I was picked up by a policeman because I was crying and he took me to the police station and I remember that they put a police helmet on my head. They had to send somebody round – there was no question of telephoning, of course – they asked me where I lived and I knew where I lived, and my mother arrived in a terrible state of fear because it was the police.

Emanuel Litvinoff

I remember once, I'd got me youngest brother – he was two more after me – and I used to dance to these barrel-organs; oh, I loved dancing, you know. Anyway, we was going on, going on and night-time came on and we stopped at all the pubs and I was still dancing and the man said, 'You'd better go home,' and I'd lost me brother in the pram – I'd forgot all about him. So anyway, they took me to the police station and I was in one police station and me little brother in the pram was in another police station somewhere else.

Hilda Bunyon

In 1920, a golden eagle got free from Hamlyn's and had a lovely time flying around the district; from the steeples of the churches and the roof of the dock warehouses, it would swoop down and soar into the sky. For some days it made its perch on the roof of number six warehouse, by the main gate of London Dock. Men tried to catch it, but to no avail. The local children gathered in the roadway to watch the bird fly and stretch its wings, and the police had great difficulty in clearing a path for the traffic coming in and out of the dock. Tales went round amongst the kids that Goldie had snatched a baby from its pram and hid it up on the roof, as well as several dogs and cats.

Try as they might, the PLA and Metropolitan Police could not shift the crowds of children, even when they moved in swinging their heavy rolled-up capes. Sometimes the eagle would fly down towards the crowd and there would be a general stampede to retreat, but crowds soon gathered again. The bird had its freedom for nearly a week and no wild pigeons were seen around, and the local racing pigeon fans kept their lofts closed the whole of the time. It was eventually captured, but not before it had snatched Mrs Creamer's hat, which had a plume with birds, as she crossed Gravel Lane bridge, and dropped the hat in Wapping Basin. This is true, because Alec Creamer was the welfare officer and I spoke to him about it. 'That's funny about that eagle,' he says. 'My mother was crossing the bridge and the eagle swooped and picked her hat and dropped it in.'

Alexander Gander

Fighting for Work

Around the turn of the nineteenth century, the trade union movement was booming, growing from three-quarters of a million members in the 1880s to six-and-a-half million by 1918. The East End was at the forefront of this movement, its workers inspired by the successful 1888 strike by women match workers at the Bryant & May factory in Bow, and the gasworkers and dockers' strikes of 1889, where dockers demanded a minimum wage of sixpence an hour (the 'dockers' tanner').

In 1909, after the Port of London Authority, headed by Lord Devonport, took control of the docks, a strike aimed at ending the use of non-union labour led to a downing of tools in 1912. The dockers' leader Ben Tillett addressed a massed meeting on Tower Hill, urging the dockers to 'Repeat after me: "Oh God, strike Lord Devonport dead",' to which the men responded, 'He shall die! He shall die!' During the strike, the Jewish tailors came out in support of the dockers, and it is said this forged a bond that was still remembered by the dockers nearly twenty-five years later, when they fought side by side with the Jews in the Battle of Cable Street.

The Transport and General Workers Union (TGWU) was established in 1922, a founder member being Ernest Bevin who headed the Dockers' Union. For many manual labourers, the period directly after the First World War represented the boom years, as the loss of a large portion of the workforce meant that there was almost full employment. But in the run-up the worldwide Great Depression in the late 1920s, the fall in Britain's economic output led to attempts to restart the economy by cutting wages, resulting in the General Strike of 1926. This began with the miners, and spread to the electricity and gas industries, the railways and the docks, where some of the most dramatic scenes occurred. In order to stop food rotting on the quays, the army was called in to unload ships

Army, navy and police prepare to escort a convoy of food lorries destined for London markets from the Royal Victoria Docks during the General Strike of 1926. Clashes between the 'blackleg' civilian drivers and striking workers were common.
John H Avery, 1926

and man the dock gates, and riots took place among the strikers and the blacklegs. After the collapse of this strike, dockers were forced to accept lower pay and longer hours. The poverty and political unrest continued into the Thirties with marches and protests, including an invasion of the Ritz Hotel, and in 1936, East Enders welcomed the Jarrow Marchers as they arrived in London after walking three hundred miles to draw attention to the lack of work in the north east.

My mother was made an orphan at a young age, and her own mother had taken on that plight in them days, as most widows had to, of bringing up five children. Her own mother worked very hard – she used to make matchboxes for Bryant & May's in her own house. Not by gaslight either, by candlelight. And I think they used to get about a farthing a gross for making the shells. At one time she had to go to the parish for a certain amount of relief; it was refused and she finished up doing six weeks in Holloway because she set about the parish council. She took part, as a very young woman, in the Bryant & May's matchgirls strike.

Maurice Foley

My first memories must have been the 1912 strike – I remember me father and me mother and meself standing at the top of the street, just a few yards, as the railway went by, and they was all booing the train for the blacklegs. And I believe a policeman told my mother off. The point was, as the train pulled out, everybody was standing along the Victoria Dock Road booing the train as it pulled out of Custom House station. See, 'cos it picked up the blacklegs to take them out the way.

Charles Beck

When the 1912 strike was on, six of us out of the family, we was only youngsters, and we was taken to the back of Watney Street, name of Planet Street, and they used to give us soup. That was laid on – there used to be great big forms along this Planet Street and we'd get soup and a lump of bread, something like that.

Sidney Bell

About the 1912 strike, the Price's bakery used to have a house van used to come round. It was a single pony van with two wheels and a flap at the back. I remember that stopping in the middle of Lowder Street and the driver got off, took the catch off the back and let the back down and loaves of bread fell and people just helped themselves, and the driver stood on the pavement like that. Probably he went back and said, 'They've pinched all me bread.' But you see, there was community feeling. You know, 'Well, here you are. Don't go hungry, have it,' see?

Jack Banfield

There was an English person who lived in the top flat and he worked in the docks. And when the strike was on – there was a big strike on, years ago – my brother worked there as a blackleg. The other men used to wait for him and they wanted to give him a good hiding 'cos they was on strike and my brother was doing their job – he got paid well for it. As he came home, they used to throw bricks through the train windows because these men, they were all blacklegs. Course, my brother was glad of a job.

Mrs B

My father, all those donkey's years ago, when I was a baby, went on strike – it was a sensation, you know. I don't know what they came out on strike for. I know my mother kept telling me how he came out on strike for three or four months

– and in those days, they were terrible times to come out on strike, weren't they?

William Mather

My father took part in all the major dock strikes that took place over the turn of the century, and they had a few bashings; the 1911 strike over the question of sacking white crews and employing Asiatic crews, the 1912 strike that went on for fourteen weeks.

Maurice Foley

I think my father was rather unusual – he resented this boss relationship with the worker, and he questioned it. I believe he used to lead strikes. I seem to remember my mother saying that all the women were angry with her because he'd led the strikes – but people in the street were angry with her.

Miss M

I was born in 1910, and in those days, things were bad. My dad was always regularly employed because he was a good tradesman, but there was times when, on the shipping, the ship was finished, and I'd come home from school and behind the door was Dad's travelling case or his tool bag full of tools and Mum'd be crying. Because when you were unemployed you didn't know when you was gonna get a job; there was no dole. When things got really bad you were given relief tickets. Mum knew about it because her dad was a coalman, and people would have a ticket for 50p for coal – no, it wouldn't be as much as that – and a ticket for meat and a ticket for bread.

Walter Dunsford

The main source of work was casual, docks or riverside work. The exception to that were the men on permanent jobs – the postman and the policeman, the road sweeper, people like that. But the majority were casual work in the docks and along the riverside. Now, in the early days, they used to call on at six o'clock in the morning, so men would be there in hope of getting a job. Also, the pay was by the hour, so the result is, although they might get a job at six o'clock in the morning, they may be paid off at eight o'clock, because then what they called the 'blue-eyed boys' would come. So they would pay them, half a dozen or so, off, to take another half a dozen on who came at eight o'clock.

Jack Banfield

He'd shout to his friends; he'd have perhaps thirty to forty tallies, according to the amount of work that was going. And he'd throw that amongst the men and then they used to fight and scramble for these tallies. It was bad. That would be in the morning and it would happen again at one o'clock. That was for half a day's work. They didn't get a full day, no guaranteed day, only what they fought for. And it was real nasty to see it. There was no friends; there was fight for half a day's work.

Walter Dunsford

In 1926, we had the General Strike, and we had dockers come down from East Ham and they must have been a rough lot because they caused a lot of damage. On one occasion, just outside Grays, in some cottages called Flint Cottages, there was two shots fired from a train and went through the windows of these two people in Flint Cottages. We had the Manchester police horse division come down and they took over to keep law and order. The dockers were naturally incensed at the blacklegs, as they were called, coming down, and they pulled the gates at Grays station down to get at them as the trains came through. Things got very ugly at times.

Herbert Hollingsbee

The General Strike, my parents had been to the Queen's Theatre in Poplar High Street, which was a music hall. And when they came out, they got caught up, there'd been a march and my mother was hit by one of the policemen on horseback, hit by a truncheon. She wasn't seriously hurt, but she had a bit of a whack. But that was when things were really bad in the East End, you know, because to get work, the men would try and climb the dock gates to get in before they came out, and the head stevedore would choose who he thought he wanted to work that day, and men would just be climbing over the gates.

Lucy Collard

There's an old iron bridge at Canning – we called it the Iron Bridge at Canning Town. On that old iron bridge there was more cars turned over than anywhere. You'd go along and see cars on their roofs, you know, with the people going to work, legally going to work, and the people on strike used to turn them over. And outside the docks was the miners with their lamps collecting money, you know, from the dockers or anybody that could help them. Always see the miners outside Charlie Brown's 'cos he was always sat there on his big white horse. His son had the Blue Post, opposite.

Walter Dunsford

I left the West India Dock and went down the Royals. We had the 1926 strike and believe you me, blimey we didn't half have a good time; we was getting fags on the cheap and everything, you know, all the navy boats. And we used to be able to walk in and nobody took no notice of us lads, you know. But it wasn't half rough. Christ, they had to have soldiers laying on street corners, laying there with machine guns, you know, at Canning Town. Yes, fights coming over Canning Town iron bridge. Oh, terrible it was.

But we had a good time because there wasn't no work for us. We used to go in there and play cards and all that, see. We was only messenger boys. They knew we couldn't do their work – well, we wasn't allowed to – so we wasn't legging or nothing like that. See, being messenger boys they didn't take no notice. They used to ask us, 'What's it like, who's in there, anybody in there?', that sort of thing.

This bloke Tebbit, he's a bloody liar he is. He said that when the 1926 strike was on, his father got on his bike and rode around getting work. Well, he never done nothing of the sort because nobody was at work, so how could he get a bloody job when everybody was out of work?

Alfred Green

When I came out of my cooper's apprenticeship in 1929, that was the bad old days when there was very little work about and we used to get a fortnight's work, a month's work, all over the shop, and we were sent there by the trade union. We never dealt with the dole people in those days, it was always done through the trade union – the National Association of Coopers.

Henry Harington

You used to sign on three days a week, and the unemployment clerks, they were very tough and very hard. If you were late, perhaps just a minute late, you lost a day's pay. And outside the Labour Exchange in the Walworth Road, the unemployment queue would be about a quarter of a mile or half a mile long.

One day, a lad was late – two minutes late – and they wouldn't let him sign on, and the lad was desperate, he had three kids, and of course, in his anger, he grabbed the clerk by his tie, and he was going to drag him over the counter. One of my friends, who was a member of the Unemployed Workers

Movement, Patsy Hicks, he dived in and released him. Then they brought the law in – they Old Bill as you call them today, the word we used in those days was the filth – and when they brought them in, out came penknives and everything. But of course Patsy Hicks, very cool lad he was, he went and appealed to the police, and he appealed to the Labour Exchange manager, saying, 'We're going to have an ugly scene here,' and so it was all quietened down, and finally he was allowed to sign.

Jack Dash

In the 1926 strike, I remember – I should imagine it must have been somewhere near the end of the strike, when I was only six – I remember a lady coming along, knocking at the door, known to my mother, and she said, 'Oh, I'm glad you're in, love. I made too much bread pudding and it seemed a shame to throw it away, and is it any good to you?'

And I remember my mum saying, 'Oh lovely, my hubby loves a bit of bread pudding,' you see? And she said, 'Yes, I will take it, I'll return the dish.' And when she'd gone, we ate the lot. Because we were – we weren't starving, but we had good appetites because we didn't have too much to eat in those days. And in my six-year-old mind, I remember thinking, Well, if Dad likes it so much, why didn't we save him any?

Edwin Hunt

And I vaguely remember, because I was a child in the Thirties, when it was the Depression, young chaps out of work came in, and Mother would sell them a cigarette for a ha'penny, and five of them would be passing it from one to another. And children not being able to go to school because their one pair of boots was at the snobs.

George Adams

I remember as a kid when they came down from Jarrow. Marched along the Barking Road and we had a public meeting in the Canning Town public hall with them. The local people put some of them up. You know, it was exciting times, when you realise it now, but it was times of dire poverty.

Maurice Foley

I don't know how Tate & Lyle treat their employees in the West Indies but they treated them pretty badly in Plaistow and Silvertown. It was terrible, slavery, there. Men would be fighting at the factory gate for work, you know. Really clawing at one another to have their books taken and to be taken on, in the days before the National Dock Labour Board. It was like a cattle pen – they called it the pen. And men who hadn't eaten enough for some days would work until they dropped and they would be carried out and someone else would take their place. And I'm talking about the Thirties.

Edwin Hunt

We invaded the Grill Room of the pinnacle of elite hotels, the Ritz Hotel. We invaded that and pulled our posters out, 'Relief for the Unemployed', and of course the manager of the hotel came down, and wanted to know what it was all about, and we demanded to be served. And I remember the manager, he said, 'Well, we can't serve you, you're not the sort of customer we serve here.'

So we said, 'We give your customers the greatest courtesy, when they come down from Park Lane and Grosvenor Square, come down to Aldgate and the East End, slumming it. See, nobody refuses them food if they pay the money for it, so we want you to show the same courtesy to us – we've got the money, we want tea and something to eat.' And of course, he refused to do it.

Jack Dash

London in the 1930s, you got more beggars in London. My dad was a carpenter at Shell on the corner of Kingsway, and I met him on the Saturday when I was up there. As we walked along a man says, 'Got the price of a cup of tea, guv?' My dad give him tuppence. So Dad said, 'Come on, we'll follow him.' We went back and the bloke went into a cafe, and my dad said, 'If he hadn't gone in, I'd have hit him and took that tuppence back.' 'Cos the bloke was genuinely hungry or thirsty – in those days, they had soup kitchens all along the Embankment.

Walter Dunsford

The Battle of Cable Street

Periods of economic hardship often lead to a search for scape-goats, and the riots that broke out around various British ports in 1919 were a manifestation of this. Soldiers returning from the First World War found that their jobs had gone and the country had nothing to offer returning heroes – particularly in the East End where the war-battered housing stock was more overstretched than ever. The sailors' unions began campaigning to keep black, Arab and Asian sailors off British ships in a time of high unemployment, and a series of race riots broke out across the country. In Cable Street, a cafe was set on fire and gunshots were fired.

In the following seventeen years, particularly during the worldwide economic crisis now called the Great Depression, the issue of race did not go away. In 1932, inspired by Mussolini in Italy, Oswald Mosley (who had sat as both a Conservative and a Labour MP), founded the British Union of Fascists, adopting a black shirt as the party uniform. Ideologically opposed to Communism, the party claimed that the Jews were in league with the Communists and set out 'to challenge and break for ever the power of Jews in Britain'.

The East End, with its large Jewish population, became a target for its speakers, and for undercover assaults against Jewish businesses. When a vast march through the area was proposed for 4 October 1936, the local mayor and 100,000 petitioners begged the Home Secretary not to allow the march, but he declared that a ban would be 'undemocratic' and the police were obliged to protect the authorised march. On the day, local people – Jewish and non-Jewish, and members of the Communist Party and the Independent Labour Party – gathered to prevent it. They adopted the slogan associated with Spanish anti-fascists: '*No pasarán!*' or 'They shall not pass!'

———•———

There was the young Communist League – along Whitechapel Road, New Road, Vallance Road, and in Commercial Street, by Spitalfields Church, there was all these people spouting about Communism. I joined the Labour League of Youth; it was in Brick Lane and we used to go along to the meetings. But the blackshirts used to start things first, around Haig Street and places like that. We used to see them marching through; they had meetings in Club Row every Sunday, and at night-time, they'd march through the districts. Of course, Jewish people were worried about it; they had the worry all the time that it's going to happen to us again – not to us, because we'd been born in this country – but to our parents, who'd been through it.

Mr U

Blackshirts, they used to come down the road, they had meetings on the corners and all that. People just used to stand and listen – but like any meeting, you get one starts shouting and hollering and then you don't bother no more. People didn't see much in it 'cos they was going against the Jews, they wanted the Jews out of it. But up here, about three or four turnings, that's all that it consisted of, was Jews. I was all right with Jews – I had nothing against them. The blackshirts said they didn't want the Jews there, that they was greedy and all that, but they weren't. They was entitled to be there, they didn't interfere with anybody.

Dolly Cooper

And they used to have rallies, the blackshirts, and they'd go to places to incite trouble, needless to say. And I was forbidden. 'You are not to go up there because it's dangerous.' 'Right.' So I'd go up there. Some of us went up there and I remember standing about that high, and the railings was there. We got up on this little ledge so as we could see. And it did get nasty 'cos they brought the police in. And there was all these blackshirts handing out this literature and me mum said, 'Where you bin?' 'Nowhere.' 'Didn't go up there?' 'No, never went up there.' But we did, we went up there.

Joanna Roberts

I remember once having gone to a meeting of fascists. I was at the time a great garlic eater; I was a vegetarian and I used to flavour my salads with garlic. I was at this meeting with a friend whose family were Irish; he was a big strong chap. And we went to this meeting and some girls in front of us started to sniff and one of them said, 'Who's been eating Jew food?' So this friend of mine puffed out his chest – he looked very Irish – and he said, 'I have – what you gonna do about it?'

Victor Leigh

It was at that time, the middle Thirties, there was a civil war on in the East End. Really – there were fascists – Mosley's crowd – and there were Communists. And they were fighting each other – literally fighting – every night. People today have no idea of the history of that period: it was a civil war; they were really battling it out, night after night after night.

Graham Rutherford

There were all these different kinds of people, the red-and-white shirts, the blue-and-white shirts, the red shirts, the green shirts. I joined the blue-and-white shirts – it was a kind of left-wing liberalism, although I was much more left wing. So all these people were battling for supremacy, but it was very enjoyable; all the kids were banging drums, anything – saucepans – when they tried to put out their chairs and it was just a lark, a great lark. Whoever turned up first with a platform was entitled to have that place for the day, so people were there at three o'clock in the morning to set out their platform. Most often, the fascists were there first.

Bernard Kops

At the time there was a rising Fascist Party who wore black shirts, and they were led by a man called Oswald Mosley. Mosley was what I would call an opportunist. He had been a member of almost every party, but he realised that Hitler had got in through his anti-Semitism, so he thought he could use his anti-Semitism to gain power. He turned his party anti-Semitic.

Victor Leigh

There's a general feeling that the whole of the East End was against Mosley. This was not so. There was a fundamental background of people who were conned – and were paid – and who accepted the Mosley element that the Jews, and anybody else that was foreign, were enemies of society. This was accepted in the street where my wife lived – where you couldn't be much bloody poorer and where most people supported Mosley. So Mosley did have some support. He had an overwhelming support against him as well.

He used to march along Roman Road to Victoria Park – he had quite a number of big marches. The strange point was that they'd march along with their uniforms and all make a dash for the Jewish shop – it always used to amuse me that they used to line up to get ha'pennyworth of fags at a Jewish shop – the anomaly was rather funny. But probably if you're a fascist, you're devoid of a sense of humour.

Bill Crook

When Mosley formed the new party, and then later the BUF, one place where he did obtain a great deal of support was Bethnal Green. And there were meetings at Victoria Park, particularly on a Friday, and we would go there, and fights would break out, and arrests made, but there was no doubt that he gained a considerable stronghold.

Jack Miller

Oswald Mosley declared, 'We are going to have a march and we are going to march through the East End.' Everybody knew they were very anti-Semitic and hated Jews, and he was going to impose this march through where we lived. So we decided we would oppose him there, which meant having a bust-up on the street. So we did. Cable Street, at one end, went down to the docks. And the dockers when they heard of this fascist wanting to march through London, turned out on the street to stop him.

Victor Leigh

It was on a Sunday and we were in a Jewish restaurant opposite the London Hospital, and we were having some dinner there in the early afternoon when someone walked in very agitated and said, 'Do you know what's happening? There's mobs at Gardiner's Corner.'

Anna Tzelniker

I remember the big day in October, the fascists, thousands of them, said they were going to march through the East End of London, and the Communists said, 'Oh no you're not. They shall not pass.' We had a million people on that day in October. There were a million people, round Gardiner's Corner, Leman Street, Cable Street. Many spectators came for the fun. But a very large number of them were the rioters, and we had a tremendous battle.

Graham Rutherford

I'd been out that Sunday, I'd been to the Bernhard Baron club with some Jewish friends of mine and we didn't actually get caught up in it because I've always hated crowds and when I saw so many people I decided that I didn't want to go through it so we really got away from it.

Lucy Collard

The morning of the Mosley march, I walked with another man I knew towards Leman Street, which is along Commercial Road, that's where the blackshirts had assembled on the other side, and the anti-fascists were assembled at Cable Street and all the streets this side. Now we were walking towards Leman Street, me and this other fellow and lots of other people, and all of a sudden, the mounted police started coming towards us on their horses. There was an old lady in front of us and we could see she was going to fall, so me and this other man picked her up and carried her out of the way of the horses.

Philip Bernstein

My brother did inform me that there was a special lot of what was called 'the toughies' – those that did boxing, all-in wrestling – they had certain plans to stop them getting through, to attack certain vehicles and let down their tyres. But I should say that it was the mass response that surprised us all. There is no doubt that a lot came out of curiosity – but the very density of the crowds made the march, for the fascists, a very difficult task.

Jack Miller

At the time, whenever there was something going on, on the streets, it was supported by the police, either walking alongside of you, or on their many horses. A lot of these horses were trained to rear up on their hind legs and kick out at you, which was very dangerous.

Victor Leigh

I was in charge of policing Cable Street – I would be right in the bally middle of it all – and it was a tremendous affair. Fortunately, as far as I know, no one was killed. Nothing was set on fire. But the physical violence was terrific. Hand-to-hand and brick-to-brick. I remember in Cable Street, they got behind us, turned some vehicles on their side, and pulled up stones from the road and made a wall, and we had to attack them that way. And as we were running up to them to get over this bally wall there was a barrage of bricks thrown at us, and I looked up and saw milk bottles coming down from the top of an occupied building. And we bust the door down and went in, and there on the window sill were a row of milk bottles and half a dozen youngsters chucking the bottles down on the police below. They got the shock of their lives of course when we balled in and carted them off.

Graham Rutherford

Even during Cable Street, kids were meant to join in and throw marbles under the horses' hooves so that the horses would be brought down and the policeman above couldn't swing his truncheon and was brought down and could be attacked. The police were largely on the side of the fascists; in fact the Commissioner of Police allowed it to go through at first. The Irish dockers were largely against fascism, and they were on our side. The Irish were there before the Jews, when they built the Metropolitan railway, and there was a great affinity in poverty.

Bernard Kops

And we were there the whole morning till late afternoon when it quietened down, and it was known that Mosley will not march that day because they all had the boiling water on the rooftops and everything ready for him. A friend of mine who I knew very well, he performed an act that day, he drove his car right into the middle of the fascists, he knocked down about three or four, then he jumped out of the car and left the car, and he went to the police and reported it missing. But he never knew that the cameras were taking pictures of all this from the rooftops so they saw him drive in. But they couldn't see his face, so he got away with it. That was the beginning, when we knew we were going to have trouble.

Philip Bernstein

It got so terrible, the march, that the Commissioner of Police had no possibility of letting it go through, so he stopped it, and that was the victory. Because it was blatantly provocative – there was no reason for that. He just wanted the oxygen of publicity, did old Mosley. He was a chancer really; he would have jumped on any wagon, had he thought he could gain power. He started out left-wing – but it's dangerous, when you go into the circle of things. You realise that extreme left goes all the way round to right.

Bernard Kops

We were defending the community from civil war. No doubt about it, the police did an enormous amount of good and

saved Britain from fascist domination or Communist domination. Which was the worst is a matter of political argument,
but both were unpleasant. The fascists were disciplined, and
you could get some sense out of them. If you said, 'You're not
going there,' they said, 'Yes, sir.' But the Communists, of
course, they fought their battles as much against the established order, against the police, as against the fascists. They
were a difficult lot. A lot were locals, but they came in tens of
thousands from all over the country, in coaches. Both sides. It
was an organised battle.

Graham Rutherford

My uncle was at the front line down Cable Street when they
all marched down Cable Street – 'cos all my family worked in
the dock, me uncles all worked there and most of 'em were all
together when the docks were closing. I remember them all
running down Cable Street and all the police – I don't know
who they were fighting but the police seemed to stop 'em –
and my uncle, he's in a newspaper, in the *East London
Advertiser*, giving some policeman a punch on the nose.

Julie Hunt

They stopped 'em. I had an aunt who was very sort of like
Labour and she went up there. And they used riot police
horses and to stop the horses getting through 'cos they were
doing the horses charging and whacking people over the
head with their truncheons, they threw marbles, which
meant that the horses were slipping. So it really was a terrible
day. It was 1936 and I can remember it and I can remember
my aunt coming home with her hair all down and her hat
half off 'cos she'd been in the thick of it. She said, 'They
didn't get through.'

Joanna Roberts

The Patriotic Worker's Paper *gives its own slant on the Battle of Cable Street. 'Britain belongs to us', it claims, reporting that among unbelievable scenes of enthusiasm, the streets rang with the name of Mosley, and the workers' cry was 'They shall pass!' Unbelievable, indeed.* 1936

PART 2

The Second World War

CHAPTER 7

Britain's Phoney War

Gathering Clouds in Europe

'There hasn't been a dictator in the history of the world who hasn't talked peace when he's been preparing for war.'

— ERNEST BEVIN

The Battle of Cable Street was the East End's personal conflict but it was closely linked to events taking place in Europe. Two days after being routed by the Jews and Communists of the East End, Mosley got married in the home of Dr Goebbels, in Berlin. Hitler was a guest and came to dinner after the wedding, presenting a picture of himself in an eagle-topped silver frame.

Since being elected German Chancellor in 1933, Hitler had transformed a country that was bankrupt and humiliated by the end of the First World War into a proud and economically successful totalitarian state. While Communists and blackshirts were battling for prime public-speaking positions in the East End, Hitler was forming alliances that would help him in his territorial ambitions, sending military aid to General Franco in the Spanish Civil War, and supporting Mussolini in his expansion of the Italian empire in Abyssinia. Mussolini then supported Hitler over the Munich Agreement, under the terms of which Czechoslovakia was forced to surrender some of its districts to Germany.

The deal was also supported by British Prime Minister Neville Chamberlain, who claimed it would guarantee 'Peace in our time'.

The events in Europe brought a new influx of refugees into the East End, and the new residents were kept aware of political developments overseas through families and friends. Many debated whether armed conflict was the only way to stop the rise of fascism, and certainly they understood Hitler's cynical non-aggression pact with Stalin, in August 1939, for what it was. It was as if Mosley had formed an alliance with Brick Lane's Jews. If Hitler-hating Russia and Communist-hating Germany were marching together, it could be for one reason only – so that they could carve up poor old Poland and share it out between them.

———— ·•· ————

Nineteen thirty-three, that was the year Hitler had come to power in Germany. We, being Jews, even as far as Romania, we felt it. And when Father got the engagement to go to England again in 1933, he said, 'Well, this time I'm taking you and Mummy with me. If, God forbid, anything happens in Europe, we should be together.' The rest of my family perished in the Holocaust because they stayed there, but Mother, Father and I left Romania in 1933, never to return.

Anna Tzelniker

After Hitler came to power, in 1933, my mother left Germany – she had to leave because she was working in an organisation that was in character very much like National Association of Civil Liberties. This is my first really nasty memory – I remember a knock on the door, and it was two Gestapo men who came and asked for her. Of course, she wasn't in, and my grandmother said she didn't know where she was. I was then nine, and it was my first realisation of things not being as they should be.

Suzanne Samson

My father had come from Amsterdam in 1902, as a boy, trying to find a job. The rest of the family were in Holland, and just before the war broke out they sent a message saying, 'Please come back to Holland, we're going to be neutral.' But my father couldn't raise the fare. That's how we survived – all the others died in the gas chambers.

Bernard Kops

We didn't want to travel through Germany, because we had heard of incidents of Jews being taken off trains and never being heard of again. We were very much afraid; we didn't speak to each other, we didn't gesticulate as Jewish people like to do, we were frightened all through. But then a miracle happened: an English schoolteacher, travelling from Austria home to England, entered our compartment. My father, having learned a bit of English through his plays and working in England, struck up a conversation with her somehow, and she was only too pleased to have someone to talk to and that made us one little English party which gave us some comfort till we crossed the border out of Germany.

Anna Tzelniker

There was a very popular expression: 'Don't buy German goods.' And I approved of the boycott of German goods. But I didn't believe in any war except in a war of liberation, like in the civil war in Spain. I knew lots of people who fought in the British contingent of the International Brigade in Spain and we were very proud of them.

Victor Leigh

In Italy, the propaganda we got, as far as Abyssinia was concerned, was so horrendous – looking back, from what I was told in school, and in the papers, there was no way I could get a balanced picture of what was going on and I developed a hatred of the English. Then the Spanish Civil War, in 1936 to '37, the propaganda was so awful that I certainly developed a hatred of Communism that was quite extraordinary, because of the tales we were told of what the Communists were doing to people – like tearing nuns' tongues out, things like that.

Suzanne Samson

My first lesson in socialism came from a Quaker who was a bricklayer. I was waiting on as a hod carrier and it was the time of the question of Mussolini coming into power, and the war in Abyssinia, and of course as a young man then, I had a lot of imperialism in me. In the course of my talks with him, it was then he began to enlighten me how wrong war is. He said that the only war that could be honourable was a war of defence against the invasion of another country – so with Mussolini's situation, it was quite different, and it was a Quaker that started me on the road towards socialist thinking.

Jack Dash

The Communist Party were active at the time, very active, in trying to explain how the Nazi parties were torturing the Jewish population. I began to disbelieve in Labour Party politics emerging into socialism. I could see that the only way to do that was the way the Communists planned, to seize power for the benefit of all. This guy I met in Victoria Park invited me to a meeting and I joined the Communist Party. So gradually, politics was instilled into your life. I remember that at home, they used to ridicule me for believing in politics.

Victor Leigh

Soon after Hitler started marching and making his fatuous promises – 'I have no further territorial ambitions,' he said, then straight away invaded Czechoslovakia – we realised that we couldn't trust a word that he said. And yet there's Neville Chamberlain flying over Munich and talking about 'Herr Hitler'. Everybody in the country, I think, except a few of his cronies, realised that the alarm bells were ringing.

Cyril Demarne

The Battle for Cable Street was in 1936. After that, it quietened down, because it was obvious to everybody that war was imminent. After Chamberlain came back from Munich, we were much too busy preparing for the inevitable war than fighting one another. And then the war came.

Graham Rutherford

I was evacuated eventually. When it all came down to it, Mother insisted that things would get a bit hot. She said to me, 'Well, things look a bit sticky, Russia made a pact,' and I'll never forget this, Russia made a pact with Germany and my mother was absolutely scared. She said, 'It's all finished now.' A non-aggression pact; I didn't know much about it then, but I do now.

Dick Allington

There had been these rumblings of what Germany was doing, and then of course when he went into Poland and took over Poland we knew that the war was imminent, we'd have it sooner or later, because the next step, he'd cross the water and try and take Britain. So we knew it was coming.

Violet Kentsbeer

For some time we sort of had at the back of our minds, you know, that the war was coming, the political situation was getting grimmer and I can remember thinking being in oil, and

Barrage balloons stored in dock cargo sheds before the out-break of war. British Balloon Command began distributing these in 1938; when deployed, they forced aircraft flying at low altitude to climb higher, allowing anti-aircraft guns more time to track them. 1939

being on the river, we were vulnerable. Just prior to the Munich crisis, out chief chemist had bought a barge, an iron barge, and was gonna float it out on the river. I was, by this time, the head typist, so they told me and my reaction was, I said, 'What, you're gonna put us all in a barge and float us out on the river when we get an air raid?' Course, we had no idea what an air raid was gonna be like – or air raid warning, come to that, although I think they did sound it occasionally so that we knew what it was. And the horror of it, of about fifty people, or a hundred people, getting into a barge and floating out. I said, 'We'll all be caught like rats in a trap.' I said, 'I wouldn't go. I don't care what happens, you'll never get me into that barge.' So, of course, he knew that if I wouldn't go, he couldn't get the other girls, and there'd be panic. Well, we didn't have the war that year. So I presume he sold the barge.

Dorothy Shipp

About 1938, I recollect a big German in his uniform, jack-boots, high cap, and a little old cockney chap, old man, he come up to him and he says, 'I fought your old dad in the last lot, you know.' And the German's looking down on him, and you can imagine, a four-foot-high old cockney man, with a six-foot-odd German looking down – he made no remark, of course.

Dick Allington

Britain Goes to War

War was coming and during the months leading up to September 1939, Britain was preparing itself. With the likeli-hood of war at sea disrupting the imports that made up two-thirds of Britain's food supplies, plans were drawn up for rationing. The government knew the London docks would be a target from the air and there was an attempt to distribute stockpiles of food round the country. Public parks and open spaces were turned over to growing fruit and vegetables.

Factories churned out armaments at such a rate that iron railings were removed and melted down to produce metal. Blackout rules were issued, dimming car and street lamps, covering every window with thick curtains or blinds or even a layer of cardboard; kerbs, lamp posts and roadside trees were given a coat of white paint to help them show up in the dark. Britain's first blackout took place two days before the declaration of war.

After the widespread use of gas in the trenches of the First World War, one of the greatest fears was of aerial attacks using poisonous gas. Some thirty-eight million gas masks were given out, house to house, and special drills held in schools and workplaces to make sure they could be deployed quickly in the event of an attack. By September 1939, one and a half million Anderson shelters had also been given out and dug into back gardens – these were free to any household earning less than £5 a week. Public shelters were built for those who were caught out on the streets during a bomb attack.

At 11.15 am on 3 September 1939, Chamberlain spoke to the nation on the radio and said that we were now at war with Germany. He finished his speech by telling the British people, 'I know that you will all play your part with calmness and courage.' Just twenty-eight minutes later, the first air raid siren sounded.

———•———

We only had one big scare, that was on the morning when Chamberlain said 'I'm sorry to tell you we are now at war with Germany.' And I can remember him saying this and I can remember 'em all sitting round our old Philips radio. And the people from next door had come in. It was very much that you all shared this with one another. And it was a gorgeous day. It was a boiling, lovely, brilliant, lovely, sunny summer's Sunday. And we sat there and we listened. And my mum must have said 'Not again Ted'. I can remember my mother, 'cos she'd been through the First World War, as my dad had. 'Not again Ted,' she said. He said, 'It'll be all right. Be over by Christmas.' So that was it. 'Oh it's September, it'll be over by Christmas.' And little did they know.

Joanna Roberts

The day that war was declared, I was on night duty, and we were going to go to bed – we were in the sitting room, where there was a communal radio – and then of course, we heard the prime minister say 'Britain is at war' and we had cold shivers, because we'd got brothers. My brother had already joined the Territorials with the talk of war coming, so I knew he would go straight away. My friend had got two brothers of army age, and we all knew that we were involved. We got a message from the matron – all the nurses must go and gather in the outpatients department, and she would talk to us. So she gave us a talk about our responsibilities and everything else, rather a serious talk, but at the end of it, she said, 'I shall understand if you want to return home, if you want to opt out of the nursing scene and go back home to parents. It's your choice.' I think only one person did that – she went back to her mother – but everybody else stayed on.

Elsie Edwards

We left Cape Town to come back to England in August 1939, and on September third, war broke out. We were on the ship, coming back to England, and we arrived here at the outbreak of war and all theatres and cinemas were closed – it wasn't allowed for a large congregation to be in one place at one particular time.

Anna Tzelniker

First thing that I know of it, in 1939, they impounded a German boat in the West India Dock. They kept fifty ton of cargo in it and they wouldn't take it out and they kept him in the dock. This German went mad, this officer, this skipper. He wanted to get out and get back to Germany, see, 'cos we'd started the war with them. And we held him in and held his ship in so that they confiscated it, see. People in uniform went aboard and it might have been the customs, but as they went up the gangway, he stood at the top of the gangway and the first bloke he just went 'Pop', knocked him back with the others, this German skipper. They impounded his ship and they kept it. That was in the West India Dock.

Alfred Green

When the Phoney War started, one could go down to the pier and see all the shipping, with Denmark as neutral countries, Holland, Belgium – one of the last ships to go under the swastika – plus the British ones.

Dick Allington

Everyone thought we were going to be gassed to death, you see, we were all carrying gas masks. And we were building shelters, constructing shelters in the streets. In the Undergrounds, they were putting up bunks: thousands and thousands of bunks. All the Underground stations had bunks where people, when the war did start, went down there every night and slept in these bunks in the most appalling conditions.

Graham Rutherford

We moved from Poplar at the very, very beginning of the war, because they built an air raid shelter right outside our door, and my dad was ill and he just couldn't see daylight – he would sit at the front window and he just stared at the brick wall of the air raid shelter, and so we moved.

Anne Griffiths

The whole of the population had been issued with gas masks, the firemen who'd be on the streets during the air raids were given service respirators – the same as what the armed forces were given – and the ordinary civilians were given the civilian type. Mothers with small babies were given a pouch-like thing to put the infant in. She was expected to put the baby in there and sit and pump a pump to put air into the baby during an air raid. Can you imagine?

Cyril Demarne

The council provided everyone with a shelter, an Anderson shelter, so we dug a hole in the garden and put the shelter down there. They provided everyone with a gas mask because they thought that's what was gonna happen, and in due course everything was on rations, so we had ration books, and we was shown how to put out incendiary bombs – there was buckets of water everywhere and stirrup pumps and we were shown how to use those to put the fire out – that's what the fire-watchers did. If you wasn't in the forces, and you was home, you was taught how to do that so that if a siren went, you went out on duty and you watched everywhere for these firebombs and you put them out. Some people were wardens, the men especially, but the women were fire-watchers.

Violet Kentsbeer

Poisonous gas attacks by planes were one of the greatest fears before the start of the Second World War; a government adviser predicted up to quarter of a million deaths from gas in the first week of war alone. Gas drills such as this one became a routine part of war preparations in every school and workplace. 1939

My father was a costermonger and used to have a barrow in Chapel Market; we sold fruit from it. Then when the war started, you only got fruit if you had allocation papers, and you only had allocation papers if you had business receipts. And being ordinary barrow-boy type of costermongers, we never kept business receipts, so we never got no fruit. So the business closed down.

John Beattie

They made Mudchute into a gun site and where my mother lived on Stebondale Street, at the top of the house you could see them preparing it all. My grandmother was alive at that time and she used to say, 'I'd like to know what they're doing over there taking all those boxes down.' And my mum used to say, 'That's tea, Nan, they're storing the tea there.' And that was the ammunition.

Annie Pope

The defence of the dock at Tilbury was non-existent. They placed wooden guns around the quays – they were sort of made to look from the air as if they were gun emplacements, but they were only wooden structures shaped in the form of a gun emplacement. That's all we had. So the reconnaissance planes would think that the dock was bristling with guns – but we hadn't a thing.

Elizabeth Garrett

In the particular area where I lived, the flats were completely dug up to prevent enemy aircraft landing. As I say, for us kids, not realising the danger, it was a great big adventure.

Albert Patten

When the war started, it was really chaotic, you know. I went over and they had soldiers in the dock – they had a soldier on top of our station, marching up and down. Didn't last long – it only lasted a couple of months, but it just shows you what went on. They thought we was gonna be invaded.

I used to go over there, eight o'clock at night, dark. And all of a sudden, I went across the bridge. 'Halt!' It was the bloody soldier – he'd got a bayonet. I'd got my little cycle lamp, and it was an oil one – well, you know how much light that showed – 'cos everything was blackouts and 'put that light out!'

I mean, when it's blackout, it's black. You can't see a thing, and I mean, there's a dock there, and the water. So I said, 'No, you bloody fool,' and I said, 'Come on over here,' and he marched left, right, left, right over to the police station, and the police looked at me, you know, he knew me – so they got this book out, and they couldn't find anything appertaining to a bicycle oil lamp. Needless to say, he got told he was too conscientious. But as I say, after two or three months, there was no soldiers at all. They did without them. But I nearly got done for a German spy.

William Mather

Early in the war, trains were extremely crowded and uncomfortable, and I started to cycle to work, which was quite breathtaking when you allow for the amount of light that was allowed until the regulations came in for masked headlights later on in the war. I cycled in the blackout at times with a pen torch as my headlight, and my reflectors for my rear. The wonder is that more people didn't get killed.

Eric Cropper

I remember when the war started. My sisters, they went to Oxford – some place took them in. And I remember me and me brother put paper on the windows, and all that sort of thing. The warning went about eleven o'clock – it was a false alarm, but everybody was screaming and shrieking – it put the wind up. And then I remember going to bed that night, pitch black, first time we had a blackout. And it went off again about two in the morning; another false alarm.

Charles Beck

On the Sunday that war broke out, the sirens almost immediately went. And my mother went across to a billiard club that had already been earmarked as a shelter. But then there was the all-clear. With my friend Johnny Walker, we went to St James's Park, and I noticed air raid trenches that were dug there.

Jack Miller

The siren went off then, and everybody thought, Let's run for cover, but we all got our gas masks on and went over to the ward, because we thought we'd better get the patients down to the basement. So we got them all down to the basement, and of course, the next thing, the all-clear went, and it was a false alarm. So then it was gas masks off.

Elsie Edwards

At eleven o'clock we was putting up the shelter, you, know, the Anderson shelter in the garden. Becontree was where I lived then and that was the first Anderson shelter I put in, and the wife was helping me. When the warning went off, I was just putting the end down, and it got caught, and the wife went to stop it and cut all her hand – they was sharp, the corners. I soon put her right, but she was the first wounded of the war, I think.

Charles Lisle

The First Evacuations

For the first eight months after Britain declared war on Germany, very little happened on the home front. Despite the shock of Chamberlain's radio announcement, many British people thought the ensuing conflict would never amount to much anyway – after all, the enemy was far away in Poland, and hadn't we beaten them in one world war already? In France, this period became known as *drôle de guerre* – 'a joke of a war'. In Britain, it was the Phoney War.

However, the idea of evacuating vulnerable citizens in the event of war had long been under discussion – by 1938, London County Council had agreed in principle to the evacuation of all schoolchildren, under the care of volunteer teachers – and this policy was put in place early, some would say prematurely, with the first group of women and children being dispatched to the countryside on 1 September 1939. Accommodation had been organised for 4.8 million people in safe areas away from major cities and in the following three days, 1.5 million people were moved. Many families also made private arrangements to stay with friends and family.

Businesses also began to think about how they would protect their workers and profits, with a number relocating some or all of their staff. The Port of London decided that the docks were unsafe for female workers and sent them all home.

At the start of the war the government also rounded up 74,000 Germans, Austrians and Italians who were living in Britain, and these were interned in prison camps while their political sympathies were checked. Most were later released, having been judged to be 'friendly aliens', but about two thousand remained in camps, mostly on the Isle of Man, until the end of the war.

———

For the first year or so, although the war was on, there was no activity of bombing, the war didn't seem to be on. The only thing that did start that particular time was rationing

– you know, you had clothes points for this and points for that and your ration books. And then you was given gas masks from school – you had to carry them about with you everywhere. But there was no bombing at the time, so it didn't seem to be on.

Wally James

I wasn't evacuated with the first lot that went, the majority of the schools closed and for quite a few months, during what we classed as the Phoney War, we was running wild.

Dick Allington

Actually, we got evacuated before the war started, down at Wells, in Somerset. It lasted six weeks; come back before the war had started.

Len Faram

In the month of my arrival at the Roan school in Greenwich, we were getting ready for evacuation at the beginning of the war – in fact, war hadn't broken out, and all we did was that every morning we went to school, and we sat in our house rooms with our house captain and house masters and virtually chatted all day – waiting for the call. Eventually, the word came through, and that morning we were evacuated, just like that.

John Earl

I wouldn't become evacuated, neither would the other two. The thing that turned me was that there was a recruiting film of ARP in the cinema and we saw this, and you could see the rooftops of a town and the planes coming and the spurts coming up and that – and I'd seen H G Wells's *War of the Worlds* and *Things to Come*. I was sitting there listening to my mother and father talking. They had a little general shop

Evacuation did not just apply to children; many companies sent members of staff, particularly women, and also key documents out of London. These PLA payroll girls left their dockside offices to spend the war in the panelled safety of Littleworth Lodge in Esher. 1940

which my mother ran, which they'd bought from Dad's compensation, in case he couldn't work.

There was a little back parlour, which fronted on to the shop, and it was just a wooden partition that was wallpapered, with a window so you could see into the shop, see anybody coming in. Then the other side of the counter was the shop window again, so it was just glass. And they was talking about putting sandbags up, and I can visualise this coming in with a bomb and them being killed. So it's really nothing courageous on my part but frightened of being separated from your parents. So I said, 'I'm not being evacuated,' and they didn't need much persuading. They said, 'Oh, OK, that's it.' So we stayed. Of course, all the schools shut down.

George Adams

I wasn't evacuated. I wouldn't go. I was given the choice. My father said, 'What do you want to do?' He said, 'You're old enough now to sort it out.' He said, 'You're fifteen.'

So I said, 'Are you coming?' 'No.' 'Will Mummy come?' 'No.' 'Will anybody come?' 'No.' 'Well,' I said, 'I ain't going.' So it was all right for the first year. It was just like – and people were bringing the kids all back home. Quiet – what was we worried about?

Joanna Roberts

Poplar Hospital took over the Barnado's Children's Home. They were evacuated, of course, and we took over the houses and lived in them, and we had the hospital. The patients used to get shipped out to Barkingside, and we used to get soldiers who'd got influenza or whatever, and they used to be in the hospital. It was a sort of twilight time, where you were waiting for something to happen, but you were busy. It was all waiting for the big bang.

Elsie Edwards

My third brother was in the firm until they were evacuated to Oxted, where he caught pneumonia and nearly died. Things were so primitive down there at first – no fires or anything, and they used to have to walk nearly a mile for an evening meal, through the village in Oxted. Having caught pneumonia, he had to come home and we, for many weeks, we took it in turns to be by his bed with a piece of string attached to his fingers and to ours so that we could replenish the ice bags. Eventually, he contracted tuberculosis; he never worked again.

Charlie Gubbins

When the war broke out, they sent all the girls – the typists, the secretaries and the calculator operators – home because it was felt that London was going to be blitzed and the docks would be a prime target. Some of the girls, incidentally, went out to Thames Ditton, where they established a sort of secondary head office and ran things from there.

So we men had to fill the breach. We had to operate the central wages office and I can clearly recall the first time we produced the wages. We had to make, I think, six copies of the payroll and we started, I think, turning out these payrolls eleven o'clock at night. At three o'clock in the morning, I think we'd just finished. And to our horror, we found that the person who should have put the carbon paper in had put it in back to front, so all we had was one copy of the payroll. I won't tell you what we said to this colleague of mine, but in about 1943, we were going out through Italy, and who should I meet but this said gentleman who was then a budding second lieutenant. It just shows that if you can't put duplicating paper together properly, at least you can become a second lieutenant.

Dick Butler

My sister had been sharing a home with my parents before the war. Because although she was married with a small child, she was evacuated, because her husband was never a naturalised citizen. He was Austrian and he was interned in the Isle of Man and then when he was released, he was sent to work in an aircraft factory in Portsmouth. She went to live in Chichester.

Vicki Green

I was regraded because my eyesight wasn't quite up to the mark, and I did mainly prisoner of war camp duties at Kempton Park and the Isle of Man. The Isle of Man was a thrilling place – there was a great deal interned, among them some Jewish people. I remember one occasion when I escorted a bearded Jew that looked like someone who could have done the role of *Fiddler on the Roof* – you know, beard and black cap, and all that. They even had some from the British Union of Fascists interned.

Jack Miller

My guardian decided to move to Canvey Island where we used to have our holidays and she got a shop in Southend. Then the war broke out and we had to come back – because she was married to an alien, and although by then he had died, because she married at the Chinese embassy, that made her a Chinese national. And all aliens had to move away from the coast – they were not allowed to live on the coast, so we came back to London. And to the air raids.

Connie Hoe

CHAPTER 8

The Waiting is Over

Dunkirk

> *'Dunkirk has fallen... with it has ended the greatest battle of world history.*
>
> *Soldiers! My confidence in you knew no bounds. You have not disappointed me.'*
>
> – ADOLF HITLER, 5 JUNE 1940

In Germany, the Phoney War was referred to as *der sitzkrieg,* 'the sitting war'. And after the *sitzkrieg* came *der blitzkrieg* – 'the lightning war'. In its shortened form, the English adopted blitz to mean heavy bombing by German aircraft, but originally it was used to describe a military tactic of sudden, lightning-like assaults on all fronts. First, heavy aerial bombardment would disrupt communication and transport systems and destroy morale; this was immediately followed by a massive invasion of ground troops. The army would keep pressing forward, driving helpless civilians before it to frustrate attacks by the defending forces.

These tactics required vast amounts of military equipment, and Britain's efforts in the early stages of the war concentrated on using the navy to intercept and disrupt the flow of raw materials being shipped to Germany. To protect naval routes and secure a supply of iron ore from Sweden, Germany invaded Denmark and Norway in April 1940 and gained control of both. In Britain, the only man in the government who had foreseen this and tried to put in place a plan to prevent it was the First Lord of the Admiralty, Winston Churchill. He replaced Chamberlain as prime minister on 10 May 1940, just a few hours before Germany invaded Belgium, France, Luxembourg and the Netherlands.

British troops had been in France since 1938, mainly deployed along the French-Belgian border, known as the Maginot line. They were expecting a drawn-out defensive war, but were swiftly driven back by the German army's *blitzkreig* as Panzer divisions bypassed the Allies' defences and smashed through the Ardennes forest to attack their weakest point. The Allied forces were driven back through northern France towards Dunkirk. Reports from the Continent were heavily censored, but by 26 May, when the Archbishop of Canterbury led prayers from the pulpit 'for our soldiers in dire peril in France', everyone knew that the British Expeditionary Force was in trouble.

I remember it was a glorious summer's day and it seemed very quiet. We rounded the Victoria Dock entrance and Jimmy Smith, one of the lightermen what worked boats, come out and he said, 'France has fallen.'

And, well, they was ablaze; they was gonna fight with broomsticks, they was not turning it in – they was really keen to have a go. But I remember that he just sort of appeared over the top of the brow of the wharf of Victoria Dock and said 'France has fallen'. And that was it.

Then we saw them take the lifeboats, but we didn't know anything about it, the lifeboats being towed down in strings from the ship – robbed all the ships in the docks of their lifeboats and took them down below, and small boats going. But they never asked for us, though I think some barges were towed across, but we didn't go across with them to Dunkirk.

George Adams

When Dunkirk was on, they collared everything that could float, and all the ships in the dock had all their lifeboats stripped. They took all the lifeboats off the ships and towed them down the river. I worked all night in the joiner's shop making ladders – sixteen-foot ladders, to put over the sides of the ships so that the soldiers could climb up the sides of the ships, and there was hundreds and hundreds of ladders made, so they could hang them over the sides of the ships.

Stan Bryan

My father would have been in about his early thirties and I think he took *The Tigress* up for Dunkirk. I can remember that so well and it always made me feel quite ill – you get the same shiver that you did in the war. I was taken down, coat over pyjamas. Now, when I see photographs of the little boats going off to Dunkirk, that photograph is in the daytime, but it wasn't when I saw it, it was in the evening. It must have been the second tide because, of course, in the war it was double summer time and it was really always light... It was absolutely terrifying because, I mean, one knew absolutely what the war was about, all those boats and it was not dark, it was just evening time and they were all going very quietly, with no lights on so that the Germans didn't see them. It had been rumoured for weeks that something terrible was happening and nobody really knew because it wasn't put in the papers. My dad, we waved to him, and he went up with all these little boats, all in company more or less locked together in a block up the river, and that was one of the most frightening and moving things I ever remember. I don't know how many boats went but the river seemed full of them.

Freda Hammerton

Between 1932-38, the Royal Eagle *paddle steamer took about three million holiday-makers from London to Southend, Margate and Ramsgate. In May-June 1939, she made three trips to Dunkirk, coming under fire forty-three times, eventually rescuing 2,657 men from the beaches.* Unknown, 1935

My father's friend George Wheeler had rung up and said, 'I don't know what's happening, but the Admiralty have been in touch with all boat owners and people who own pleasure boats and so on, requesting that they get together and make their way down to Sheerness as soon as possible.' I said, 'Well, what do you think's going on?' He said, 'I don't know, but could you fit out a bag with one or two things, whatever you can, and report to me at Westminster Pier.' Which I did and eventually I found myself in a small convoy moving down from Westminster Pier and we eventually arrived at Sheerness the following morning. We did stop that night on Southend Pier and we all moored up there for the night – there was not much of it left – and had a little bit of sleep and then we all went over to Sheerness.

And that was when I learned that there was something going on across at France – we still didn't know what it was, but all we knew was that the navy wanted us to go with these boats and take people off the shore. Well, of course, I'd never been to France – I didn't know what the shore was like, but we were told that all we had to do was get in convoy and we would be shown what to do, so off we went. It was an absolute marvel that there was no wind, the sea was very calm indeed and the *Queen Boadicea* could take about a hundred passengers and she was twin screw – a very handy craft. She wasn't all that small but her draft was only about three feet and she was, after all, a river boat.

Anyway, we arrived off a place called De Panne, and it was a very, very frightening period: five days and five nights I was off the shore there, going in and picking up people. Some of the lads never made it. What would happen is this: that I put my nose into the sand and there was not a lot of water, it was pretty flat. We got a lot of trouble from the destroyers racing up and down because they caused a hell of a wash and it would sort of knock the vessels about a little bit, specially whilst your head was on to the sand, but I had twin screws and therefore you could pull her off quite easily, that wasn't difficult. But some of the lads would get on and you would have to say, 'Well, that's enough,' and then they'd hang on to these rubber tyre fenders round the vessel and of course that was all right until you got alongside the paddle steamer or whatever it was.

I never went backward and forwards from Margate or anything like that, I only just took them off the shore and put them on another vessel, and of course it was very difficult, because how would you – what would you say to them? You know to me, as it was, the vessel was probably lying with a list to one way or another, and it wasn't easy to handle. I can assure you that I was never so frightened in all my life and nothing has really ever frightened me since, nothing at all.

I mean, you could see boats sinking all round you, and of course the old Focke-Wulfs were sort of coming down and dropping bombs and machine gunning and it was chaotic and miserable and not very nice. People always say to me, 'How many people did you save?' I've got no idea really, no idea at all.

Alan Spong

As regards Dunkirk, on the second day, when the Royal Navy ships came back into Sheerness harbour, we were sent round with a naval officer to try and scrounge as much ammunition for the *Tedsworth*, which was a sloop, to go back on the following night. And there was no ammunition ashore to give her, and on going round all the ships in the harbour, we managed to raise five hundred rounds of .303, and .25 tracers, and the *Tedsworth* went back to Dunkirk that night with just that.

John Henry Arnold

My mother's brother was in the East Surreys and he was in France. He'd kept his Bren gun carrier throughout and they loved it – I mean, it was their life, their little anchorage, and in the end they had to abandon it and that was terrible. He was a Catholic too and he spoke of coming back along those roads, roads empty of people by then, when they got there, because I suppose they were bringing up the rear guard, and seeing rosaries and holy medals thrown down in the road, and talking about being on the beach, and mostly they didn't talk about it much because it was too awful, I think. He was lucky, he was in one of the last boats brought back, and my mother and her sisters of course were all going to church and praying that Ted would come home and he suddenly turned up at home – no word, he just turned up – it was marvellous.

Ever since the war, that uncle has been very fastidious about his food and we think it goes back to that, about what he had to eat and how he's ate it and how it was cooked, and we think it was the things he saw.

Freda Hammerton

Our cockle boats went from Southend and we saw the men come back. Some had got no trousers. Some had got top coats. If they had got trousers, they hadn't got top coats. And they came back and they were on the railway station and as we passed, all the little bits of food that I had collected and bought to put in my cupboard to help me go through the war, I thought... I was so flabbergasted to see all these men, I went back and I got me last half a pound of marge and I got me loaf of bread. I buttered it all and I wrapped it up and I just went like that. And they were like a load of wolves, tearing it apart to eat it.

I didn't know that night that I would have to give up my bedroom in my house and go down with my landlady. And we had forty-three men in that house, because it was a big house.

And we fed those men. And we never got a sausage for it, for three weeks we fed 'em. Then they came and took them out. I used to curse 'em, but I used to think to meself, poor fellas, they've got nowhere to go.

Ivy Cobbald

It was before Dunkirk, but already the Germans had broken through the Maginot line, and suddenly, I thought to myself, What am I going on dreaming about? If the Germans conquer Britain, who are they going to kill? They're going to kill my family – all of us. I wouldn't be able to arrange for all of us to escape to America, or Canada. I've got no business being a conscientious objector. So I wrote a letter to the War Office asking to be called up immediately.

Emanuel Litvinoff

The Battle of Britain

'The Battle of France is over. I expect that the Battle of Britain is about to begin. Upon this battle depends the survival of Christian civilisation. Upon it depends our own British life, and the long continuity of our institutions and our empire. The whole fury and might of the enemy must very soon be turned on us. Hitler knows that he will have to break us in this island or lose the war.'

– Winston Churchill, 18 June 1940

Dunkirk was hailed as a victory; its name is now shorthand for a plucky, never-say-die British spirit. Contemporary cinema newsreels made much of the rescue of 226,000 British and 110,000 French troops in what was codenamed Operation Dynamo. Churchill called it a 'a miracle of deliverance'. The little boats and the common man coming to the rescue of a mighty army was a hugely emotive part of that miracle. However, in private, Churchill called it 'the greatest military defeat of our time'. Much of our army had escaped, but thousands of tons of essential equipment was now under German control.

When Churchill told the British public that the fury and might of the enemy would now be turned on Britain, he urged, 'Let us therefore brace ourselves to our duties, and so bear ourselves that if the British Empire and its Commonwealth last for a thousand years, men will still say, "This was their finest hour."'

Hitler had set his sights on conquering Britain, and the first step towards his invasion plan, codenamed Operation Sealion, was to beat the country down with air strikes. The Führer issued a directive stating, 'The English air force must have been beaten down to such an extent morally, and in fact, that it can no longer muster any power of attack worth mentioning against the German crossing.' The first bombing raids were concentrated on shipping in the English Channel and strategic coastal defences. A series of strikes on airfields and supply organisations followed, and the battle in the skies began in earnest. At this point, Hitler was still insisting that 'every effort should be made to avoid unnecessary loss of life amongst the civilian population'.

Then during August 1940, several German planes dropped probably unplanned bombs on civilian areas in east London, and the RAF retaliated by bombing Berlin. Hitler now issued a directive to the Luftwaffe to turn its attention to disruptive attacks on the population and air defences of British cities, including London, by day and night. The docks, with their warehouses and wharves, together with the surrounding railway lines, factories and power stations, represented the commercial heart of the capital and were chosen as a main target. On Saturday, 7 September 1940, shortly after half-past four, more than three hundred German bombers, escorted by some six hundred fighter planes, began raining devastation on London's East End.

The official first date of the Blitz on London was the seventh of September 1940. But West Ham was bombed on the night of the sixth. Hitler had given the Luftwaffe orders not to bomb London, but it's difficult to avoid London and they came over the south-eastern approaches and they strayed over into Silvertown, and they bombed part of the dockland area, the tidal basin, and that was on the sixth of September. That kept the fire service up till the early hours of the morning, and we were up again at seven o'clock the next morning. We'd had a little taste of it and we were quite apprehensive – we knew that more was coming.

Cyril Demarne

I was in Chrisp Street Market once again with my mother looking round the stalls and I went to buy some ribbon and she said, 'Can you hear anything?' 'No.' She said, 'It's that siren.' 'Cos we had sirens warning us. Sirens at the all-clear and sirens to start it all off. And it was on the top of the local police station, which was very near to the market. And I could hear this. And I said, 'It's a siren, Mum, it's the warning.' She said, 'What's that? Why have we got that going?' Someone must have started it off and before you could say rabbits you could see coming up, following the line of the Thames, you could see the planes.

And, you know, it was absolutely gobsmacking because there we were, standing there minding our own business. Nothing had happened and all of a sudden, this Saturday, it must be about five o'clock, and I can remember, I can hear them. And if I sit and I hear a plane coming over and it's loaded – sometimes you get them transport planes and the mmm, mmm, mmm, you get that load – I can get taken right back to that.

Joanna Roberts

I stood out in the garden and we watched the bombers going, because I remember my elder brother saying, 'Oh, I don't know where they're making for – they're making for the centre of London.' But of course, it wasn't, it was the East End they were bombing.

Dorothy Shipp

The worst experience I can recall is of seeing the bombers going to bomb the docks on a Saturday afternoon in 1940, I think it was, in September. It was just like seeing swarms and swarms of bees going over, with this tremendous droning and heavy feeling in the air as they went over. And everybody was terrified, wondering when they were going to stop and drop their bombs. To most of us it was a relief that it was the docks and not us, of course. All civilians were ordered to stay indoors and in their shelters.

Eileen Brome

War came on my fifteenth birthday, and for the first year, you know, nothing much happened. But the seventh of September, that's a day I'll never forget. My sister and I had gone to work for a friend of my father's who had three tobacco kiosks, one at Stratford Market, one at Canning Town and one at Custom House. I had a very peculiar feeling on me all day, and it sort of grew worse as the day grew on, on this Saturday. My sister was at Canning Town and I was at Custom House; my sister is six years older than me. And I thought, We've got to get home. I just had this feeling that something terrible was going to happen, and I phoned through to the booking office and said, 'May I speak to my sister?' And she came to the phone. I said, 'You've got to get the next train out, and shut up, and hide the money – we've got to get home.' 'Oh, we can't do that,' she said, 'we'll get into trouble.' I said, 'I don't care, get on the train.'

And in the end, she said she would, and I locked up and I hid the money – I think under some boxes in the kiosk – and she came on the next train. We hadn't been home more than about ten minutes when my sister looked out of the window – the air raid siren had gone – and she said, 'Oh Dad, look, up there,' she said, 'there's aeroplanes and all little things coming from them.' My father hurried us all down the stairs into a big strong room, and that was to become our bedroom for what seemed to be years after that.

Joan Shaw

It was a glorious September day, sun was shining, cloudless, blue sky, a magnificent day. Round about five-ish, half-past five in the afternoon, the siren sounded. I was in the yard and I looked up and there in the eastern sky was these great squadrons of German aircraft, bombers, twenty-four, I think it was, in each V-shaped squadron, and flying above them were hordes of fighter aircraft, hundreds of them, tiny midge-like things with the sun shining on the aluminium skins, glinting in the sun. The anti-aircraft guns were going with great bursts in the centre of them, and they must have hit one of them because it came down quite close to where we were serving, with a screaming zoom and a bang. I bolted for the control room – I knew the calls would be coming in; we could see the bombs coming down. We heard that the Woolwich Arsenal, the Royal Docks, the Ford Motor Works, and the Beckton Gas Works – which then were the largest gas works in Europe – all prime targets, were being bombed. Within a matter of minutes, every fire pump in the West Ham district was out attending fires, and more pumps were being called for.

Cyril Demarne

The first day they bombed, I was at Hyde Park swimming, and I got to Aldgate to come home because I was on at ten o'clock, on night shift, and I got as far as Aldgate and I didn't know all this bombing had been going on in the afternoon. And there was fires everywhere, and I started to walk; course, they pushed me down into a dugout because you couldn't get any further.

William Mather

The first night of the Blitz – I think that really frightened you – it's got to stick in any child's mind. I was four years old. We used to live upstairs in this house and I remember sitting in the, well, we used to call it the kitchen, but it was the living room, we used to have a kitchen in there where we done the cooking, and I can remember the screaming bomb. But I didn't know what it was, you know. There was your mum and dad trying to protect you, and this horrible screaming noise. Eventually we was told it was a screaming bomb. And you know, I think if they'd have used that, that would have sent everyone barmy. I think they dropped that in Mile End some- where. But I can always remember the noise of that bomb, it seemed to go on and on. The screaming noise.

The terrible anxiety there must have been – and my parents never showed it. We had an Anderson shelter in the back garden – well, most people did. And the siren went and we went down the shelters and bombs dropped everywhere. I can remember looking out and seeing all the fires burning, and Lusty's was alight. Lusty's always loomed across the cut where I lived. That was all going up in smoke and sparks and it was like a big fire- work display. As a kid, there was not a lot of fear, really. It was more being dragged back down the shelter then trying to stand out and watching incendiary bombs come down, you know. And the next morning, our house was gutted.

Len Faram

Now when they came over that Saturday afternoon, they came first, didn't they, dropped the bombs like the flares and set so much alight, and then they came over in the night-time. Well, we had a little shelter in Custom House, out in the yard, me and my missus and three kids, I think we had then, and that's where we had to sleep and during the night as each bomb thudded – 'cos we were only a hundred yards from the dock – and as every bomb thudded into that ground, all your shelters, bang, bang, and I really thought any minute now we're gonna have one ourselves. In the morning I thought when I went out there ain't gonna be a bloody thing standing, this is how I really thought because it was all night long, you know. And then we got up in the morning, everything seemed to be the same, but they'd got it over there – the island got it very bad, didn't it?

Stan Rose

The first siren came, the first warning came, and the bombers came up the river and they shut the gates when the air raid warning went, they shut the gates – and this is true – the poor Millwall people knew that Snowdon's had got this great big shelter and they're battering on the gates to get in, and of course, they wouldn't let them, you know, they had instructions not to let them in, because if you let them in once... And so they had to stay outside. And I thought, it's like the French Revolution, I thought to myself when I heard about it. And they literally were battering on the gates to get into the air raid shelter.

Dorothy Shipp

Dad had shut the shop, and the shop linked with our house so he come in from the shop, turned right into our house. So we were very sort of joined up. So he came out. So Mum said, 'What's the matter?' He said, 'Got planes coming over. You'd better go and sit in the shelter.' She said, 'But the shelter ain't ready yet.' He said, 'Well, we'll sit in the back room.'

So we sat in the back room. 'Where's the dog?' So the dog was sitting in there. So the people from next door knocked on the door and they said, 'What's happening?' 'Don't know.' So then we began to hear, you know, mmm, bump, mmm, bump and from then that whole day really, it's so much in your mind. It is so much in your mind as to how you felt. Terrified. We weren't brave. My mum wasn't brave and I wasn't brave, I feel sure. My dad was; he just took it as it come.

And then we went – there was a little lull and it was a bit quiet so he went in and made a cup of tea. And he said, 'We'll have to get that shelter done for tomorrow.'

Joanna Roberts

I was there when the East End was set on fire, and you could see it – you could actually see the whole place, the fire was so red. I remember the next morning, some of the firemen who lived there coming back, all black and, oh dear, exhausted. That's how I remember the start of it.

Elsie Edwards

The first raid was over during daylight and as the night drew in, the sky was a great blaze of red – first of all pink, then pink and red, and it was reported that people as far away as fifty miles could see the glow. People in Reading noted, strangely enough, the phenomenon of a sunset in the east – that was the fires burning in London.

Cyril Demarne

Smoke billows from fires still raging in the London Docks on the morning after the first night of the Blitz, when more than a thousand bombs had pulverised the East End. Behind Tower Bridge are the Surrey Docks, on the left, and West India Docks in the distance. 1940

The Fire in the Docks

After a night when many felt that the world was surely ending, the morning of 8 September dawned, and the people of the East End found that London was still standing, although it had taken a terrible battering. In one night the capital had lost 436 civilians and suffered 1,666 casualties. More than a thousand bombs – some strapped to oil drums – and many thousands of incendiary devices had fallen in an area concentrated on the docks.

The ensuing firestorm raged throughout the following week, covering 250 acres. The largest fire, at the Surrey Docks which were storing two and a half million tons of timber, much of it recently arrived from North America and the Baltic, required three hundred pumps to bring it under control.

The different goods stored in warehouses in the docks burned in different ways, posing all kinds of hazards to firemen. In the West India Dock, flammable spirits from the rum warehouse formed blazing rivers and barrels exploded, sending boiling contents flying. Burning pepper produced eye-stinging, lung-scorching smoke, and paint and rubber gave off poisonous fumes. Rats poured out of the burning buildings. The flames ran up the ropes tethering barges to the docks, burning through them and setting the flaming barges adrift to float away on the tide. South of the Royal Docks, the area devastated by the Silvertown explosion in the First World War had once again been flattened.

In Canning Town, several hundred bombed-out families had to be temporarily housed in a school in South Hallsville Road. A convoy of buses was organised to take them to a safer area but, hampered by blocked roads and possibly poorly instructed, the driver got lost and failed to reach the school before the returning Luftwaffe bombed it again, killing about four hundred people.

But if the intention of the German *blitzkreig* had been to crush the spirit of the British people, that first night failed. In the Port of London, firemen worked day and night, without sleep, to extinguish blazing warehouses, and dock workers returned to work showing no signs of being crushed. At midday on Sunday, Winston Churchill himself came to inspect the damage, and the crowd greeted him with shouts of, 'We can take it, Winnie. Give it back!'

———————

We'd cleared London Bridge coming down and we saw these planes up in the air and then we saw something which puzzled us at first and we realised it was bombs dropping. As we were under Tower Bridge it seemed as if the German planes was turning at the edge of the City and going back over the docks. And we ran downriver and the Surrey Docks was afire then, and there was barges ablaze.

Then, as we ran down, we were going from side to side because the bombs were dropping close and we could hear the shrapnel frapping on the sides of the boat. And the skipper was up there in the wheelbox and he didn't come down, he just sat and we were a light boat, that is, we had no craft, we was running down light to Blackwall Pier.

As we went by the Commercial Dock, a petrol tanker ran up, the small ones, and they had their gas masks on, and they went 'What happened to us?' and we got this acrid smell and – Jesus Christ! – it was gas! I always brought my gas mask, so did the skipper, so did the mate, but the Scotsman didn't, nor his son. So I said to his son, 'You'd better put water on your handkerchief, put it over your mouth.' And the two of them down below, crying. The Scotsman had been in the trenches in the First World War, so I could understand his agony.

Prime Minister Winston Churchill and his wife Clementine visit the East End, accompanied by his chief military adviser, General Ismay. The manager of the Port of London is taking them on a tour of bomb damage, including this seamen's hostel near the docks. 1940

As I say, the Germans came back and we was in a silly position, really, the bombs were dropping close. We could see the dock, an absolute ball of flame silhouetted against the air, and on our boat we had the scuttle open, and there's the Scotsman sitting there rocking backwards with his son in the dark – he wouldn't have the light on – and the mate and the skipper was sitting up on the wheelbox, and I knew we had no water so I said, 'I'm going across on the other boat for water,' which I did do, and I looked up at the skipper, Uncle Jim Chew, and he could see the gasometers in the Leven Road gasworks silhouetted by a ball of flame behind them, and his house was a couple of streets behind that. I can see him now, and I really, you know, admired the man there, you know sitting there. I mean, his wife was there, and his child.

George Adams

I never thought I would survive when on that first Saturday, when the planes come over, it was terrible – everywhere, right the way round the island was in flames. No buses or anything could run, the firemen put all the hoses across the main roads, one mass of flame all the way round.

Annie Pope

We knew the docks would be a number one target so we put five fire stations in there and they were housed in warehouses. We'd got the docks to work from for our water supply but one of the points we were told was that if food warehouses were involved, we had to use clean water from the mains, we couldn't use contaminated water on foodstuffs, otherwise it couldn't be used again. If you use clean water on food, once it dries out, most of it can be salvaged. And practically four-fifths of our food had to be imported. So dirty water for dirty fires, and clean water for food. Everybody understood this, but the fires that occurred in the first blitz of the docks, we had to order five hundred fire pumps for the docks. There was eleven miles of quays there, all lined with warehouses filled with combustibles, fifty ships in there, all combustible, so you can see how five hundred pumps wouldn't go very far.

Cyril Demarne

We came home from Spratt's, where we'd taken shelter. My dad used to do fire watching on the roof. And he came down and he said, 'It's terrible out there.' He said, 'The whole city's ablaze. They've got no water.' They couldn't run the pipes 'cos there wasn't enough hose. The EWS – he used to call them Edward William Samuels, 'cos that was his initials, but it was Emergency Water Service – so the EWS had tanks in various places, fairly big, full of water, and they all ran out. And so everything just burned, there was nothing you could do about it.

Joanna Roberts

The first night, I was playing cards down in the shelter, down below with the superintendent, four of us, quite happy, when the warning went. And then somebody shouted out, 'The stores are on fire, come out!' Out we came. Just as we came out there was such a blast it blew me helmet off, see. And I looked around. I couldn't find it. Course, you're all het up. And the superintendent looked around at me, he said, 'Where's your helmet, son?' I said, 'I don't know – it blew off, guv'nor.' So he said, 'Find this man a helmet, quickly.'

We went around and I knew the stores, having worked there. The old printing shop and the typing shop were all made into one then and they had rows and blimmin' great coils of rope in there and they kept it as a rope store. The incendiaries had come right through there – it was burning with the ropes. We managed to get them out, we saved that store, but we didn't save a lot of the other dock.

Charles Lisle

And the next time we came in, which was the Sunday, it was like a scene from H G Wells's *Things to Come*, after the war: you couldn't see any sign of life on the shore. I mean, as far as we were concerned, we were the only people alive, and smoke and barges drifting about everywhere. Then as we passed Woolwich we could just see a lorry going along, I think it's Church Road, it's up high at Woolwich, and we went back to Blackwall Pier and we tied up.

And then we walked home, 'cos Jim Chew lived in the general direction that I did and we parted and as I walked up Slimmer's Road, at the bottom, my grandmother's turning, there was Rosenblatt's Jewish bakers, that was flat. I walked round the corner to my own house and I could hear them crying inside because they didn't know what had happened to me. Me grandmother was there, me father's mother; she'd been bombed out of Culloden Street, and that was the start of the Blitz.

George Adams

And then early on Sunday morning, I think, there was a request on the radio for anybody who had anything to do with the docks to get down there as best they could. So my husband went immediately – of course the devastation was absolutely dreadful, he said it was ghastly. It was all burning and everything reduced to rubble. They all got on with it, the clerks and the dockers, everybody, the bosses, they all went in and helped to get all this mess cleared up, and they stayed there for about three days, without having a change of clothes or anywhere proper to sleep.

They continued somehow to operate those docks. They were very keen to do so, because everybody was very patriotic of course and it made you feel very cross indeed to see all this devastation that we couldn't help. So in spite of it all, life went on.

Eileen Brome

I remember on that Saturday, we looked over the roof garden when we came up from the shelter and there just seemed to be fires all the way round, and my little brother said, 'Will we ever get out? Will the fires come and burn us?', because you turned round and there was just fires everywhere, and it was really frightening.

Joan Shaw

The Surrey Docks was full of timber, it was well alight – you could read a paper by it. And at that time, I used to smoke, and the warden's come along and said, 'Put that fag out, they'll be able to see it.' Honestly, you could have read a paper by it.

Dennis Pike

The sight of the burned-out Surrey Docks was one of the most depressing things I've ever seen in my life. I had an inkling of it, of course, when at my house in Sidcup, some eleven miles distant, we saw the smoke and flames. But I couldn't believe that it could happen. On the Monday morning, when we got there, there was absolutely, literally, nothing – the sheds, the corrugated iron on the sheds had all been melted and carried away. The girders were either burnt right out or just bent over into tangled masses. Even the stones of the quay, the granite stones and cement had all been cracked and fused. The floated timber in the water alongside was burnt down to the waterline. There wasn't any ashes either – it was absolutely unbelievable, the updraught had carried the whole lot away.

Laurie Landick

And on the Sunday morning, when the all-clear finally went, there was this big pall of smoke coming up from along the river. And our neighbours – who we knew extremely well – loaded up and going. They were just going to get out. I presume they went out Brentwood way. I know some of 'em went to Brentwood, 'cos I kept up with one of them.

Anywhere to get away from near the docks. 'Cos being near the docks you were a target. And we had the Blackwall Tunnel which they were aiming for, and the docks, the East India Docks, all the way along. I mean, we were a sitting target there.

Joanna Roberts

When they hit London on that Saturday, the first Saturday, we were at Manor Park, but I had to go into work on Sunday and I went in but you couldn't do no work. Terrible state down there. Hallsville Road School, they had six hundred I think it was, women and children in there. All the houses in Custom House, they didn't half get a hammering, you know. And all you could see was people crying and all that sort of thing. In the night-time, they hit the school and killed the lot in there. 'Cos it still had a light from the incendiaries and all that sort of thing. But it was terrible down there.

Alfred Green

I knew that my call-up was very close so I took a day's leave on Monday and went away to Kent for a youth hostelling weekend, and people in the youth hostel on Saturday morning said, 'You ought to go to the top of the hills and see the fires over London and the docks.' I just said, blasé, 'Oh, it'll still be burning when I get back to the Rum Quay on Tuesday.'

And it was, and the firemen were there. They had started from the north side of the quay, just pumping water from the dock, and spraying the water across the dock, and by this time they could move across to the Rum Quay side and play from a little closer, but they were the same men who had been on duty, without relief, since Saturday evening. I don't say that they'd actually stood up the whole time, but I'm sure many of them were fast asleep and held up by the pressure of the water in the hoses. There were a mere seven million gallons there to burn and it was still burning quite cheerfully.

Eric Cropper

We hadn't really had time to instil into the auxiliary firemen's minds the dangers from falling dangerous buildings, so we had to be their eyes and ears. Down in the docks, you'd be fighting in clusters because there were fires all round; you weren't fighting one fire, an isolated fire, they were all around. There was the roar of the flames, the banging of the bombs, the noise of the anti-aircraft, every now and again you hear a plane swoop down and bang, bang, bang – machine-gunning – and that sort of thing, so there was lots of distraction. We had to keep alert to so many various things. I felt my responsibility deeply – men's lives were in my hands. It was a very tense time.

Cyril Demarne

The next morning, one could see the shattered remains of the warehouses and we trod along roads covered in squashed currants and dried fruit which had burned the night before, and there were various smells of burning fruit and burning cheese. The smells remained for some months, hanging in the air, as the ruined buildings stood, you know, unattended and unusable really, and that situation remained until the end of the war.

Rose Bater

In Millwall, there was a bomb dropped on a barge laden with powdered milk – imagine a bomb in a barge of fifty tons of powdered milk? Poplar was bathed in white for a week, and wherever you walked, you were walking in what looked like flour.

Cyril Demarne

Dockers shovel up precious sugar from the remains of West India Quay's number seven warehouse after a night of heavy bombing. This is not just a clean-up job, this is vital salvage work to conserve precious food resources. 1940

My department, North Quay, was very heavily bombed and we had tens of thousands of tons of sugar went up in flames. One offshoot of the burning of the sugar and the firemen's efforts with their hose was the formulating of a very nice thick layer of toffee over it.

One thing we didn't realise was that it absolutely jammed up the drains, I mean to such an extent that they became useless. Another thing I remember was that since there was hardly any sweets in those days, the labourers used to come in and chip lumps of the toffee off the road and take them home.

I often remonstrated with them about that, saying it was unhealthy. Two or three of them told me, 'It's quite all right, we washed it when we got it home.'

Stanley Tooth

CHAPTER 9

In Which We Serve

Serving Your Country

The First World War was called 'the war to end all wars', and the attitude towards the armed forces after it ended was based on that assumption. From 1919, the ten-year rule, which was renewed in perpetuity by Winston Churchill in 1928, kept the armed forces at numbers that assumed that Britain would not be engaged in any great war during the next ten years. In 1939, the army (including reserves and the Territorial Army) numbered less than 900,000, but by the end of 1941 it had increased to 2.2 million. Conscription was introduced in 1939, initially only for single men aged between twenty and twenty-two, who would undertake six months' basic training and then be on active reserve.

At the outbreak of war, the National Service (Armed Forces) Act was established, with conscription for all men aged between eighteen and forty-one, except for those in reserved occupations. These included merchant seamen, railway workers and dockers, which accounted for many of those in the East End. There were still shortages in some industries, and some conscripts ended up as 'Bevin Boys', working in the coal mines in a scheme devised by Minister for Labour, Ernest Bevin, to keep the country supplied with fuel. Men who were too old or unfit for conscription joined the Local Defence Volunteers, better known as the Home Guard.

Conscientious objectors had to attend an interview panel which had the power to grant exemption from military service, and many 'conchies' went on to serve in the ambulance corps or the land army.

The usual performance was they would come out of the pub any time between eleven or twelve, make their way down the street, probably two or three of them or more, sing one or two songs – as the war was on, they would obviously be patriotic songs, *Rule, Britannia* – but they would sing these patriotic songs until somebody aimed something out of the window at them and then they would gently evaporate. But one morning after a bit of that, my father, when we were having our breakfast, casually said, 'I've joined the army.' My mother looked at him and said, 'No self-respecting army would take you.' He said, 'I've joined the army. The only problem is I don't know where.' He'd been on a binge and he'd joined the army, and that was that. That morning, accompanied by the wife and the daughter, they went on a round of recruiting offices.

Bill Crook

Ronnie Egleton and Crane, they said, 'Charlie, we're going to volunteer.' I said 'Good luck' and they both volunteered for the air force. Anyway, poor old Ronnie was shot down over Brest, in a bomber, and Crane, he survived the war. He was a magnificently built chap and he survived the war and he used to fly the Emperor of Ethiopia in his private plane but he came down one Saturday on a jaunt on his own in the Tasmanian Sea, and it was shark-infested, and that's where he lost his life.

Charlie Gubbins

Immediately war broke out, I gave up my job and joined the ARP, and that was in Gunthorpe Street. I was there about five or six months before I got called up. It was very pleasant, one day on, one day off, and we had various drills.

I was looking forward to my call-up – I was one of those – it was something I wanted to do. I took to it like a duck to water; I loved the open-air life, I loved the drill. I became the captain of the boxing team.

Jack Miller

My first husband, as I say, stayed in the Merchant Navy and that's where he got killed. He was killed in the Merchant Navy on a trip to America – it was early in the war and it was whisky they were taking to the States. The whole ship was lost. There was no one saved at all. It was a brand new ship.

I was very ill after that. I just couldn't stand everyone, all their boyfriends was coming home and they was having leave and I didn't feel like I could cope. I'd had my mother home with me – she had diabetes. I was looking after her and doing the three shifts, doing fire-watching in the street and in the end I just sort of ran out of strength.

Anne Griffiths

I'd been on reserve for twelve years, I think, which would make eight years in the army, twelve years on reserve. If I'd been called up directly then, it would've meant I was in line for a pension. Unfortunately, my wife sent back my last payment – the war had been declared so that I was waiting, unconsciously, to be called up. I was never called up. I wondered why I never got my last payment either, because my wife has sent back the envelope and had put 'Not known' on it. So I didn't get my pay and I didn't get called up. Until I got two gentlemen around here, who politely questioned me. On showing me the envelope, I realised that my wife had put 'Not known' on it and sent it back.

Bill Crook

My brother Reg got shot down, the fifteenth of May, 1944. He won forty-two operations – he had three more to do, because Pathfinders did forty-five ops, the main force did sixty. But he said to me, 'I'm going to do another fifteen and become a flight lieuie, so I can have another few bob.' Mum was in hospital and me dad and I used to go and see her on Saturdays, and he asked the sister to tell her – don't think me dad was a coward, but he couldn't face her.

Dennis Pike

My father died when I was ten, in 1940. My mother remarried when I was twelve, and was widowed again within three months; he was torpedoed at sea and all life was lost. She was only thirty-nine when she was widowed the second time, but she said she'd never marry again.

Jean Cunningham

My husband was in a reserved occupation because he was in the docks, and he had to be in the docks for about three or four nights a week on fire fighting and everything else, because the docks were far more important than anything else.

Bevin had called his dockers the flying squad – say Liverpool had had a bashing the night before, with the bombing, then London Dock would have to send so many dockers up there, you see. The majority of them did not want to go – I mean, Bevin gave out that they were willing and happy to go.

Well, Bill said to one fellow who had volunteered, he was quite unusual, so he said, 'Why have you volunteered?' He said, 'I'll tell you what, governor, I've got a nice little woman up there.' He said, 'I enjoy going.'

Florence Mugridge

I met a load of our blokes at Penarth, and one of them was a bloke I fought three times, Tommy Buckley out of Bethnal

Green. He beat me twice and I beat him once. And he used to love me – he see me down there, he said, 'Ah, tiddler, come here.'

But he went out to Africa and he was working on an ammo boat out there and they hit the boat and blew the lot up, killed him and all the blokes that was on it. I never see him no more, old Tom. Good boy he was, lovely fella.

Alfred Green

We was up and down the coast for six months or so and I was on the gun, and we were often left by ourselves, being last in the convoy, and we had plenty of action from the German planes who'd be coming over, and having a few bombs to spare would drop them on the tail of our ship.

One period, they dropped them so close I thought they were men jumping out of the plane on top of us, and I was firing the gun, and eventually a destroyer came up and as we were firing at this German who was diving out the clouds, on the semaphore they shouted out, 'Cease fire, it's a friendly aircraft.'

All of a sudden, there's a few bombs dropped round him, and immediately the Oerlikon guns got cracking, and when it died down, we shouted across, 'They weren't so friendly, were they?' We could hear the chuckles of the sailors on deck, you know, it was really funny. I came home towards the end of the year and I had some eye trouble and I went to the Shipping Federation doctors and they said I wasn't to go on the ships again, so I finished off, and the ship got sunk the weekend I left it. The captain and quite a number of the crew lost their lives, so I was really lucky.

Alexander Gander

I was delegated, by the time I was old enough to work, to be a Bevin Boy. There wasn't the usual occupations you could put a young lad into because there wasn't the tradesmen about – ie, carpenters, builders, electricians – they was all in the army. It was a government thing for young men, it was more or less, if you like, a forced labour. Obviously, you got paid for it, and you was allocated to the pits, the mines and trained in such work.

Albert Patten

I was appointed signals officer at the Home Guard – this was quite interesting but entailed quite a lot of work, running out at night on a motorbike to the different sections all around the countryside. My wife helped me then, doing the telephone work. Her job was every other night to go on the local telephone exchange to do night duty, and I used to pick her up at ten o'clock on a motorbike – I was supplied by the army with a motorbike to run around the different places.

Herbert Hollingsbee

We were in Wormwood Scrubs – there was a hundred conscientious objectors in at the time who illicitly ran their own prison magazine (which can be found in the Residual Museum in London, having been brought out of prison by devious means which no one would record).

At my trial, a Liverpool Irishman who was a pacifist came and said, 'Gentlemen, I have known Eric Cropper for twenty-three years and I am quite convinced of the genuineness of his conscience – I have come over a hundred miles from a busy provincial parish to say this, and if you have any questions to ask me, will you ask me them.' And he said no more, but we were all given recommendations to undertake agricultural or forestry work. So I came out and went on the land.

Eric Cropper

I was a Quaker. I had become a Quaker by working with the Quakers and I joined what was known as the Friends' Ambulance Unit. We went with the army but we only did ambulance work; field rescue work and that sort of thing, picking up the pieces and patching them together and bringing them home. We made one mistake which we rectified later: when we picked up a wounded soldier we refused to handle weapons, so we left his gun lying, and we discovered later that the poor damn soldier was charged not only for the weapon he'd lost, but for the new weapon he was issued with. So after that we just used to sling the rifle in the ambulance – but you had to compromise a great deal.

Louis Dore

Up on the Roofs

By late August in 1940, with German plane losses estimated at around six hundred to the RAF's 260, it was clear that the RAF Fighter Command, despite starting out with far fewer planes, was succeeding in holding off the Luftwaffe. Britain's success was due to her secret weapon – radar and the extraordinarily speedy and effective Spitfire. Germany was forced to change tactics and Operation Sealion was abandoned until further notice on orders from Hitler.

But the Luftwaffe continued to focus on British cities, and particularly London, which was blitzed for fifty-seven days without remission. After the early daylight raids led to heavy losses of German planes, Herman Goering ordered that all attacks would henceforth take place under cover of darkness. To avoid giving guidance to the planes, the blackout was rigorously enforced by the ARP wardens, who are still remembered for their catchphrase 'Put that light out'. However, the distinctive loop of the Thames was an unmissable target, especially on a moonlit night.

Volunteer fire-watchers were out on duty every night on the capital's rooftops, watching for the first wave of planes,

Volunteers are always needed in wartime: in addition to the well-known ARP wardens, the Port of London had its own brigade, called River Emergency Service volunteers, seen here posing with blankets and bandages as they take a break from civil defence duties. 1940s

dropping incendiaries in their thousands. Designed to set fires that would guide the bombers to their targets, the incendiaries were packed up to a hundred at a time, in seven-foot-long bomb cases known as 'breadbaskets' that scattered them over a wide area.

The fire-watchers' equipment was a low-tech combination of a bucket of sand, a bucket of water, and a stirrup pump; the King and his two young daughters were helpfully photographed trying out these items, just like any normal London family. But this simple equipment proved invaluable in putting out thousands of fires, and thus helping to avert the following bombs. By law, all businesses had to provide fire-watchers, with men doing a maximum of forty-eight hours per month. Women were later added to the compulsory rotas, and for many, the experience of being recognised as part of this vital work, alongside men, as equals, was both novel and satisfying, although it could also be extremely dangerous.

During the Blitz, the RAF had established such a supremacy over the Luftwaffe, they packed up raiding by day and only came at night-time. When they went off in the morning, we knew we'd got the day or so – what we used to do was to round up our troops as quickly as possible, get them back to the fire station; they'd take off their wet clothes and get changed, have a meal and then get their heads down. Winter time, as it started to get dusk, some of the air raids in the winter time started at four-thirty in the afternoon and kept on till eight-thirty the next morning.

Cyril Demarne

In the Blitz, you went to work and you came home and if it's firefighting, that'd be on, go up to the roof, incendiary bombs along the street. That was until they made explosive incendiaries and then, of course, it was dangerous – when you went to tackle an incendiary bomb, it'd explode. But in the first instance, they'd just come down in clusters and could get a stirrup pump or douse them with sand. We'd organise our own voluntary watch of a night-time, and we did two hours. I used to go with my father, and then someone else would come along and relieve you, and we'd go through the night like that.

They did fetch in compulsory fire-watching at factories, but my father was socialist and also he detested Morrison because Morrison was a conch in the First World War and when they said he had to go and fire-watch at a factory over in Mile End somewhere he said, 'I'm not. I'll go to prison. No conchie's going to tell me what to do.' But we did fire-watching in the street. So that life carried on more or less as normal, you just did your work and if there was an air raid, you had a disturbed night, that was it, and you went to work next morning wherever it was.

George Adams

They bombed the docks for eleven months, and I used to go up top and there was a bit of a dugout, and I could see all the incendiary bombs falling on the sheds, and they was like a lot of idiots dancing around all these lights. Many's the time I picked up an incendiary bomb that hadn't gone off.

Between you and me, I was crazy; I got two or three incendiary bombs that hadn't gone off, you know – it's amazing what you do when you're young. And I took them down the station, unscrewed the bottom. They were made of aluminium – they polished up beautiful, you know. Got this powder off several of them because, as I say, several of them never went off. Souvenirs, see – and they had a little fin on the end of them. They used to open up a canister or something, they said, as the plane came down.

William Mather

The Germans used a navigation system that threw out a radio beam from a couple of places – one of them was Kleve in Germany, and another from Norway that bisected the Kleve beam over the Royal Docks. So what the Germans did was to fly along the navigational beam and they got a different signal when they were over the target. And for three months, that target was directed over the Royal Docks.

Cyril Demarne

When war was declared, we had to sleep in the docks for four nights to start with. And then it was every other night, unless it was weekends, and then it went to one night a week. We were paid about a shilling for going on this particular duty.

Kevin Chandler

On one occasion we turned up for work after an air raid – I was working on Canary Wharf, which was approximately one-ninth glass in its roof, and we counted some 380 incendiary bombs burned out on the roof. No glass was broken, although I'm sure some had been hit – it was quite small bombs then, and presumably the angle of the roof was such that it could shoot the bombs off on to the concrete, covered with three inches of gravel, without being burnt out. But numbers three to nine warehouses were burnt out one of these nights and it must have made a good blaze with the amount of sugar that was stored in them.

Eric Cropper

It was because they was after the London docks – they followed the river up, specially if it was moonlight, and they'd come up the river, you see. Now, outside our station, there was three barges there – I remember it well, and they had copra on them, you know, the insides of coconut? And they got an incendiary bomb on those and they were alight. You know, they burnt for about three days, couldn't put them out. In the event, they came along and the firemen flooded them with the hosepipes and made them sink to put them out, because the light was bringing them over.

William Mather

I had experience of the First World War. I'd belonged to the warden service and I had the training for gas and incendiary bombs and all that. When they dropped the incendiary bombs at Manor Park, all the houses at the back of us were all empty houses where a land mine had dropped and blasted a hole in all the houses. The wife and I were on our own and we could see flames coming through these. I said, 'That lot's gonna all go up.' I said, 'They're all gonna burn. I'm going over there to try to put them out.' She said, 'I'm coming with you.'

Climbed over the fence with me – she was a little brick. I found a shovel in one of the gardens and I went upstairs where I see these bombs burning, and shovelled them out. I said to the wife below, 'Stand clear,' and I shovelled the bombs up and out the window where I could find them. And saved those houses, because it was burning holes in the floor, you see. Oh, we put out umpteen fire bombs, the wife and I. As long as she was with me, she was happy.

Charles Lisle

The whole of the staff were involved in a rota system of fire-watching duties. According to the number of staff, it could be one night in twelve or one in ten, or as the staff decreased, one night in eight for every person to remain at the dock after working hours and to each be responsible for some object of books or other important documents, to take these down to a shelter which was mostly under the main offices in each dock. During these off-duty periods, when we had a quiet night, we played darts or a game called Lexicon. That was the only time I beat my guv'nor. I beat him at darts and again at Lexicon.

This would never have happened in the daytime. It was just a night-time occupation, where we were all equal. There was a period during the war when the German raiders were coming over half an hour earlier each night, until it began to be air raid warnings at six o'clock at night. One person on the staff in turn had to wear the earphones and plot the course of the bombers as they neared areas of the London docks and to write these directions in a book at the side of the location maps so that reports were telephoned to other areas the next day, for reports in the press and so forth.

Rose Bater

If the alarm went during the day, we all went to our respective shelters. But there was a control shelter for the docks, because they were working all through the night in those days, and the superintendent had to know what was going on from each point in the dock – from the dock master's end, southern department, northern department, jetty, landing stage. He had to know just what was happening. So all the phones were based in the control shelter and each representative had to phone in just what was happening, and we girls had to be there to man the phones, and we had to do that once a week. So if your turn was Monday night, you worked all day Monday, you were there all Monday night, you worked all day Tuesday, and then you went home.

Elizabeth Garrett

My sister was in the Royal Albert Dock and I was in the Royal Victoria Dock, and we really quite enjoyed our work there. We were doing men's work but about every ten days we used to have to do a night duty, ARP, and there was a shelter for the girls and a shelter where the men were. If the sirens went, you had to get out quickly and my sister and I had to go to the men's shelter and they had a big map there and you used to plot the aeroplanes coming in, and you were in touch with Barking gun battery, and you had to give out a yellow alert warning and a red alert warning to people concerned, like the fire station and the Port of London. So really you felt you were doing a good job.

Joan Shaw

I happened to be standing at the door one night, fire-watching, and a bomb just fell down, hit the shop and spur of the moment – fortunately, it was an incendiary – I just kicked it in the road. And the air raid warden gave one hell of a shout and said, 'You silly fool, you could have blown your leg off!', which was right, but my main thought was to get the bomb away from the shop, otherwise I had visions of the shop going up.

Opposite, there was a store which was the whole length from one corner to another, Brick Lane to Cygnet Street, which was originally about ten to twenty shops, and the whole thing caught alight. The flames were going from one shop to another and the firemen came out and unfortunately there was no water, and the men were just crying to watch the place burn down in front of them. Now if you go down there, all that is there now is a petrol station on the corner and a small block of offices they've built.

Sylvia Silverston

There was myself and another nurse on duty of a night-time. And this nurse come in to me and she said, 'Oh, Violet, I'm ever so frightened.' She said, 'I can see a light shining underneath one of the doors outside – I think there's an incendiary bomb been dropped.' Because it was getting a bit noisy. So, looking much braver than I felt, I said, 'Well, we'll have to find out, because we'll need to tell someone,' and I opened the door very gingerly. What it was, we had to put food tins, the big tins that had been used, outside to be collected because everything was collected and saved, and the moon was shining in on this tin making it look alight.

Violet Kentsbeer

We had air raids all the afternoon, and in the evening, my husband, my first husband, this is, said, 'Come to have a drink.' It was only just around the corner, in The Albion. So I said, 'Yes, all right.' So I went round there with him and then we'd just got a drink and then there's someone called in the door, 'All bombs are dropping everywhere!'

It was the night they dropped that Molotov cocktails, they was called, and they was just like a big basket of bombs. 'Hurry up, Anne,' someone said, 'one's on all around where you live.' So I came running out, and my husband, he run after but he had his pint in his hand – 'I'm not going to leave that, I've only just got it'. And anyway, when we got home here, this house was alight, like third storey, and next door was alight in their kitchen, and all around they was just falling like starlights. Water supply was very poor in those days because we only had the one tap downstairs – we didn't have water upstairs or anything like that. Anyway, we managed to get the fires out – and I've still got that pint glass.

Anne Griffiths

The night bombing was the worst and the officers took turns in being in control of the air raid precautions of night staff. I stood in that square between the offices, just inside the India Millwall Dock, seeing the flames from burning offices going right round in huge circles.

One of the more emotional times was when I was in charge at night and the place had thousands and thousands of incendiary bombs rained down on it, two or three nights running, and our first aid staff was essential to them. I told them not to go out of their dugouts, unless they were called out, but some of the ARP staff whose duty it was to try to put out these incendiaries, weren't so keen on doing their job. One of our first aid men who was leading his group, he got to the top of the dugout stairs and saw so many incendiaries threatening a certain place that he thought he'd break the rules. It was some distance away, and the first I knew about it was that I was told that a high explosive had fallen completely on that dugout, would have wiped the whole lot out – and it was one of my best foremen, on my own department and a chap I was really friendly with.

So I went out, and lo and behold, I saw just the hole where the dug was and, you know, felt – I didn't know what I felt, and then a voice behind me said, 'Lucky we weren't there.' And he'd been right down the other end of the quay.

Stanley Tooth

It wasn't a bomb that injured my family, it was the shells from the guns in the park. They didn't explode, they just came down in the middle of the road, and the shrapnel, it was only small pieces, but it hit them right in their groins as they was standing in the porch, ready to go on their duty, fire-watching. That's what did it, all these small bits of shrapnel came out and hit them as they stood there. When I got home, the three of them were in hospital. You could tell my sister was dying – she was grey. My mum was unconscious, and my other sister had her arm in traction. I'll never forget going in that ward and seeing the three of them like that – it's an experience you never get out of your mind, it's always at the back there. Nina, she lived for a day, and she died in the night when I was there. She was nearly twenty-one, she'd been married six months, and her husband was a sergeant in Italy. He couldn't come home on compassionate leave – they said, 'No, she's dead, you can't do anything. You'd better stay where you are.'

Violet Kentsbeer

In the first part of the war, in the Blitz, we had more casualties in Britain through the fire service and the ARP than they had in the front line of the armed forces.

I think the working class of our country took the Blitz like workers in all countries would take it, when their towns are being bombed – it brings out the courage and the loyalties of the nation. It was in Hamburg, it was in Berlin; the people they was being bombed and starved and blitzed, they showed tremendous courage. I don't think it was just copyright to us.

Jack Dash

Evacuation – Again

Since the Zeppelins of the First World War, the government was aware that any future war would be likely to feature concerted bombing campaigns against British civilians. Just before the start of the war, estimates of up to four million civilian casualties in London led the authorities to devise the largest-ever mass movement of the British population, and in early September 1939, nearly three million people joined the exodus from cities and towns into the countryside. Most were children travelling without their parents, accompanied by some of the 100,000 teachers who volunteered to be evacuated with their pupils. It was an astonishing feat, but looking back with twenty-first century sensibilities, seems to have been arranged without much regard for, or understanding of, the needs of children. The matching of children to host families was haphazard and many evacuees were desperately miserable through homesickness. Some were resented by their new families, many were overworked, underfed, or ill-treated. It is little wonder that over the course of the eight-month Phoney War, three out of every four evacuees returned home.

Once the Blitz began in earnest, the government started a second evacuation programme, supported by the Women's Voluntary Service for Air Raid Precautions. Nearly a quarter of the population were evacuated from London. 1939–40

In September 1940, with the start of the Blitz, there was a second attempt at evacuation. Once again, the government encouraged families to send the vulnerable to country areas, and free travel and a billeting allowance were offered to all children, the elderly, the disabled, pregnant women, and those who had lost their homes, as well as to those making their own arrangements to stay with friends and family. About a quarter of London's population now took up the offer and moved to a place of greater safety. Not all had bad experiences – for some, it was a chance to experience an entirely new way of living, and to make connections that would last a lifetime. For others, it was a further ordeal on top of all they had gone through during the bombings.

———•———

That seventh of September, we had a right old blitz, everything was alight down Silvertown; it was a real good night, it was. And everybody all on the run then, because they'd started evacuating – they'd done a bit of evacuating of the kids before that, took them out of school, but it wasn't all good stuff, because I remember my eldest nephew went in a house and the old lady there used to threaten him. And then my sister would send him stuff – new boots and like that – and the old dear used to threaten him, make him wear the old stuff her kids left off, and she'd take the new stuff. Course, you heard all this afterwards but I know he had a rough old time when he was away. He was threatened all the time, if he said anything, they would... you know.

Charles Beck

I went away from the school, although I didn't attend the school; it was the school of engineering in Poplar High Street. I went to Somerset, approximately eleven miles from Taunton.

There were schools out there but we never mixed with those. We weren't allowed to go in their school. So they got all the remainder of these evacuees, me included, shunted on a train and went to a place called Wellington, in Somerset. And there we were sorted out; the biggest lads actually went on the farms. I, being a titch, nobody wanted me till the end. I got a very good billet; she was very strict but marvellous food for war time, grew all our own food. And our school was in a Liberal Club, in the skittle alley. I was evacuated approximately a year and a half. There's a place called Norton Fitzwarren which is near Taunton and it was being built for the invasion, for the troops' stores.

I went and worked in a garage as a basic – my wage then was five shillings, but being so small, I could get on the local bus and go into Taunton for a child's fare. The pool petrol was the mode then. I used to get a gallon or two drainage out of the pipe and put it round the back, and hide it – use my integrity on that – that is basically a London cunningness.

Dick Allington

We were evacuated, as I say, to Barford. We all ended up in the village hall and people came and chose us like we were cattle on a stand – we all had our names on our coats. Of course, we didn't appreciate any of the bad bits of this at all; for us it was a bit of an adventure, although for us it was the first time we'd ever been away from our parents and we were scared. But people came and they looked at us and they kept wanting to choose one or the other, but we would not be parted, we kept clinging to each other and saying, 'No, no, we've all got to go, we've all got to go.'

Eventually, a young woman – she was only twenty-one herself and had a young baby of two months – she decided she would take all three of us. So we went to live with her, we laid on palliasses in the house. We thought it was fun – she never worried if we washed ourselves, if we didn't wash ourselves, if we cleaned our teeth, if we didn't clean our teeth; we thought it was marvellous.

My mother came down and she spent some time with us, and eventually she thought, this is not good, this is not how she wants her children bought up, so she brought us back to London. We were down there about two years – from about 1941 to 1943. We came back in time for the doodlebugs.

Julia Lewis

I was evacuated with Stepney Jewish School, from Stepney Green, to a place called Denham, which was literally about twenty-five miles away, near Uxbridge, a peaceful village. But I got fed up with being away, and it was too quiet.

The first day, when the war broke out, I was picking black-berries. I saw rabbits running through a field for the first time; I'd never seen the countryside. I was with my young sister. We heard sirens and we rushed home. A policeman at the cross-roads, he had a tin hat, and he said, 'You kids don't you know there's a war on?' So I rushed inside and Mrs Thompson was cooking, and I said, 'There's a war on, there's a war on,' and she said, 'Yes, isn't it terrible. It's time we had lunch.' So she brought out a cold lunch, and she said, 'Try one of those tomatoes, they're really nice and sweet.' And I said, 'My parents are gonna die, we're all gonna die 'cos bombs are gonna drop.' She said, 'I shouldn't worry about that; would you like some brown bread?'

Bernard Kops

I spent some important formative years – my early teens – in Wales. If I'd stayed any longer I'd have ended up a Welsh speaker. And I finished up with two sets of parents. The first people I stayed with in a little village in Wales were really unsuitable to have children; they had no children of their own and the woman was rather neurotic. Nice man – collier. And so when a friend found a home with these people in Ammanford, which is a medium-sized town, he said, 'They can take another one – would you like to come?' So the two of us went and stayed there. They were very amenable people, and they were very much younger than my own parents, which was a strange experience because I looked at the lady and thought, You're pretty. Now, I'd never thought of looking at my own parents that way. Perhaps my mother was – she certainly was when she was a very young woman. But suddenly I was part of a family where the surrogate parents were very young. They had no children and apparently couldn't have and they were very anxious to keep me – oddly enough, my wife had exactly the same experience. She was only six when she was evacuated and at the end of the war, the people she was staying with desperately wanted to adopt her. And when I left, the people I was with adopted a daughter, and so did the ones that my wife was with.

John Earl

I was evacuated to Suffolk and I was on a farm and I loved it. I didn't miss anybody, I was terrible. My father died on Christmas Eve. The people I was with were very good, they just told me he was ill. Because they were going to come down for Christmas – I wasn't really worried about seeing me mum, I wanted to see me dad. When they told me after Christmas – well, I felt broken down for a long while, but I got over it, like you do. And I loved every minute of it down there – I used to go and fetch the eggs in the morning, feed the chickens. Her daughter and I used to wash the eggs at night and pack them all ready to go away. I don't remember ever being hungry there – it was a dairy farm and there was plenty of milk, plenty of eggs. Didn't seem to be a shortage of meat in the country. There was always something on the table. I had a hike to school though – three and a half mile I used to walk, every morning. But I loved it because we used to walk across the field and see something new every day. I used to pick wild flowers and see the lambing season, pick up the lambs when they was first born, see the young calves being born. I didn't want to come home really.

Jean Cunningham

So my wife and her sister, they got browned off with this bombing every night so they decided to be evacuated. So she goes to see the brother-in-law – his wife's a Welsh lady and she come from Ebbw Vale in Wales. So they were billeted in with this postman in South Wales. She had to do a job at a munition works there. Being in London, you'd go to the shelter right away, as soon as you got the siren – well, the Welsh couldn't make it out, 'cos they hadn't been bombed.

Well, one weekend, they were making munitions there, so they got the warning through, see, and they drop a few bombs. Well, Mag, she's in the shelter, she don't want to know 'cos she knows all about it. Then they found out why she went to the shelter – course, they hadn't experienced it. Once they'd experienced a few incendiary bombs coming down, then they knew what it was all about. She stuck it out for a month – just over a month. She said, 'I'm coming home. If we get any whatsname, we'll be going together.'

Sidney Bell

Well, I was unlucky that I was terrified. Some people they didn't, it didn't matter to them. They slept in their beds and they said, 'Oh well, if a bomb drops, it drops.' But I was absolutely terrified. And when our house got – it didn't get destroyed, but it was unliveable. When it became unliveable, and also where I worked was destroyed and we were given a letter which said that we were employed by Woolworth's and if we went to a Woolworth's they would probably would give us a job. The local school was evacuated to a little village north of Oxford, and nearly everybody followed them, because their children was there. So when they got bombed out or had to go somewhere, they naturally went to Oxford. My husband, who was my boyfriend then, his mother and sister was at Oxford, so I packed my bag and went to Oxford. Being seventeen, I wasn't an official evacuee. So we knocked on every door in the village and asked, did they want to take in an evacuee. Because they were in an area where they had to take in evacuees. Wolvercote was a typical little English village and it had all these Chinese children running about there.

Connie Hoe

We stayed in Bournemouth for a little while with some neighbours of my grandmother's who were very anti-Londoners. We were called bomb dodgers by the people of Bournemouth; they didn't want us down there, they told us to go home again. They did make life a misery.

We spent the time walking round the streets with my stepdaughter – and my sister had a baby and a friend had asked me to look after his daughter as well, so we'd got three children living in one room. Eventually it became so unpleasant that we realised that the best thing to do was go home – we really thought bombs were better than people, and they were.

About a fortnight after we got back, I went to a little jewellery box to get some jewellery to put on. I had a few bits and pieces of opal and platinum that my husband had given me, because I like those things, and they were all missing. And a silver pencil my father gave me, and my mother had given me a silver thimble – and they were all gone, and a heavy silver bracelet. And so I went to the local police and told them, and they made enquiries at Bournemouth and said we'd been staying in the house of the biggest thief in Bournemouth. But the problems of going back and trying to prove they'd taken them were insurmountable so we had to sort of say goodbye to all that stuff, which was rather a shame.

Eileen Brome

By that time, I had three children, one first, then twins. And that was no fun being at home with them. I had a school friend who lived at Bourton-on-the-Water in Gloucestershire – I couldn't stay with her because her sister and family were there, but her husband owned a butcher's shop and one of the men who worked in his shop, his mother could take me, which was wonderful to take somebody with three young children.

Well, you can imagine what it was like. Children, when they are young, they all wake up at about six in the morning. She had three adults to get off to work, so I had to tie my son to the bed to keep him upstairs, and I've lived a day by half-past eight. I was an absolute wreck.

And then we were trailing around with this great twin pram, and Janet the girl at the side, trailing away to get out of the way. Then you'd get on with doing your washing and what have you at night. But she was wonderful to take me.

Also, you see the country is different now, but then, there were flies everywhere, you see. Of course, in the town, we never let the flies get in the sugar or anything, but as she said, 'My dear, if I spent all my day worrying about a fly I'd never get anything done. We don't take any notice of them.' There was a manure heap outside the door, for the garden, things like that. You can imagine, we'd been brought up to believe that flies were instant death, kind of thing. Well, I know people cannot believe it, but I swear this is true. In the little village was the baker's shop – now, it was a single mass of flies. You would go in and point to what you want. This girl had a fly swat she'd go swish, swish, and get what you want. I was mesmerised – I couldn't believe it.

Well, it was three weeks before Bill came – I said to Bill, 'It would be so easy to die, but to live…' I said, 'I'm coming back. I don't care.' I couldn't live – it was like living on the edge of a volcano.

Florence Mugridge

The next place, Ross-on-Wye, I was there a year, and my mother came down to see me and I was so hungry – I was always hungry down there. The person I was staying with, she starved us, she was a horror. Young married couple, and they had vegetables in the garden, they had chickens in the garden and we never saw an egg, never saw nothing. We used to have a slice of bread and butter for our breakfast, or marge, cup of cocoa and that was it, weren't allowed no more. We used to have school dinners, so that was all right. Come home in the evening, half-past five, we was allowed two slices of bread and another cup of cocoa and that was it. No more.

Saturdays, she used to give us sixpence between me and this girl called Rose who was billeted with us and we were expected to go out from nine o'clock to six o'clock on this sixpence, so we used to gorge ourselves on chips, that was about all you could get. Sunday, we'd have the minutest bit of meat and her husband would have the rest; he had everything on his plate.

I came down one night and I was so hungry I stole a slice of bread, and she went and told the headmaster that I'd stolen. We had to go to bed with candles and it was freezing cold. Anyway, my mother came down and she was so disgusted that she brought me home – and she didn't even have the money for me to go on the train.

Jean Cunningham

My youngest sister, Beryl, she's a war casualty. After the war, she began lots of mental trouble. She was here when the bombing started – the others were evacuated, but Beryl being only a baby, she was about four or five on the first day of the bombing. On the first day, she was in and out of the bath about four times with Mum trying to bath her. So she had to go – even though she was a baby, she had to be evacuated.

We found out afterwards that she said once, 'Well, I have heard God.' What happened is the first person she was sent to was an old spinster woman who had had nothing at all to do with children, and she'd been beaten with brass curtain rails because she wet the bed. She'd been held upside down over a sink with a tap turned up and the water going down her nose, and she heard God. She said, 'Somebody said, "What are you doing to that child?"' She said afterwards she realised it was the man next door looking over his fence, and she was put in hospital.

All that we heard was that she'd been put in hospital because she had a little trouble with her waterworks. So there was another war casualty.

Dennis Pike

My mum had a sister up in Peterborough and my dad said, 'Well, I think you ought to go up to your sister, like.' He said, 'Have a bit of a holiday up there.' Well, typical East End family, sisters never got on, they was always rowing. So we go to Peterborough, take my cousin Ronnie out of Oban Street, and my sister, and my gran, and we all go up to Peterborough. Well, my aunt wasn't that clean – you know, they had fleas and things like that – she had about six kids anyway. She had two lodgers – two kiddies, young boys, who had been evacuated to Peterborough. I felt uncomfortable, obviously. Because my mum, she used to grab us and she used to look through our hair, looking for fleas and nits like. And she used to do my cousin as well, Ronnie.

And my gran used to say, 'You can't do that in front of Ann' – that was her sister. 'I'll do it in front of anybody.' And she'd have a right go. Anyway, I started school there – went for a fortnight. I got picked on because I was the youngest one, and I got picked on by the locals and there was a right battle between the Londoners and my cousins in the local school, so it was the best thing to keep me away from school. That was only disrupting the school. So the main time up there was playing in the brick fields.

Len Faram

I worked on a community farming project in Lincolnshire where we received refugees from the bombing of the Isle of Dogs and even became foster parents of one of them who was left behind when the rest went back. The Isle of Dogs bombing was doodlebugs, and this girl Iris was stripped down to vest and knickers in the kitchen when a bomb struck between her and the air raid shelter and buried the shelter, and left her unconscious, destroying the whole house. She and her sisters, who were in the air raid shelter, they were in quite a state of shock when they came to us for a holiday – they would not take any clothes off in any circumstances, even to wash or bath, until after quite a time.

The other girl had lost both her parents in the bombing and two brothers in the forces were her only relations. We were clothing this little girl out of our own second-hand clothes and the whole community came forward with coupons, and thus for the first time Iris found she had shoes in which she could walk the three miles to school if the school bus didn't turn up or, more likely, if she hid behind the hedge and missed it.

Eric Cropper

I was living as an evacuee and there was a blizzard on. And my child was expected late in December. But I woke up this night in pain and the person that I lived with thought that I had rheumatics or something like that. And it wasn't until it was obvious that the baby was being born that she went out in the blizzard to phone for the midwife. And it was dark and when she came back the baby was born. I had her alone.

And it was in a house similar to this but there was no central heating, no fires, no nothing. And nothing arranged for the birth or anything. And then of course the poor woman when she came back she had to go out again to cancel the midwife and call the doctor out. But they couldn't come out because there was a blizzard on, you see. So I had to lie there until the doctor could come, which was the next morning. I forget what the odds were, but the fact that both of us were healthy and survived everything – one main thing being the cold, you see, and the baby being premature as well. But we survived, so that was a good thing.

Connie Hoe

Sooner or later, in that school, I felt very uncomfortable, so somehow or other, I thought I would go. I got on a bus to Uxbridge and I got on a train to London, I think it was on the Central line. When I went to London; I could hear noises – this was when the Blitz was starting, but it was before September seventh – and so I walk in on my parents, who were absolutely astounded to see me there. I was thirteen. They said, 'What are you doing? What are you doing?'

Oddly enough, I think it was on that day that I became a writer – or wanted to become a writer – because I told such lies, but they revealed imagination. I said, 'I had to come because the school was bombed, and a master was killed, and three children,' and I said I'd been injured. My mother said, 'Where, where?' and I said, 'No, I can't show you, it's private.' That was it. That was the end of my education, and the beginning of my imagination.

Bernard Kops

There's a war between us three elder brothers and the others because they were evacuated and we weren't. And there's a big division between us. For instance, me sister Edna, that's three down from me, her boy was very ill, and Percy, him and Edna are holding hands. We don't hold hands in our family. We don't. That ain't our lark.

I said, 'What's all this holding hands lark?' So he said, 'Well, we're special, ain't we?' 'What are you talking about?' He said, 'Well, when we was evacuated during the war, there was only us two in the world.' Makes sense, don't it?

Dennis Pike

Courage, Cheerfulness and Resolution

The bombing campaign against Britain continued during 1940 and 1941, but at the same time, Hitler was considering other countries that could be conquered by land; Germany was not a sea-going nation, and taking on Britain's powerful navy was never going to be easy. America was yet to enter the war, but if it did, and if Russia chose to attack at the same time, Germany could find itself fighting two major powers at once. To avoid this, Germany invaded Russia in the summer of 1941, the non-aggression pact proving to be no bar to this change of tactics.

As Hitler had declared an intention to put an end to the Russian state in *Mein Kampf*, published in the 1920s, the attack on Russia was always a matter of 'when' rather than 'if'. Yet the continued bombing of Britain led Stalin to believe that Hitler's intentions lay elsewhere, and that the Soviets were safe for a while longer, despite a build-up of troops on Germany's eastern borders. Hitler was sure that once the Soviet Union had fallen, Britain, finding itself alone, would be prepared to negotiate.

In London, the bombs kept falling, and with many of the children evacuated, the focus was on keeping key sectors of the economy – the railways, docks and factories – working as hard as possible so that the country could continue to function. Much more famous at the time than the later, better-known poster exhorting the public to 'Keep Calm and Carry On', was one that assured the nation '*Your* Courage, *Your* Cheerfulness, *Your* Resolution Will Bring Us Victory'. The sense of unity in adversity was only increased when Buckingham Palace was bombed, and the Queen declared 'I'm glad we have been bombed. Now I can look the East End in the face'. Britain might have been standing alone, but London's workers were standing shoulder to shoulder to get their jobs done.

I always remember the famous time when London was really blitzed, really, really – we had such a job to get to work – I don't know why we even attempted it. But my dad and I, we walked almost to London. Now and again we managed to get a lift on a lorry that was going that way, but when we got into London, it was all aflame and firemen were everywhere and water and hosepipes; we was treading over hosepipes and all that. We didn't even know if we'd have any work when we got there – it might have been bombed but we got there finally, I think it was nearly dinner time, and then we could only do a few hours' work, then we had to come home before the Blitz started again. You just went to work because otherwise the whole country would come to a standstill. You just led a normal life, as far as possible.

Violet Kentsbeer

We went down to this peanut factory one night at Custom House, and when we arrived, there was flames through the roof. They'd evacuated the people who lived around the factory, and we knew what we were doing so we got stuck into this fire and very soon knocked it out. This was a very poor area, right in the heart of dockland; most of the people worked casual, but out came the old ladies with their jugs of tea and a few cups and the station master said to me, a couple of you go in that doorway, have a cup of tea. So I went round with a cap, with the boys, and they put tuppence in the hat for the tea, and when this old lady came out to collect the jugs, I put this couple of shillings in her hand, in coppers. 'What's this?' she said. So I said, 'To pay for the tea and sugar.' 'I don't want that,' she said, 'Gawd bless you firemen – I don't know what we'd do without yer.' Straight from the heart. The East End of London; she couldn't afford to give us a cup of tea, really she couldn't, I'm sure she couldn't – but she wouldn't take the money.

Cyril Demarne

The last horses I dealt with was when the war was on. And they had to start getting rid of them. One Saturday afternoon, I went with a chap, took a pair of horses up the paddock – they must have got rid of them from there. But that was the last time I dealt with horses, taking them through the City during an air raid. There was an air raid on but we were supposed to get out, take the horses out of the van and tie them on the back and hope for the best. Over the top of us in Oxford Street, danger – wallop! All the different things you had to put up with.

Charles Beck

At Tilbury, during the Second World War, it was quite hectic at times, but we carried on our duties as usual. On receiving the air raid warning, course, all work was stopped – my job during this time was to raise the red flag after receiving instructions from head office, and once the red flag was hoisted, all work stopped and everybody went to their shelters. As soon as we got the air raid clear from head office, we used to take down the flag and everybody carried on.

Herbert Hollingsbee

We used to come along singing *We're the heroes of the night* and all this sort of thing, and there's shrapnel going ping, ping. And you're walking amongst it – ping! I picked up a lump, a big lump it was, red hot, cor! But they knocked the sheds about a lot, you know, they done a lot of damage. But we still went to work all the way through it, you know.

Alfred Green

You was young and you regarded yourself as a coward if you went into the shelters with the elderly and all that – you didn't really use them.

John Beattie

It got so that we really couldn't pack up every time the warning went, and go to the shelter. So in the end, we had a flat roof and we used to have a watcher up on the roof to tell us when they were coming near, and when they got near enough, he would blow the whistle and we would go down.

Winifred Herbert

It took us a little time to reorganise after the terrific wave bombing for so many days consecutively, but sooner or later we did get our department working for ship discharge purposes again, and we'd even got to the stage where we would work after an air raid warning until we could hear the aeroplanes coming up from Tilbury way.

Stanley Tooth

Very early on, during the Blitz – there was still daylight raids then, that'll tell you how early on it was – a delayed-action bomb went in the church which was right opposite us. There was only me, Mum and Dad and we'd got to get everything out of the church. And we was all carrying stuff, and the next thing I know, I heard a 'whoosh', no more than a whoosh, and I've lost a shoe. It had gone off. I don't remember a flash, just this sort of whoosh. I'm flat on my face and my shoe had gone.

Dennis Pike

As I went into the dock there was the ships lying all askew where the bombs had dropped in the water and laid all the ships, you know, askew. Number thirteen shed in the middle row, as they call it, that had a direct hit on the shed where they stored all the cargo which comes to go on the ship discharging or loading, and it was in a bit of a state, but work must go on, so we just simply carried on.

Stanley Rose

In 1940, one Saturday afternoon, we had nineteen bombs drop on Millwall that afternoon, at low tide, which cracked the Greenwich Tunnel and it was flooded. Of course, we couldn't get over and we had to climb down the edges of the wharfs with bicycles into a row boat, and it used to cost us threepence to go to Greenwich. One of the bombs dropped on the Manganese Bronze and Brass Company, right next to our place, but it shattered the laboratory itself and they wouldn't let us go back to work because they said there was a danger of an unexploded bomb.

Charlie Gubbins

When they bombed the tunnel at the early part of the war, in the big air raid up the river, I think, the tunnel was bombed, the Millwall side of it, was bombed so you couldn't get through it. So we first of all used to go over by rowing boat – somebody did it for tuppence, I think – and we lived in wellingtons for, oh, I don't know, it couldn't have been very long, but it seemed a long time, because you had to plough through, if it was low water, you'd have to plough through the mud to get on to the row boat, and they put us off the other side, opposite Greenwich Tunnel.

Well, then after a little while, this chap that lived at Grove Park, he was a bit of a bright spark. He goes to Mr Rowlatt and says, 'If you lend me a car, I'll drive the south-east London people in.' So, of course he thought that was a jolly good idea. So they gave him one. Course, by this time, some of the travellers have been pulled up so we were reduced in number; we had one or two spare cars. So he took the car and picked up Mrs Smith at New Cross and two from Grove Park, and he used to come round here for me, and he used to drive like a maniac. I don't know what was worse, whether to be frightened of him or the bombing.

Dorothy Shipp

We used to have to bag up all this National Dock Labour money for the labourers and we used to do it in the shelters. We used to have to take the money down in the afternoon. I was always given the pound notes to count; the other chap counted all the silver, another chap counted all the copper; there was a team of three. Bombing got a bit heavy one day and we all ducked under the table and knocked the table over and we upset the lot, and we spent the rest of the afternoon picking it up.

Elizabeth Garrett

Beer was terribly short and Dad used to say 'no waste, no waste'. We borrowed off of each other, all the pubs, 'cos so many places got bombed, and breweries. And this little soldier came in, and I thought he said 'Twenty pints' and I thought he'd got a darts match arranged so I'd got them lined up, and he was standing there, and I said, 'You did say twenty pints, didn't you?' And he said, 'I asked for twenty Woodbines.' And there was these twenty pints on the counter.

And Dad came out and he said 'What's this?' and I said, 'I thought this soldier asked for twenty pints, but he wanted twenty Woodbines,' and he said, 'I can't waste all this,' and he smacked me round the face – he was so cross. I ran in and cried, it was such a stupid mistake. But that silly little soldier – he watched me pour twenty pints – he could have stopped me.

Mary Ridgeon

We were being bombed to hell, night after night, non-stop. I was working by day on my job as detective inspector at that time, and by night on fighting bombs and things. But you'd see these East Enders in the evening, with their costermonger's barrow laden with a few bits and pieces and a mattress; they'd push it all the way down the Mile End Road out into Epping Forest, spend the night there, then push their little barrows back, with their babies on the barrow, the next morning, not knowing whether they'd find their houses there, or not.

Graham Rutherford

Buckingham Palace was bombed, I remember, and the King and Queen – George VI and the present Queen Mother – came out. We'd had a hell of a raid in the East End, not far from St Paul's, and they came out. And these poor East Enders, who'd lost their homes; lost their mothers, lost their fathers, lost theirs sons – lost everything – they painted the few doorsteps which were left red, white and blue for the Queen and the King to walk round and shake hands with them, because they'd been bombed too. That was one of the worst, stupidest things that Hitler did – bombing Buckingham Palace – because we were one together then, you see. And they wouldn't leave London, the Queen and the King – they stayed in London. They sent their children away, but they stayed in London throughout the bombing and that put on a very good show and gave a very good impression indeed.

Graham Rutherford

I remember the King and Queen coming down to Poplar and walking about, having a look, and Churchill coming down. All that sort of thing – it seems unreal now that you could have been involved in it at all.

Elsie Edwards

CHAPTER 10

War on the Home Front

In and Out of Shelters

As early as 1924, the Air Raid Precautions Committee began to consider how best to protect UK citizens from air attacks. Enclosed underground spaces are extremely vulnerable to build-up of gas – then still the most feared weapon – and perhaps because of this, progress was slow. Eventually several options were approved. The cellars and basements of buildings such as schools, churches, hospitals and factories were to be made available to the public, and during the war, these were widely used, although not having being designed to survive bombs, they were liable to both flooding (from burst water mains) and collapse if the buildings above received a direct hit. Large companies built communal shelters for their workers – the Port of London Authority provided two hundred earth-covered concrete dugouts equipped with benches. Brick and concrete communal street shelters for fifty people were set up, divided into sections, each containing six bunks. However, their rigid structure was not ideal for withstanding shock waves, and after the roofs of several had collapsed, the public rather lost confidence in them.

Anderson shelters were much more successful in design – the curved corrugated steel shell gained stability from being dug into the ground (most East Enders referred to them as dugouts) and they flexed with bomb blasts instead of collapsing.

Unfortunately, they were also extremely cold in winter, and being below ground level, almost constantly wet. For this reason, at the end of 1941, the Morrison, or table shelter was introduced – families could sleep in these, inside, in the warm, and they were strong enough to survive a collapsing upper storey. In fact, short of a direct hit on a building, properly-sited Morrison shelters were shown to be almost totally bomb-proof.

The most well-known form of shelter, the image that endures in popular imagination, is the London Underground. So it is something of a surprise to discover that at the start of the war, the government was adamant that no Underground stations should be used. Rational worries about people falling on to tracks, the lack of toilet facilities, and the possible spread of disease, combined with the stranger beliefs that once people were down there in the warm, they would simply refuse to move and would stay there night and day. In the event, both the progress of the war, and the will of the people, forced a rethink, especially after a group of Communists from Stepney led a hundred East Enders into the Savoy Hotel to demand that they be allowed to use its basement shelter. But over the course of the war, only about four per cent of London residents sheltered in Underground stations, and even they were not always safe. A major disaster took place at Bank Underground station, on the night of 11 January 1941, when sixty-nine people were injured and fifty-seven killed by a bomb that dropped through to the ticket hall and exploded, sending shockwaves down the escalators and along the platforms deep underground. The bomb left a massive crater in the middle of one of the capital's busiest road intersections, but within a few weeks, the rubble had been cleared and a temporary bridge created, with the station returning to full use within two months.

During the coming year, I think they must have got a government grant, but they built a very good air raid shelter at the bottom of the yard, big enough to take us all. That was finished before the big air raid came up the river, September 1940. Every now and again, we'd have a rehearsal; we got the warning and I remember dear old Mr Murray, he had a list of names of all the office staff and he was gonna call out the names and tick them off, just imagine, tick off the names before we all marched down to the shelter. It was quite a long yard – can you imagine all going orderly – it's amazing really, how you imagine people would behave under those circumstances.

Dorothy Shipp

And Dad was caring, sensible, looked after his bits and pieces, loved his garden. It broke his heart when he had to tear it all up and put an air raid shelter down there when the war came. They said, 'You got a shelter, you have to put it in your back garden.' But he said, 'It's me garden.' They said, 'Well, you know, we've issued it out to you, you do it.' Anyhow, he must have thought, you know, this is – he'd went through the First World War. He must have thought, This is something I've got to do. And all the neighbours helped one another to put the shelters up. They was very good.

Joanna Roberts

Then you had air raid shelters built at the back of your flats where you had to go. You'd come home from school, you'd have your tea, by about seven or eight o'clock the bombers used to come over. You'd all be in the air raid shelter and all the community of the people used to get in there. There'd be singing and cups of tea would be floating about and all around you, you could hear the thuds and blasts and the banging. And you was only too pleased the next morning, say about seven or six o'clock in the morning, then they'd be

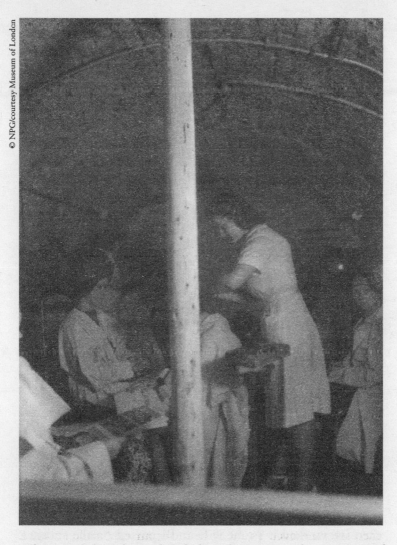

After a while, life in the shelters began to echo aspects of the world outside, with cups of tea, impromptu sing-songs and, in this instance, hairdressing provided by T Vasco Ltd to take the occupants' minds off the destruction outside.
Bassano Studio, 1940

finished and out you'd come, go back home, hoping your home was still there.

Wally James

My father was so pig-headed, he wouldn't have an Anderson shelter. 'We will never have no air raids here,' he used to say. When it came to it and we did have air raids, he used to go to my sister's air raid shelter in Seyssell Street.

Annie Pope

My husband was an air raid warden and my dad was a warden – he was getting on, but he wanted to be in it. I was a warden but when I used to go outside they used to say 'Sling your so-and-so hook home, 'cos you're more nuisance than you're worth, all you women', and that was it. So as soon as the warning went, we all used to down Oxford House; we all used to have our own blankets – they supplied the blankets, beautiful blankets – and the beds they used to supply and all. We all had our own bunks. And they used to have a beautiful canteen down there. It was like one big happy family down there – all in there together. Used to have concerts down there, used to be smashing. Somebody would get up and sing, and somebody played the violin – you didn't know there was a war on down there when you got in there, because it was so noisy.

Dolly Cooper

We were in the old dugout, night after night. We had to work it so that, the oldest baby, I used to run down with it first, and then we worked it so me wife and I passed on the staircase with the second one, so the first one wasn't left too long, and then I used to run in and get the youngest one, who didn't notice things. Anyway, we worked it all right. In fact, the dugout, we lived in there all the time and it used to be lovely.

Charles Beck

We had no room to put an Anderson shelter. At that time, they didn't have shelters you could put inside underneath the table, so we was all in the family shelter next door, the Lovelands, husband and wife. He hadn't worked for years; he was gassed in the First World War and had some form of palsy and we could hear this rattling on his gas mask case.

George Adams

When the war was really bad, we was having a bad blitz, it used to be, oh, terrible in the dugout – tension. I'll let you know now, I'd say, 'That bleeding Hitler.' And they all laughed, 'cos they never heard me swear before. So there's a good thing. After that, anytime we had a bad air raid, having to go there, they'd all be laughing.

Charles Beck

At work, we had shelters underneath the buildings, but we never used to use them much. It was a nasty feeling; you got a three storey brick building and you've got a shelter all under-neath the footings, no wider than this room, and seats all down there, dark, right down the whole length of the build-ing, perhaps two hundred, three hundred foot, and very claustrophobic. It wasn't nice – I didn't like it. So a lot of us, we never used to go there – we used to find our own place where we used to go to. Afterwards, well, we got contemptu-ous; we didn't bother except for shrapnel falling about. We'd have a tin hat on.

Henry Harington

That night, my dad came down and he said, 'You'd better get out.' So we all got out and I can remember hanging on my mum, my mum took the baby and we went round to her mum's in Leven Road, where they'd all gone down in the gas works in the retort houses. There was a shelter. But they was all bombed out and the houses was on fire and everything, it was a complete and utter mess. We didn't know where we was going.

We get to Oban House and it hasn't got a window out. Everybody sleeps in the first, ground-floor flats; there was no shelters or anything.

We got down and comfortable there and then they said there's a bomb in the grounds and it hasn't gone off. So we all get out of Oban House. We finished up in Monar House where there's a brick shelter. My dad appeared then. I don't know where he'd been but he appeared and when we get there, a woman gave me mum a cup of tea and she thought that was fantastic. It was amazing: people would pour a pot of tea out in the middle of everything falling down around them. 'Have a cup of tea, darling.'

Then we got slung out of there because it was overcrowded and sent to All Hallows, back of the Tavern. When we got there, there was no roof on that building – it had never been finished, that shelter. So that was useless. And a woman took us in Abbotts Road. There was a house between Oban Street and Monar Street and it didn't have any damage – to me, it looked perfect the other houses were all damaged. I was soaking wet because I'd peed myself in fright, being a kid, and my sister was in a state and everyone was – but the woman took pity on us and took us in for the night.

The next morning, we all tramped round the streets looking for relations and you know all the windows was out and people sweeping up glass and clearing the mess of the night before. We got back to our place eventually, and it was damaged. Mostly fire damage, it was incendiary bombs, and the windows was all blown out. It had caught from the sparks from Lusty Oil and the whole of the area was sort of like that.

Len Faram

And I remember coming out from the Spratt's, it was this underground, it was where they stored all the dog biscuits and things, and we used to sleep under there. We all got very cootie 'cos there was lots of lice down there. Itchy, nasty, filthy, but you took shelter there.

Joanna Roberts

We were stuck in air raid shelters every night, hoping and praying that we were not going to be the next victims. It was terrible, every night, and neighbours used to come in and we used to spend the night in our cellar which was really the coal cellar. We used to have the coal delivered down a chute through a hole by the front door, and that was a boarded-up section, and we put boards across and we used to sleep down there. We were newly married but we stayed with my parents because you wouldn't go and buy furniture and that when the bombs were falling every night.

Vicki Green

We were all in the air raid shelter and my mum said, 'I can hear somebody saying we've all got to get out.' So I said no, but she said, 'Listen.' And all of a sudden a police put his head in the air raid shelter: 'Come on out, all out, all out.' So there was my sister, heavily pregnant, and my dad was ill, and a couple of other people we were giving shelter to for the night, and we all had to go around to the school. There was a big tree and there was a land mine hanging on it – the tree is still there. And we all had to go around the corner to the school outside the post office at the top of Brenn Street, and the girls next door, they were running along – there was a house full, mostly all girls, there was hardly any fellas. And she had a bag and there was a bra hanging out and her knickers and everything, and her father was saying, 'Look, at your bag, you're showing your knickers.' 'It don't matter about my knickers,' she said. 'Come on.'

And her mother, she was a lovely lady, she had snow-white hair, and on that day, her daughter had set it all nice, and anyway bombs drop, all the incendiaries, so we all had to run out and get sandbags to put the incendiaries out, and she put her sandbag on her head to carry it and it was all full of dog muck. She cried her eyes out. She said, 'Oooh, just look at my hair. It was all lovely and clean.' But it was different things like that, you know; you was crying and laughing at the same time.

Anne Griffiths

It was terrible. It used to fill up wi' water. It was, you had, a puddle. So you had steps coming down, then you had to keep your feet up, and then you had a couple of bunks that side, a couple of bunks that side. And very cold. And a candle, or a torch. And we all got in there and we all sat in there. And from then on it was continual bombing each night. You didn't get away from it.

Joanna Roberts

My mother had a particular system of organising the family for raids. She invariably filled the bath up with water and put it at the bottom of the stairs and we sat round and the instructions was that when the bomb fell, whoever was nearest to the bomb would kindly pick it up and put it in the bath. The only thing we ever caught was my father who was on leave and having a doze – he ran down the stairs in a hurry, so at least we did get one victim.

Bill Crook

In the morning, when the all-clear went, you'd come out of the dugout, as we called them, and you didn't know if you was going to find a house still left – your house might have been blasted to smithereens – you didn't know what you was gonna find when you come up.

Violet Kentsbeer

And a land mine that was intended for the soldiers on Mudchute, that landed on an air raid shelter right opposite Seyssell Street – they never ever found the bodies of the people. My dad wanted to come home to see if his house was all right – he put his hand on the front door – it was all glass, the door – it was all right till he put his hand on it but when he went to open the door all the glass slid out. If he'd been in that Anderson shelter, if he'd had one, he'd have felt the blast of that bomb.

Annie Pope

We kept our valuables, such as they were, in a tin box which we put in the cooker. Because we knew that if the house got hit, we could recover the cooker and open up the door. We had a little box with our marriage certificate, insurance certificate, birth certificates and things of that nature, personal things. So Alice had instructions: she and the kids used to sleep in a shelter – we had a Morrison shelter in our room and the kids and her used to get in there of a night-time – and if they had to get out, they would put on some clothing, go to the cooker and get out the box of valuables, put them in a bag she'd got ready and then off. She was always the first out. She had to get out this night, and she walked along the street with her hands over the children's heads to protect them from shrapnel coming down from the anti-aircraft guns – not that it would have done if a piece had come straight down, but it was a modest protection.

Cyril Demarne

Then we had a Morrison shelter in the back room there which was lovely, because you put the children in there and then you could creep in yourself beside them – 'cos Bill was very seldom there, and that was so much easier.

During a day raid, they'd bash on the door and anybody, whoever it was, would come in and get under the table. You never knew who they were, never saw them again, kind of thing – but that was the kind of thing that happened then. Everybody worked for the one reason; to do as you're told, do what you could, and to get the war over. And that has never ever happened again – not that feeling of everybody was in it together, and strangers, you'd pick up any kind of conversation with them, and it was all how we were going and what we were doing. Course, it was a pretty grim time one way and another, but it's amazing what the human body can stand and survive.

Florence Mugridge

We used to have the buzz bombs come over; it was always then my daughter would decide to have a bath. The warning used to go and I used to say very often she's run to the air raid shelter with a bath towel round her.

We had an Anderson shelter – I used to have bunk beds in there, we had electric lighting in there, and in winter we had a fire in there. Because we felt more safer in that air raid shelter than what we did in the house. And we had very good neighbours. If we had a bad air raid, everyone used to come out after the all-clear had gone. Everyone right along the road used to shout out, 'Are you all right in there?'

Annie Pope

We even got to a stage that it was a waste of time going to the shelters, you know. My mother used to say that the best thing to get under is the table. Like, if you ever go into bombed houses, you always see a table standing up.

I remember once we was going round, we'd just come back from hopping – anyway, we lived in Cable Street at that time and there was a heavy raid going on. We said we'll go round this certain shelter, big shelter, it was, in Stepney. And we was walking round there, and all of a sudden, me mother bumped into a friend she knew. 'Ah,' she said, 'it's terrible down there;

it's jam-packed.' So I said, 'Oh, come on, we'll just go back and sit indoors, and get under the table again.' And unfortunately, that night, the shelter got a direct hit and there was a hell of a lot killed in that thing. So it was just fate – one took it as it came.

Joe James

You always had this fear of being buried alive – everybody had this fear of being buried alive – you all said, it didn't matter if you got killed, as long as you didn't get buried. My vivid memory of that flat was my mother standing in the passageway, with her chair, all night long, so she knew she was near the door, so that if the place got hit by a bomb, she had it in her mind that she could get out.

John Beattie

When the Blitz started, the government didn't want us to go down. They even had armed guards covering the entrances, like at Liverpool Street station. And I remember my father going there, and of course, it was political as well, and there were all these people pushing against the gates, and the soldiers, and suddenly, we were let through. And my father shouted, 'It's a great victory for the working class!'

What it was really, was that Churchill had said, 'OK, we have no choice, we have to let them down.' But it was very sporadic and difficult. It was first-come, first-served – but I was called 'the snake' by Mother – I could always get in and out of things. So as soon as the air raid sirens went, we would go to the nearest tube station, or prepare for it and go earlier and wait outside. What happened was, when they opened the gates, people would rush down, and my mother gave me lots of scarves, so I'd have them all round me, and I'd go down three at a time on the stairs, rushing down, getting on to the platform, because you'd grab your place. I opened up all the scarves so I'd have enough space for all the family. And then, after this fury, everyone would start to talk, friendly.

Bernard Kops

Through its leadership, the local Communist Party led to the opening of Underground stations which became air raid shelters, because there was no deep shelters, and it was the march at Aldgate East station by members of the Communist Party and members of the Labour Party collectively, that marched down the stairs, and from the following morning, all over London, the Underground became open.

Jack Dash

My older sister Phoebe and I were on our way, jumping in and out of trains in both directions, and we were on our way to Marble Arch, but before we got there, we got out at Bank, walked around the place, looked at the people, got back into the next train, and as we drew out of the station, we got into the tunnel, there was a kind of a rocking feeling. And my God, had we not got that train, we would have been dead. Because a bomb went right through the lift shaft. We didn't know what had happened till the morning.

Bernard Kops

The bloodiest event was what was called the Bank incident; there were about two hundred, or 190 fatalities there, and literally hundreds of injured. It was when I was at Bethnal Green fire station, and the first fire crew that they could contact was there. We'd just come in from about twenty-four hours' continual fire-fighting and we were soaked to the skin, frozen and very hungry, and all our carefully-made arrangements were found useless when the event happened. Not completely, but to a great extent useless.

The army clearing the huge crater resulting from a direct hit on Bank Underground station on 10 January 1941. Many people taking shelter in the station were thrown under an oncoming train by the force of the explosion, or killed by shockwaves from the blast. Arthur Cross/Fred Tibbs, 1941

And we had to go out. My crew – I was driver with six crew under the charge of a leading fireman – were the first ones on the scene. It was our job to climb in, over the dead and the wounded, on our bellies, dragging lengths of hose and foam to deal with the burning gas main before we could start on the rescue operation. Things like that... they weren't all like that, I'm glad to say.

Charles Poulson

The first year there were no air raids, but when the air raids started, it was quite bad because we spent every night in the shelter. And my husband's house was destroyed on the first day of the air raid, and so that was opposite where I used to live, and also one of my friends got killed in that same air raid. So it was, it brought, the war to our doorstep. And also there was no water, gas or electric or anything. We was just existing for days on end in the shelters or out of the shelters.

Connie Hoe

A Changing World

By the end of 1941, with Continental Europe under Nazi control, the war had became truly global. British and Commonwealth troops were fighting Mussolini's army in North Africa, the Germany army was pushing on through Russia, and British and Soviet troops had invaded Iran to secure its oilfields. On 7 December, infuriated by a US oil embargo, the Japanese attacked American ships in Pearl Harbor, and America entered the war. Japan then invaded the Philippines, Burma and Hong Kong. The first day of 1942 saw the US, Britain, the USSR and China, plus a total of twenty-two Commonwealth, European and Central American nations come together to form what would eventually become the United Nations.

On 10 May 1941, the first London Blitz came to an end with a massive raid that saw 550 bombers drop more than seven hundred tons of bombs, which damaged the chamber of the House of Commons, Westminster Abbey, St James's Palace, the British Museum, the Old Bailey and almost all the major railway stations. Following this, London had a respite from the continuous air bombardment.

Between September 1940 and May 1941, more than a million London houses had been destroyed or damaged. Dealing with the practical reality of being bombed – not just once or twice, but night after night – had been deeply traumatising and, in the East End, there can not have been a single person who had not experienced the loss of a family member, friend or neighbour.

There was genuine unity between the people who went through those long nights together, packed in basements and shelters as the bombs fell outside – whether listening fearfully, or singing cheerfully to keep worries at bay. But once the all-clear had sounded, each family and each individual had to walk out and face their own losses, discover what was left of their house, their street, their once-familiar neighbourhood, and pick up the pieces of their own life.

And we came out and Dad said, 'Wonder what it's like when we get round home,' 'cos we now called Granny's house home. And we got round home and we turned the corner and the house had gone. It was burnt out completely. So what my mother had laboriously saved from the first she lost. And I saw my mother disintegrate. From what she was to what she became was completely... She used to always be dusting and cleaning; that all went by the board. Give up on that.

And then we got took in by someone who let us have their upstairs. So although it's not really true about how we were

After the first fifty-seven days of bombing are over, the unrepaired damage to St Katharine Docks from the first night of the Blitz shows the level of destruction sustained by London's port area and surrounding buildings. John H Avery & Co., 1949

one and the comradeship – there was a lot, but there was still dirty things going on, like looting. People still looted if they thought there was something in a house – they wouldn't be above going in and nicking it – but there was a feel that you did do your best for anybody you could sort of do your best for, if you were lucky enough.

Joanna Roberts

Tilbury Hotel burned down during the war – a canister of incendiaries hit it. I lived in Grays, on a hill, and my daddy went up and said, 'Tilbury Hotel's on fire.' He could tell where it was, and it was like a sheet of flame in the sky, because it was a timbered construction, all oak. It was a wonderful place and I remember standing howling that night. In the morning when I went to work, the chief accountant who was in residence that night, he and his wife called at the office. He'd lost everything he possessed – they brought his wife up to our office in pyjamas and a fur coat, and we just had to comfort her the whole morning, she was in such a state of shock. I think we spent the whole morning piling coal on the fire and making cups of tea for her. A lot of naval guests staying there, they all had to escape in their nightwear.

Elizabeth Garrett

I had a succession of jobs in the City working for various small firms, but as fast as I worked for them, they were getting bombed out. You'd start work on the Monday, hope for your wages on the Friday, then on the Thursday, they'd be devastated and you'd end up with no wages again.

John Beattie

I'd been at Barkingside when I heard that the hospital had got bombed; that it had got it right in the middle. So a friend and I cycled up from Barkingside to Poplar to have a look. And we got off our bikes, and there was the hospital, with just a hole right through it, the matron's bed hanging out. Lovely hospital it was, and it went right through the middle.

Elsie Edwards

I remember, during the war, it was a terrible day of being bombed, and there was a soldier sitting opposite and they shouted out that the bomb had fallen in a certain turning, and his father lived there. And he rushed round to this turning, and he came back and his foot was all bleeding and I had to bring him in to bathe his foot and take some glass out. And he was so shy, this fellow, and I said, 'Well, you're not shy of taking your sock off? I can see where the blood's coming from.' That was terrible; there was a lot of people killed there.

Mary Ridgeon

Years later, I read in a book that there was a lot of looting, and I can testify that was true. I am sorry to say that in my platoon, the only two who did not loot was Peter Addington and myself. They went into jewellery shops and every shop: sergeants, corporals, men. I mean, I remember seeing some of the big puff trying to open the cash till, that had fused together, you know; it was that bronze metal and someone frantically trying to open it. But still, that's war time – there was a lot of looting during the war. It was only wristwatches, perhaps; I don't think it was very expensive stuff. What they primarily wanted was money, because boozing and women are the two *raisons d'être* for soldiers.

Jack Miller

My worst moment was coming home one Friday morning and turning the corner of the street and seeing three-parts of houses on one side totally demolished – I didn't think that the houses on the other side would stand up, but eventually they did. All that there was on the other side was broken glass and roofs and things like that.

John Henry Arnold

I hadn't realised that this was one of the early times when the Germans were using two-thousand kilo bombs – and at this time, the manager and his wife of the local Barclays bank were in bed in the flat at the top of the bank, which was totally destroyed, and they were found in bed a whole block away, in the street.

They were taken to hospital and discharged the next morning. I don't know if it was the right thing to discharge them – they were probably suffering from tremendous shock – but they were not found to be physically injured.

Eric Cropper

I went down the next day and you'd never seen anything like it, it was like being on the moon. All the telegraph poles were down; he'd bombed, and he'd had a whale of a time, the chap there. They'd bombed some destroyer up by the basin at Woolwich, and there was pieces of bodies around, you know. I remember putting a piece of whatever – nothing, you know, it was just, well, like a butcher's shop, you know. Not too bad, but it was shocking. And everything was chaos. It made you wonder.

William Mather

There was an occasion when one of the firemen got blown into the dock. Me, being first aid man, we got him out and he seemed quite happy and chirpy, you know. So I got in the ambulance with him, took him down to the proper hospital. And I said, 'How do you feel?' He said, 'I'll be all right.' Do you know, that man died of shock, next day. A fine, big fella. That gave me a shock, you know.

Charles Lisle

And there'd be a terrible raid, and outside various buildings there'd be lists of people who'd died, and you'd go and look at them, or hear that several hundred had been killed that night. It was an unreal situation really.

Elsie Edwards

My brother-in-law was a warden and he told me he was walking along Columbia Market and he saw someone leaning against a lamp post, and he said, 'Hey, quick, get shelter,' and he touched the man, and the man literally fell to pieces. A kind of disintegration of his body. He told me he walked into a street shelter and some people were sitting there, dead. It was the blast that killed them.

In the early 1940s, there was a police station bombed in Tottenham Court Road and lots of people were killed. I was looking in this vegetarian restaurant window and this bomb went, and I saw people looking the other way and falling – the blast had somehow sucked the breath from them. So the war stopped being an adventure, if you like, and started to become quite terrible.

Bernard Kops

One of the fellows in the general office, I remember his saying – he was quite friendly with me, as a matter of fact – and he said one day, it frightened the life out of me, 'You know what's going to happen if there's an invasion, don't you?' I said, 'What?' He said, 'Well, I've got a revolver and the first thing I shall do is to shoot you.' So I said, 'Thanks very much.' But it was meant, because they did believe that we would be invaded, and the first thing the Germans would do would be to take the docks. All the men felt very protective towards us, we never really knew what was going to happen at night, where the parachutists would land, or anything.

Elizabeth Garrett

We were billeted in the students hostel and everybody was a bit ambivalent about our status; most people thought we were medical students, and so when there was a heavy raid, we were on call from the London Hospital and nobody queried or enquired as to our status. We just did... you know, we sewed people up, we patched people together... you know.

And the first thing we had to do was we had to go round – the idea to begin with was there was going to be hundreds of thousands of casualties, but this didn't happen, and all the casualties were brought into the London Hospital and the whole of the entrance hall, that was available to us, and it was strewn with all the dead and the dying and people burnt and God knows what.

When the heavy raids started, the roof was gone and all we had were little like car lamps, run by batteries, and it was really dark, and we had to go round first and decide which of these people would live and which wouldn't. Those that we decided wouldn't live, we just gave them a shot of morphia and wrapped them in blankets and put them to one side, and then we dealt with those that we thought we could save. And that was how it went on, night after night.

Louis Dore

As the casualties from the bombing was brought in, they'd have a quick look, they'd do something for those they thought they could deal with, and the others, they'd say, 'Put them over there.' They'd get looked at if they'd got time to – most of them, it was too late anyway. And I always wondered what would happen if they brought me mum or dad in, and they said, 'Put them over there.' Never happened, but we all thought, how would we feel? 'Cos with other people, after a little while, it was just, I know it sounds awful, but they're, you know, bodies. 'Put them over there.'

Dennis Pike

And my dad said to my mother, 'I can't get anything out these wardens.' He says, 'Where's all them? Where's all my relations? Where are they?' So this warden was very kind. He said, 'Come on, old chap, I'll take you over to there. We're doing what we can.' Apparently they were killed, a lot of 'em, the whole lot went. And that was the only time I've ever seen my dad cry. He did cry. He just did.

Joanna Roberts

My friend Angela lived in the flats behind, quite high flats they were and they'd gone to powder. Angela's brother, who was on his paper round, had seen this happen and had seen where his parents had gone and they were dug out because he was able to direct them, so his mother and father were in hospital, and Angela was all right, but they'd lost their home. Old Mr Lee, whose boathouse it had been, and Mrs Lee were killed, and young Kathleen downstairs and her father were killed, she was eighteen, a pretty girl, and I can't remember who else, some people on the river front, and that was really the end of a whole chapter of our lives, changed completely.

Freda Hammerton

Violet Carr, I always had a soft spot for Violet Carr, and something had happened in Reculver Road and I'd gone round there and got through the house into the shelter. They told me where it was and I looked in there, and there was an incendiary had actually gone into it with them. And that was the first thing I ever did see. It didn't scar so much then as it did afterwards. It's afterwards you think about these things. I see other things, but you don't really remember the other things, they all become a blur, they all roll into each other after a while. But that, I can remember that. Violet Carr. She was a lovely girl. I always fancied her. Violet Carr, I'll never forget. It had actually gone in there. There was other people in there, but I only actually saw her. I could recognise her, but that was that.

Dennis Pike

Nearly every family was affected in some way or other. If they didn't have someone in the forces, they had people being injured and killed at home – there was hardly any families that weren't involved in some way or another. There was no counselling – you just had to get on with it.

Violet Kentsbeer

We weren't all together, we were all desperately trying to survive – there were lots of dark and terrible things happening, you know, on the home front. Brothers away in the army, abroad, parents desperately trying – I remember my mother taking us out of London so many times, to different places, for shelter. Seeing my own house, in Stepney, first day of the Blitz, destroyed. Moving into rest centres while you were allocated a couple of rooms somewhere – that happened to us. Moving into Arnold Circus, where the Old Nichol used to be, in Bethnal Green – the Old Nichol has a fantastic history, it was an absolute den of iniquity and vice and shit and God knows what.

Despite all that happening, we lost... imagine, down in the cellar in Stepney Green buildings, imagine all the aunts and uncles in the cellar because it was safer, and then in the morning, coming up and seeing your house not there, the top of the tenement has gone. These thing really impinge and give you a sense of – not disintegration, but being not there. A world hard to imagine, the sudden overnight loss of the place you were born into and brought up in, and suddenly it's gone. We always feel at one with refugees and people like that – it just brings back this sense of not belonging. I think many writers came out of that school of not belonging.

Bernard Kops

Living in a Strange Calm

The East End's war was not over, but between May 1941 and June 1944, bombing in London effectively ceased. The war continued in the Pacific, with the Japanese seizing the initiative, eventually taking twenty-five thousand prisoners in the fall of Singapore, many of whom later perished in the terrible conditions in Japanese camps. In June 1942, an American victory in the naval Battle of Midway finally saw the tide turn against Japan.

The East End continued to play a vital part in the war effort, producing armaments and equipment to supply those on the battlefields. One of Britain's great heroes, commander-in-chief General Bernard Montgomery, was pushing back German forces in North Africa, and East End factories were making spare petrol tanks to fuel the planes out there. The Russians were counter-attacking in Stalingrad, where a German surrender in 1943 was the first major check to the seemingly unstoppable Third Reich forces. Success in North Africa was followed by the Allies invading Sicily – their troop transport aided by Horsa gliders, also constructed in East End factories. The Allies went on to invade southern Italy and overthrow Mussolini, though German forces came to his rescue.

In Britain, code-breakers working at Bletchley Park were doing their part to stem the huge losses inflicted by German U-boats. RAF Bomber Command was under the direction of Sir Arthur Harris (nicknamed 'Bomber' Harris), who had taken a leaf out of Hitler's book and was conducting a series of night raids on German cities, in particular, Berlin. He believed that breaking German resistance was the key to winning the war, and Berlin was substantially destroyed over the course of sixteen massed attacks between November 1943 and March 1944.

Mobile canteens, staffed by volunteers, were a wartime innovation. This one in the docks served visiting soldiers and dockers alike. They were so popular that the Port of London Authority introduced permanent staff canteens that were soon serving up to 18,000 cups of tea a day. 1941

Normal life began to resume in the British capital, but the sirens still sounded whenever unidentified aircraft were spotted, so the fear of bombs was never far away. Many families now slept at home, inside their new Morrison shelters every night, but others continued to trek to air raid shelters to sleep in safety, particularly after news of any Allied bombing raid that might result in retaliatory attacks. So on 3 March 1943, after reports of a heavy raid on Berlin, large numbers headed towards Bethnal Green tube station after an air raid warning. New guns were being tested nearby and the noise made the crowd panic. Within minutes, 173 people – sixty-two of them children – had lost their lives.

I went to the Metropolitan Plywood Company, which was off City Road. It was an old building that had been bombed out. What we were making there was interesting: we were making spare parts of petrol tanks which were put under the wings of fighter planes and dropped in the desert when they were exhausted. We had a long bench and had to build these parts, which were like a huge bullet, with a nose and tail, and put stringers in – that's long pieces of wood which were inset all the way round, which we'd cover with a skin. They had to be lightweight, because they had to be attached underneath the plane. They were made of plywood, and each one was tested for certain amount of pressure when you'd finished. Lots were rejected.

Alfred Alexander

The first job I did in the war was white wardrobes and cupboards for hospitals in France. It was white enamel, inside and out – I got covered like a snowman. Then we went on to tent poles and telegraph poles; the telegraph poles were done with khaki paint, the tent poles red. Then we went on to ammunition boxes – they were khaki, with white letters on the front.

Then I went into the dope shop, where I spent the rest of the war working from seven in the evening until seven in the morning. My husband was there too, on landing craft, next to me, but he was on days. We used to pass one another in the street, me going to work and him going home.

In the dope shop, you had this material called madap, which is linen, that you put over the plywood of an aircraft. We worked on the Horsa glider, which was very big, like an underground tunnel, thirty feet across. We worked in a gang of six, first the fabric, madap and then the dope. Dope was like a reddish paint – terrible-smelling stuff. We used to do four of these fuselages a night. We were the best gang – they put me in charge.

We also made these frameworks of lorries in wood. Just the framework. It was then covered with canvas and I had to spray the windscreen, the radiator, the wheels and the numbers. They were then put on the road so the Germans would bomb that convoy of artificial lorries, so the real lorries got through.

Sissy Lewis

There's all the extra munitions and uniform, it all has to be provided. So by 1939, people like Lebus's were making gliders. My father, in the First World War, he'd worked on making wooden propellers, and my uncle had worked on the fuselage of the wooden aeroplanes – who'd have thought you'd have wooden aeroplanes in the Second World War?

Charles Megnin

Being the outside tug, we got all the dirty jobs. We used to meet the convoy destroyers coming in the harbour; they used to lay there overnight, and we used to take off the survivors of the ships that had been sunk to put them ashore. It was all right if they were naval personnel because they had places to go, but the poor walking wounded Merchant Navy, if the merchant seamen's hostel was shut – which it shut about six o'clock at night – they had to walk round the town until such time as they opened in the morning. There was no facilities at all in 1940, '41 and '42 for them, which upset me.

John Henry Arnold

We moved to Bethnal Green and that's where we lived, and the war was kind of settling down, life was quiet, but then they started up again a bit, at night. By this time, the nearest shelter was Bethnal Green. We were in Brick Lane, and to get there, we had to walk a little way to Bethnal Green Road and get a bus, which we did, every night. We were officially in the shelter.

So on that day, the radio said, 'Alert, in about five minutes, the sirens will sound.' My mother immediately took my young sister and run with her, all the way along, I could see her running, and she said, 'You're coming on, aren't you, you're coming on?' I said, 'Yes.'

So they go, and me and my father, we go about five minutes later. So we go, and we get off the bus underneath the arches that leads into Cambridge Heath Road. And we see crowds of people, and screaming, and police and the guns. The problem, apparently, was that the government had got new guns going, they were in Victoria Park, and they sounded like bombs dropping, they were so loud. Unlike the others, which were ack-ack.

Bernard Kops

In December of 1943, we had a play called *The King of Lampedusa*, which was based on a true incident in the June of that year, when a British pilot by the name of Sydney Cohen, who happened to be a Jewish boy from Hackney, East London, had to land his plane on the island of Lampedusa, because there was something wrong with his plane. The Italian islanders, having heard of an impending invasion by the Allies, when they saw this British plane swoop down on the island, they thought this was it. They came running towards this one plane with white flags flying and surrendered to this one British pilot.

A Czech journalist, who happened to be a friend of my father, took this incident up and wrote a play about it; a true incident that is transformed into a dream, where he really becomes King of Lampedusa. Now this play hit a chord with the press. They all came out roaring with applause for this funny Yiddish play in the East End of London, in this little theatre in Commercial Road. We had not just non-Jewish audiences, but people who had never been to the East End, let alone to Jewish theatre. It ran for eight consecutive months – ten performances a week we had to give. The theatre being so little, we had to accommodate all the people who wanted to come and see it.

Anna Tzelniker

In those days, there was no central rail. And apparently, someone shouted out 'Bombs, bombs!' and people started rushing down. When you went down, you reached the bottom and there was a brick wall, and then you turned to the right to go into the station ticket office. So apparently what had happened was the people were rushing down, crushing, crushing, crushing, and a lady with a baby had slipped because there was no central rail, and someone stumbled on to her, and gradually, gradually, without anyone able to turn right to get into the ticket office, they were just suffocated. In fact, their faces were black and their tongues were blue – it was a really terrifying disaster. I couldn't look – the police kept everyone away, but it all happened so fast. When I say we were five minutes after, it could have been ten minutes or quarter of an hour – a lot depended on how fast I got the bus down Bethnal Green Road – I don't remember. But we arrived to find this terrible scene of crying and screaming and ambulances and police cars.

The real problem was that we thought that my mother was in it, and my sister; and she thought we were in it. You couldn't get down. People came from the other end – it was an unused tube then, Bethnal Green, things stopped at Liverpool Street, I think – but police and other people came running in from the other end, along the tunnel, to try and get through. It took several hours – in fact, I don't think we knew until the next morning if everything was all right – which was the most terrible thing of all. As you know, not knowing is probably worse than knowing. They got there just before; we got there just after.

It was hushed up, because Churchill demanded it, because he felt it was very bad publicity. At that point, everything was going better and he didn't want bad effects like this – it sounded like panic.

Bernard Kops

CHAPTER 11

Glimmers of Victory

D-Day

For many, the Second World War began with the evacuation of Dunkirk, when the East End's seafaring men piloted a variety of small boats to help pluck the British Expeditionary Force from a beach in France. Four years after Dunkirk, Britain was getting ready to carry out an equally secret mission on the beaches of France: the Normandy landings.

This time, instead of rescuing a battered army that had been driven back to the coast of France, the movement was to be in reverse, with the army invading from England to start of the final push of the war. The actual day of the landings – 6 June 1944 – was codenamed D-Day, and was the day after the liberation of Rome by Allied forces.

As the Allies had no foothold in France, and no harbours in which to unload ships, they took two floating harbours with them, codenamed Mulberry Harbours. These were assembled from specially constructed concrete blocks called caissons, some weighing nearly six thousand tons, which were constructed in the drained East India Import Dock, the Surrey Docks and Royal Docks. The harbours were assembled in the Solent, towed to Normandy and sunk off the beaches. One was damaged in a freak storm, but the one at Arromanches worked perfectly. It was as large as the harbour at Dover and could handle twelve thousand tons of supplies a day.

In the spring of 1944, Field Marshal Montgomery, a hero after his success at El Alamein, visited the docks to urge men to redouble their efforts; victory was now in sight. The dock workers did not know the project they were engaged on would be a vital part of the D-Day landings. 1944

On 6 June, infantry and armoured divisions were transported across the channel by nearly seven thousand vessels, landing on the now-famous beaches of Utah, Omaha, Gold, Juno and Sword, spread across fifty miles of Normandy coastline. It was the largest amphibious invasion in history. Many Thames barges were converted into Landing Barge Vehicles that were used to transport supplies, and even Landing Barge Kitchens, to keep the troops fed.

The invasion of Europe was backed up by the Mulberry Harbour system, much of which was developed in East India Dock and other docks in London. And the people who were constructing it had no idea what they were constructing. They were constructing these great big concrete structures which were being towed and floated and they had no idea what was going on, of course, until after the war.

Dick Butler

Periodically, they'd bring in and you'd see the damaged barges, and along the river you would have the minesweepers going up and down. Everything was grey, and we were converting, at the time, Thames lighters. They'd cut the swim of the barge off a certain amount and put in ramps to be used, I presume, when the invasion did come.

Dick Allington

I joined another destroyer and that was involved in the D-Day landings – our particular part being to oversee the laying of the petroleum pipeline across the Channel to the beachhead.

P Satow

A very secretive type of work was begun during the second half of the war years. These became later known as the Mulberry Harbours, which helped the landing of the troops on the D-Day invasion of Europe. These Mulberry Harbours were taken out of the dock entrance at the Millwall and were seen floating down the river at this point. This was followed actually on June fifth and sixth by troop ships full of Allied troops. We had accommodated them in our canteen with cups of tea and they sung the songs of the day and then embarked for their – well, their trip became the D-Day landings. We didn't know at the time.

It was a great thrill to see them going out, going somewhere, we didn't know where, but just going in such numbers. American troops in particular, as well.

Rose Bater

I was fourteenish and we pulled up to the Mulberry Harbour where we was unloading; out in the middle, oh, about a mile off the shore, they had these rocket ships. Great big banks of rockets. Not so much aircraft but there was a lot of shelling going on, and I forget what I had to do, but I'd come up on deck when these rockets let fly. Well, what happened is a secret between me and the laundry, because I've never had such a frightening thing in my life. I mean, a thousand of these rockets. They're the most deafening noise God ever put breath into, you know.

Bob Silver

Prior to D-Day, there was a big time lapse because of the weather, and all the ships, the invasion ships, day after day, was lined all the way down past Southend, right down to the towers and just bobbing away there in the water. And the next time we went down there to see 'em all, they was all gone, and then we heard on the news about the D-Day landings.

Dick Allington

Everything was converging on Tilbury, all the little ships were in position, and it went very, very quiet – nobody spoke, we were too terrified to speak. We could see but we daren't say a word. Then the road from London, the A13, was absolutely blocked, all the army travelling, on the move, and everybody locally knew they was coming, but nobody said a word – they was too terrified.

Elizabeth Garrett

We didn't know anything about D-Day, didn't know when it was gonna take place. That night, I was on fire duty all night, and we hadn't been long back – we used to knock off at seven o'clock, go home, come back eight or nine o'clock – and I hadn't been back very long before the sirens went. Of course, our orders were, once the sirens went, into the air raid shelter. We went in the air raid shelter, the air raid went on all night long, came out in the morning, and I had the biggest shock of my life. During the night, the army had arrived, and the whole of the length of that road – King George Dock, Albert Dock, and right down to the bottom of Victoria Dock – was lined two-deep with army vehicles. And I'd been in the dock all night and didn't even know they'd arrived. Honest, it's the biggest shock I've ever had in my life. And then, of course, the penny dropped. Something was happening. But I don't think anybody knew that *that* was going to take place.

Harry Foss

We've come out of Waterloo Station, there was military police, the redcaps, there with machine guns all around. We were straight shepherded into lorries, there was no wandering off. We went over Tower Bridge and down to Poplar and then the rumour went round we was going to a camp nearby. We went down East India Dock Road and I said, 'Let me off the back of the lorry, I'll see if my granddad's there.' But we went round this camp, which was on the bomb site, and it was only tents and marquees with the barbed wire round. They weren't redcaps, they was soldiers they had patrolling inside the wire with machine guns and orders to shoot anyone that tried to get out.

We went in, had a meal, they took our English money off us; we was in there it can't have been more than an hour, then on to lorries, straight in the dock, up aboard the ship. So I thought, Oh, we're not going home tonight. Then we went across and landed on D plus one.

Dick Allington

I was on duty the night they went off, and it was eerie. All you could hear was feet, and we couldn't go up. We were kept down. The army kept us below – well, any of us could have been spies, and we weren't allowed to emerge and all we could hear was quiet orders and tramping of feet as they boarded and went. And they went in these roll-on, roll-off things. There were loads of those, and they went in anything, really. But it all happened very quickly and very quietly, and then of course it was very empty – they'd all gone.

Elizabeth Garrett

On D-Day, there we were, receiving the vehicles to go into the landing craft and it was the time of the VE bombs, the flying bombs, and we got used to knowing what lanes they came over and, of course, not to take too much notice of them while they were still buzzing, but directly they stopped you were on tenterhooks and you could gauge, to some extent, which direction they were coming from. Well, on the particular day in question, there was so much noise where I was, just superintending the lining up of these vehicles for the landing craft, that I didn't hear a flying bomb coming, but a soldier who was on guard at the pumping house and quite near to me, his exact words were 'Christ, look!' and I looked up and there was a flying bomb coming down just where I was standing.

Anyway, I ran to a place where I knew I would be below ground level, which was the superintendent's garden, and by our training, I knew to stand with my back to the wall and with my hands over my ears, thumbs over ears and fingers in my eyes, and just waited. And there was a pretty loud crash, and I went up, back onto the level, and there were several vehicles burning and the soldier and his pump house had disappeared.

And I went into the front office and asked if everybody was all right, because all the windows were broken, and there were a lot of people shrieking and I saw one of my foremen, I shan't forget this in a hurry, standing there with half a pane of glass sticking out of his nostril.

Stanley Tooth

Just before D-Day had opened, we were towing tank-landing ships, the big American jobs with the big open doors, and we was laying alongside it in the West India Dock to tow it out full of troops and equipment, and someone called my name. I looked up, and it was one of my neighbours going away. But of course, at that time, it was all hush-hush and he just said, he said to me, 'See the missus when you get home, tell her I'll be OK, and you know where I'm going.'

Dick Allington

So we went out and we just cruised up and down the Channel behind a smokescreen and a few shells now and again, or bombs. We was laying there waiting to go ashore, we was all below decks, we could hear the guns booming and whatnot, and bombs dropping, and we was all singing there and ordered not to move till we were told. Then you could hear them ordering some of the deck up quickly and the crew just looking down on us. There and then we just fell quiet and just listened to the sound of the guns. And then our orders came, up we went and just had to throw our kitbags down the scramble nets into the landing craft and it was all a rush.

When we got ashore, the navy people wanted us ashore straight away, and in we went and marched over the hill to Arromanches, went through a system of trenches. We didn't see any Germans then; they'd gone inland a bit. But we sent a corporal and a couple of blokes back to the beach for something and they went into the trenches for souvenirs and got the fright of their lives: a few Germans came out with their hands up. They turned them over to the infantry.

George Adams

Doodlebugs and Rockets

The first phase of London's bombing, now sometimes referred to as the 'Great Blitz', ended on 10 May 1941. Three years later, the bombs started again. Hitler's new secret weapon was the V-1, and the first one hit London one week after D-Day, falling on Grove Road in Bow. Its arrival caused people to scan the clear skies, puzzled by the lack of a plane or telltale escaping parachutes, unaware that the new explosives did not need to be dropped by aeroplane. The V-1's pulse engines made a characteristic buzzing sound, the insect-like noise giving rise to the nicknames buzz bomb and doodlebug. More terrifying than the noise was the silence that followed, as the engine cut out and the bomb began to fall. This gave you about ten seconds to find somewhere safe.

Anti-aircraft, or ack-ack, guns were deployed against the V-1s, as were barrage balloons whose cables were intended to disrupt their flight, although the V-1's wings had cable cutters which could cut through these. Altogether, nearly half of the

Mulberry Harbours were floating concrete structures – with about the same capacity as Dover Harbour – and were towed across the Channel to provide an unloading point for military equipment required for the D-Day landings. This one is leaving George V Dock. PLA Staff Photographer, 1944

9,251 rockets fired at Britain were destroyed before they could do any damage, but even so, London suffered 2,515 attacks over a three-month period, killing and injuring nearly three thousand citizens. Then on 7 September 1944, the government announced that London was safe; General Montgomery's troops had now overrun all the French sites from which the rockets could be launched.

The next morning, London was rocked by two large explosions, and the rumour went round that they were caused by faulty gas mains. Nine weeks, and several explosions later, the gas story was beginning to wear a little thin. On 10 November, Churchill had to admit that Britain was once more under attack, this time, from larger V-2 rockets launched from sites near The Hague. The forerunner of all modern rockets, and the first to achieve sub-orbital spaceflight (higher than one hundred kilometres above sea level), V-2s were very hard to target accurately and, being launched from Holland, most fell on the east of the capital, particularly on Dagenham, East Ham, Barking and Walthamstow. These caused devastatingly large explosions, creating twenty-metre craters. Over a thousand fell on London, killing and injuring nearly ten times that number. The worst single rocket attack killed 160 and seriously injured 108 after striking a Woolworth's store in New Cross. Altogether 9,238 people were killed by the flying bombs and rockets of the Little Blitz, about half the number of people killed in the Great Blitz.

In 1945, I fly to England, we landed in London and flying bombs were everywhere and we stay in London for three weeks. It was the war – bombs were flying, houses were burning – it was a disaster, terrible.

Zygmund Izycki

Things were changing. I don't know how long afterwards, but there were buzz bombs and the rockets – I think people were numb by then.

Bernard Kops

I came home in what was supposed to be the dying days of the war, and of course immediately, the V-1s and V-2s started. For a child my age – about sixteen – that was exciting. We had to go down into the shelters every night. I saw the first doodle-bug – the first V-1 over London – with my face pressed up against the glass of my bedroom window. What a stupid thing to do. This thing went over – an extraordinary sound – not like an aeroplane at all. And I could see flames coming out of the back of what I now know was the jet propulsion unit. And then the engine stopped. I yelled to my mother. 'It's coming down!' And of course it did come down, with a bang. But not anywhere near us.

John Earl

And we got not only the bombing, that went, then we got the doodlebugs, or the ones that phut, phut, phut and stopped, and that's when you knew it was gliding. When you heard the engine stop that was when you got frightened 'cos you knew it was gliding and coming down and if you were in the way then it hit you. We got over that and then we went on to the rockets. And the rockets were terrible. That was about 1944, September, getting towards the end of the war. And you had no warning whatsoever.

Joanna Roberts

When the doodlebugs started coming over, that was really awful, because they didn't have any airmen in them, they just were shot over and you could hear them coming – it was a terrible noise they made, and if you could hear that noise it was OK. But as soon as the noise stopped, it was gonna drop, and you just didn't know where to go to be safe. Because you wasn't always in the shelter in the daytime. That was terrible. And they made great craters in the road, and killed so many people. Great craters, not small holes; they was enough to put a bus down. And if houses were in the way, whole houses collapsed.

Violet Kentsbeer

The V-2s started, which were an extraordinary thing because there was no warning of those – and in fact, you had quite a different attitude towards them. You didn't go into the shelters; what was the point? You didn't know where they were going to fall or when they were going to fall. All you knew was that there was an explosion. Rather like a terrorist explosion. Nothing you can do about it – if you're unlucky enough to be on the train or in the cinema when it happens, you're unlucky.

John Earl

When the rockets used to come over, they just went bang; nobody knew what was happening – it was just a large explosion and you'd think, Where's that gone?, that type of thing. You got to a stage where you thought, Oh well, if it's going to happen, it's going to happen, and you didn't really think about it. You got on with your life. You went to girl guides, saw a few friends, you just carried on your life.

Jean Cunningham

I saw the first doodlebug or buzz bomb to come and hit London while I was on the tug. We were laying up at Limehouse Pier, we'd been sleeping there all night actually, waiting for the tide to go down to Sheerness, and we was filling up with freshwater, and it was a beautiful early morning, about four, just breaking dawn, and there's a terrific noise of engines. Looking out, I can see nothing; the river was quiet. The guns opened up and of course, we looked. First thing, we looked up in the air, and we saw this fire trail coming out and I said to them, 'Well,' I said, 'they've caught the bugger – look out for the parachut-ist.' Which we didn't see, naturally, as the buzz bomb had no parachutists, no pilots. And that landed – it was the first place that got bombed – in a place called Grove Road in Bow, or Mile End, right near the railway bridge.

We were chased down the river on a Sunday lunchtime by a doodlebug. I was on the engines at the time, and we was towing nothing. Whenever one was towing nothing one used to give a double ring on the telegraph, you didn't ask any questions, just ding-ding, you know, really put the throttle all the way up. So I thought it might, you know, get me down below, I've got to get up. So I goes to the top of the ladder and there's this doo-dlebug coming abreast of us. And he dropped on the Surrey Commercial Dock, but we was actually chased down there by this bug, and we went over towards the old Millwall entrance and the buzz bomb went over the other entrance.

Dick Allington

We had a land mine at the bottom of the road – my mother was making a bread pudding and it stuck on the ceiling – that was pretty close. It was only two hundred yards away. The first doodlebug that dropped was two roads away and that demol-ished a railway, and left one of my friends hanging, in the bed, on the edge of the floor. One of the first rockets fell four or five hundred yards away and demolished a whole square.

The doodlebugs started on my birthday, June twenty-first. My mother was rather scared, so for the first six months, I was in Scotland. I came back when the rockets were coming over and I started work. I went with her – so if anything hap-pened, we would both go together.

Jean Cunningham

After the house was bombed, I got very busy with the distemper, doing what was a very fashionable thing called stippling, making great big patterns on the wall with two coloured distempers, to make the place habitable again. Only for it to be bombed severely a second time – a flying bomb first, oh, that did some terrible damage. Anyway, then six months later, a bomb, a rocket, fell right at the end of our garden and the place was quite uninhabitable, you could see through to the sky.

Eileen Brome

The doodlebugs, there was no problem with them; everybody knew them, we looked at them and if they stopped over your head, you was safe because they did a complete circle and went back where they come from before. The problem is if they'd gone by you, then you watched the engine stop, and then you watched them – because they would turn round and come back.

That was the time when they come back – and run. It was all right, it was always this tale: lie on the floor, put your hands behind your head and face down, and lay flat on the floor. That was drummed into us at school. Lay on the floor, face down, hands behind the back of your head, interlock your fingers and stay there. And needless to say, the blast would go over the top of you.

Len Faram

Every time you heard one of those V-1s coming towards you, you flung your bike down and got down in the road on your face because of the blast, and you didn't feel the least bit silly about this. Of course, there were hardly any cars – if you saw a car you watched it come and watched it go because there was no petrol.

Anyway, the V-1s – by then we'd got a Morrison in the kitchen which was a shelter of steel top and mesh sides and we'd slept under it several times, very uncomfortable too, but at least it was protection.

That weekend, these things had started, there were lots of alarms all the time and they would come over, you would hear it going mmmmmm, silence, and then this enormous explosion. If you saw them, they were awful because you could see the flames going up and there was nothing anyone could do about them, it was just how the wind took it.

Freda Hammerton

I remember coming home from school at one time during the doodlebugs and we were told we couldn't go to our homes because there was eight time bombs surrounding the area, in the streets adjacent to ours, so we had to go to a rest centre and we spent about two nights there until they cleared all the bombs out of the area and we were allowed home. We did, in fact, force our way through the wardens – we had to get to our home because we had a dog there. We had to get the dog and take it to safety. They weren't terribly concerned about animals in those days, they were more concerned with the people.

Julia Lewis

One of the most disastrous things that I experienced, and I wouldn't like to see again, was when we came on to the hulk where all the boats are tied up at Limehouse. As soon as we got on there, a phone message came on from Wapping Police, send one of your boats up there to pick up some barges that are adrift. Just prior to that, the flying bomb went over the top. I saw the bomb, didn't think anything of it, you know, you got very blasé in them days about things. He just flew over the top.

We heard this crash, wallop! Next minute, well, within the next ten minutes, we're getting prepared to go out under way, Wapping Police asked to send the boat up. So we go up and there's the company tug, I believe it was called the *Nadia*, got a direct hit on that when changing crews. It had come right over Tower Bridge and it was on the Tower Bridge buoys. I knew a couple on there. And they was changing crews. I would say about six got killed. Course, we couldn't do nothing. The boat was gone. The doodlebug came straight over the top of the span of Tower Bridge and just dropped straight down on to it and that was it. And all we done, we went out and picked up the barges, drifting, which we was sent up there for anyway.

Dick Allington

Shocking to see them. We used to stand there on the riverside and watch the blessed things go up that river. Like the one that went in New Cross, we saw it go up the river, we heard the explosion. Killed about 240 people. It hit Woolworth's and the old Co-op in New Cross.

Henry Harington

After a bit, it seemed a little while, there was this great woooof – we didn't hear it at all – the ceilings came down, the windows came in, the door apparently just missed my mother and she came and screamed at me, 'Are you all right?' And I walked over the rubble and I was all right, and so she said, 'Well, get dressed, and I'll go and ring your father.' There was only one pub that had a phone and she went down and phoned Tuff's and said, 'Will you tell Fred we're all right.' And they said, 'He's not here yet.'

She said, 'Oh, that's funny, he should be – anyway, he'll be there in a minute.' So she came back, and I can remember she said 'Fred!' all of a sudden and she ran down to the river because she knew obviously what had happened, and I ran after her, and mother found him first. He was lying on that piece of shore by the big manhole cover.

As I got there, an ARP man was coming up to put his arms around her, saying, 'There's nothing you can do for him.' My

Damage resulting from a V-1 rocket hit at Royal Victoria Dock in 1944. Fired direct from the Continent, the V-1s and later V-2s were never very accurate in their choice of target, but they carried a massive explosive charge that caused widespread devastation. 1944

dad had been killed by the blast and you know he looked perfectly all right but we decided, or my mother said afterwards, that his neck must have been broken because it was at an angle.

Freda Hammerton

I remember when the V-2s come about, they were the things you had no warning of. They was rockets. All you heard was the first bang, the second bang, it was all over. The first bang was the exhaust blowing. And then the second was the explosion when it blew up.

I remember being out on a nice summer's day, kids, and heard a bang. No one took any notice because, I mean, you couldn't do nothing. You couldn't see nothing. The second bang, it was all over. We heard the second bang and there was pieces of metal falling everywhere. There must have been about ten of us in the street, messing about on bikes and skates and things like that. And this metal fell everywhere and not one person got hit by it. The rocket had blown up in the air and it just fell down in lumps, it was just lumps of metal, falling all around people. There must have been ten kids within fifty yards, and where people was on pushbikes and skates, lumps were falling alongside of them, and no one got a scratch. It was a field day picking up all the bits – mind you, it was a bit hot at the time.

Len Faram

When Peace Came

Two months after the Normandy landings, Allied forces joined with the French Resistance and fighting broke out in the streets of Paris. Despite direct orders from Hitler that the French capital must not fall into enemy hands unless lying in complete debris, the Military Governor surrendered on 25 August 1944 and Paris was liberated.

Despite the V-1 and V-2 rocket attacks of 1944, the tide of the war seemed to have turned, and many Londoners were confident that the end was in sight. Also in plain view, after the Soviet liberation of Auschwitz in January 1945, was the full extent and horror of Hitler's Final Solution. This camp, among many others, was the ultimate fate of many thousands of Jews whose relatives had been lucky enough to have found a safe haven in the East End.

In February, as Allied bombers were creating the firestorm that destroyed the city of Dresden, London was coping with an attack that saw fourteen rocket hits in fifteen hours, but this was the last major bombardment. The final V-2 rocket to fall on London caused 134 deaths and destroyed sixty flats in Vallance Road, Bethnal Green, on 27 March 1945. Two days later, the last air raid siren was heard in the capital.

In April, Mussolini and his mistress were captured by Communist partisans as they headed for Switzerland, executed and then hung up for public view in a Milan square. Two days later, on 30 April, Hitler committed suicide in his bunker.

The war in Europe was over on 7 May – VE Day – but fighting continued overseas, with the Battle of Iwo Jima and the eventually ending of the war in Japan by the dropping of atomic bombs on Hiroshima and Nagasaki.

The celebrations, when the declaration of peace was signed, were long and loud but in the East End there would be many thinking of all their friends and relatives who had not made it through to the end.

At the end, we thought we'd won the war, so if there was fear, it was momentary. I think most people felt, well, we've got them beat – this is just a horrible last phase. It makes a tremendous difference to your outlook.

John Earl

We knew it was coming. The air raids had stopped some time before, and the rockets and the flying bombs. As our troops pushed into Europe, they overran the launching sites. The word was going out and we thought it was getting near the end. So there was a good deal of elation. We could hear the women singing in the women's quarters, which they hadn't done for a long, long time – that was a most welcome sound.

Cyril Demarne

When this Victory in Europe day came about, we were told that the Americans were giving free drink at Piccadilly Circus – one of those London rumours that are always milling about – so we decided to walk there. When we got there, we found there was about a million people round there, and there was no sign of free drink. So we met some Land Army girls, they wanted to get back to Victoria and we showed them the way, and then it started raining, so we made a tent out of deck-chairs in St James's Park, and we slept on the grass.

John Beattie

And then when the news broke that Montgomery had signed the declaration of peace, at Luneburg Heath, we let our hair down. London erupted that night.

I took a liberty, I got my staff car out, told my driver she could go home, drove down to the East End and picked up my wife and the kids, and we drove around my district – I'd got eighteen fire stations to look after at that time – and I congratulated all hands on coming through, 'Good luck, lads, it's all over, you'll be demobbed soon,' and they were all waiting to get demobbed – well, not all of them, some of them wanted to stay in the fire service.

Cyril Demarne

The day war finished, 1945, I remember we had a big bonfire on the bomb sites – you've never seen such a big bonfire in all your life – I think half the houses that had been knocked down, they was raided for every bit of wood that was there. I should think the fire must have been twelve foot by twelve foot – and it went about twelve foot high. It lasted well into the early hours of the morning. And everyone, if they could find drink, brought it down. And everyone was round there singing.

Jean Cunningham

We went up on to the roof of the fire station; the scene was reminiscent of London at the height of the Blitz. It was lit up; wherever you looked, there were fires. Every street had at least one bonfire in it, some several. People used to go into the bombed houses – and there were plenty of those – and they'd tear up the floorboards and tear down the doors – and very often the firemen had to turn out because they'd built their bonfires up against combustible fences and there was a danger of a fire spreading. The sparks were flying and I looked out and thought, God, we're back in the Blitz! The noise was terrific; there was just a hubbub of people dancing in the streets and shouting – it never died down till the fairly late hours of the next morning.

Cyril Demarne

It was just the relief – as if a huge, huge stone had been taken off your back. Two things I remember distinctly – one was that we went out at night and opened the windows and tore away the blackout curtains and went outside in the street and looked into each other's windows, just for the sheer fun of having lights on – it was so wonderful after these years and years of darkness where you were hardly allowed a torch. Then this tremendous joy of everybody going dancing to Buckingham Palace – the Mall was just completely dense with people, thousands and thousands out dancing in the street from Trafalgar Square all the way up to Buckingham Palace. It was the most wonderful feeling – everybody was your friend, the world was lovely, Hitler was defeated, and this tremendous sense of freedom, relief and joy that was expressed.

Suzanne Samson

VE Day, we took so much money that it took us four hours just to undo the pound notes, 'cos they were throwing them at you. I said to my husband, 'This will never, ever happen again.' We were undoing this money, it took us ages and ages. We had a street party, but our party was later than the other streets for some reason, so the other streets all came round to us and we did double trade. We got a load of stuff in, as much as we could, and they were bringing their own glasses to get their drink. We'd serve our own customers, which was fair enough, and if you got strangers from another turning, you'd sort of walk past them and serve your own. You got called a few choice names, but that didn't matter. We sold out everything we had.

Mary Ridgeon

I can remember the day that the war in Europe was over, that it was the most marvellous thing but ever so solemn because it was only two years after Daddy died and it seemed such a pity he couldn't have made it. And I remember having a royal blue suit and a blue hat round which I put red, white and blue ribbon and we went to church and then we went in the pub with Granny and Granddad and sat in the garden and had drinks but we didn't rave because it was all very sad really.

Freda Hammerton

I've never ever, ever forgiven us, or the Yanks, for Nagasaki and Hiroshima. And I remember them August the fifth every year, where the *Enola Gay* come over and dropped. And I have terrible arguments with people about this. People who say it helped stop the war. I said, 'The war had stopped anyway. The Japs had given in, they knew bloody well.' They know, but that was a try-out. The Americans wanted to see what this little bomb could do and so they dropped it. And people were vapourised and there's people still alive now who are suffering the effects of that with bone disease. It's terrible, terrible, terrible. And they're not happy at dropping the one at Hiroshima; we had a go at Nagasaki, 'cos we wanted to make sure. And I'm ashamed of that. I think we should never have gone along with all that.

Joanna Roberts

We were still concerned that we'd finish up around Japan or somewhere unpleasant in that the war was still going on. But on a succeeding trip we went to New York, and on the afternoon of sailing from New York, we had this newsflash that the atom bomb had been dropped on Hiroshima. After the news was analysed and the commentators spoke about it, we were very much relieved, and applauded this event that quickly saw the end of the war in that sphere.

George Shaw

At the end of the war in Japan, Mother and I were on holiday in Weymouth and I think we'd been reading in the papers that it was going to happen but suddenly in the night it must have been declared because suddenly we heard all the sirens going off in Weymouth harbour and the whoops and everything so we got up and put our coats on over our nightclothes, rolled up the pyjamas and went down to the harbour. I remember the searchlights swinging round and it was so marvellous that at last it was over. No one really knew what it would mean, you'd almost forgotten what it was like not to be at war, and it was a long time before it stopped being very different.

Freda Hammerton

The war changed everything. We lost so much. We lost relations. I lost a lot of family. And that was apart from the people who actually fought in the war. I mean the blokes who went abroad and were killed. No, it was never the same afterwards. The war did it actually. The war finished a tremendous amount that ordinary people used to do yearly.

I think the war did me. The Second World War. I went in a little innocent of fourteen. I came out not such a little innocent, knowing what people do to one another. And I must have been about twenty, twenty-one. Perhaps it's those years. They're very formative years, those.

Joanna Roberts

You grow up in it and you see people maimed and you see people killed. In the intervening years, my father had died, my two grandmas had died, I'd had a cousin lost at sea, I'd had another cousin blown up in Italy. So there'd been quite a lot of death in the family. So you lived every day as it came, you don't take anything for granted. I think it's made me a bit standoffish – I think the children have noticed it more than anyone, because I was never a one for cuddling or kissing – I always wanted them to stand on their own feet, and be able to take it in their stride.

Jean Cunningham

They told us that some people were worse off, in that their mind had been injured by being in severe artillery attacks and so on, and these unseen damages that had been done to 'em were sometimes worse than the ones you could see; the mental

As a hugely popular wartime leader, Churchill's victory in the 1945 election looked certain. But with many of the returning soldiers preparing to vote for the first time, this modernist poster suggests that the Labour Party sensed a new forward-thinking desire for change. 1945

damage was far more serious than physical damage. And there were a few of those who were very much affected – shellshock, sort of situation.

Charles Megnin

People were unemployed and men came back from the army, and those men should have had counselling, but in those days it wasn't heard of. They came back from a life of communal living, and they came back home and they had to find jobs and they were living in a more enclosed environment – it must have been very hard for them.

Vicki Green

All the friends I tried to contact after the war that should have come to the same demobilisation point as I did, out of the twelve of us in the class, I could only see six, so it was a safe bet at the beginning of the war that you'd lose half. The navy wasn't a job that you were going to survive in easily.

Leslie Hoe

I had a strange feeling that many of the dock-experienced workers that worked there before the war, they'd failed to survive the shooting – and not only that, many of them had failed to survive the bombing. You were hard put to it to find someone that you knew.

Norman Grigg

There's something wrong with them all – all those blokes that came back. I don't know, they're either boozers or loners. Out of the lot of them, all those that came back, I found they're odd. Wonderful guy, what's his name, sits in a corner and hardly talks. He'll join your company and that, but he just sits quiet.

Dennis Pike

PART 3

— ◆ —

Rebuilding the East End

CHAPTER 12

Adjusting to Peace

War Romances and Setting Up Home

The devastation of the Blitz had fallen disproportionately on the East End, both around the docks and the edge of the city, and further towards the east, which bore the brunt of the V-2 rocket attacks at the end of the war. Vast numbers of houses had been damaged or destroyed, so although the peace theoretically meant that couples who'd got together in war time could now start living as man and wife, it was not that simple. Having made do with weddings kitted out on clothing coupons, and brief or non-existent honeymoons, many wives waiting for their husbands to be demobbed faced the prospect of living with their in-laws until a room became vacant; in this respect, they were much like the poorest families earlier in the century. Although some couples were able to start families immediately, others had to wait several years – perhaps one reason why Britain's post-war baby boom was so drawn out, with the birth rate peaking towards the end of the 1940s.

Despite this difficult start to so many marriages, such was the nostalgia for the war-time love affairs that there was a 1950s boom in magazines bearing titles such as *Wartime Romances* and *True War Romances*, full of handsome airmen and soldiers falling into the arms of WAAF cadets and nurses. With the rosy glow of hindsight, there was nothing to beat the heightened passions of the Blitz, but as both houses and commodities remained in short supply, in East End at least, the happy-ever-after ending promised by such stories must have seemed tantalisingly long in coming.

One of the boys who was an apprentice with me, he used to like cycling, and during the war, it was the only way of travelling about. I used to go cycling with him and one day, meeting him on a Sunday morning, his sister was at the door who was five years older, and from then on, I used to cycle with his sister. You could say that she fell for me, because cycling around the countryside at the beginning of the war, you really had to know your way. There was no signposts and people didn't want to tell you, and on this occasion we came to a patrol of Home Guard, and she was looking round and she caught the side of the grass verge and we both fell on top of one another.

Bill Pyne

Then the war started and I met my husband, who was a policeman. The police station was right along the road, on the same side as the hospital, and his friend was marrying a colleague of mine, and he must have seen me in the hospital – they used to come in for a cup of tea in the porter's lodge, the policemen were in and out all the time. And he must have seen me, and he asked his friend, could he get an invitation to meet me.

I used to go and stand with him while he was on duty because it was pitch dark, you see. It was great. Then sometimes we'd go out and I'd have to climb over the railings to get back in. At the back of the nurses' home was railings, and he'd bend down and I'd climb on his back and get over the railings, and I could get in. And there was an old porter there who used to be very kind to the nurses and he used to let us in. It was all very daring, but we did manage to see each other quite a bit.

Then of course he went off into the army and I didn't see a lot of him because he was posted in Dorset and then up in Richmond in Yorkshire.

Elsie Edwards

George seemed to be away a long time and he came to the house on a Saturday and he'd been away about nineteen months. It was lovely to see him and then I went back to his mother's to stay and we got engaged in the December time. He sailed in the January, and he came home in March and had a week's leave and said, 'Shall we get married?' So I had to ask my parents and they said 'Yes', but my mother said, 'Not Thursday, leave it until Saturday.'

Joan Shaw

Of course, I was a widow all that time. Then, like, towards the end of the war, my second husband, he came to see me – they used to do that, like just visit one another's girlfriends or wives, and he came to see me and I went out with him a couple of times and later on we married. So that was like – they were each other's best friend, so I felt comfortable with him, and secure – I did have trouble adjusting again, but I managed it, you know.

Anne Griffiths

My father and mother came down before the wedding to buy material for my outfit – of course it was coupons then, but nurses did quite well because we were in uniform, so we did have a few extra coupons, so my father brought me some lovely blue material that I had made up by a dressmaker, and some lovely camel-hair material that I had made up by a tailor for my coat. And I had a funny hat – a pillbox with blue feathers, with a round piece of felt in the middle – it was a horrible hat. My husband hated it.

Elsie Edwards

Connie was evacuated to Oxford and I came home after one leave and I said, 'I want to get married.' So we went to the Bishop of Oxford and he said, 'I'm afraid your wife is too young.' So I said, 'But I can go to a register office; I want to get married in a church.' He was very uncooperative. So we got married in a register office and I had forty pounds – my dad gave me some money and I had pay from the navy, so I said, 'We'll all go into this cafe' – rather a posh cafe – I said, 'Order what you like.' So some says 'I'll have baked beans' and some says 'I'll have sausages' and they says, 'I'm afraid they're off – there's only two sardines and one baked beans.' My forty pounds, they weren't making a hole in it at all.

Leslie Hoe

We had a lovely white wedding. My father gave me his coupon and I made a wedding dress – a white wedding dress because my mother wanted me to get married in a white dress. We got married on the Saturday, and we went to Glasgow the next day. I think it took us all day to get to Glasgow on the train and we stayed at the Central Hotel, but then at the end of ten days, George's ship sailed away again and I came home on my own from my honeymoon. I didn't see him again for about six months because the ship he was on had been in a collision.

Joan Shaw

The wedding was a quite sparse little wedding. The wedding ring cost twenty-nine and ninepence – it was called a utility ring. You weren't allowed a gold one. We had a little reception – twelve, all told, including Walter and I – and a proper cake, but the decorations were not made of proper icing sugar. Cinemas then, used to have cafes joined to them, and the reception was in the cafe of the cinema in Poynton, Cheshire, where my mother and father were then living.

It was a very plain sort of wedding, but the thing about it was that we didn't know where my brother was, which was a bit horrid for my parents.

Elsie Edwards

We got married at the town hall – it was the time of the doodlebugs, and of course, you never knew when anything was going to hit you, because you couldn't hear them – or you could hear them, but when they stopped you knew they were going to drop, but you didn't know where they were going to drop. So it was a very bad day of the doodlebugs, they were coming all day long – I think it went over our heads, in more ways than one, but I was told about it afterwards by people who were at the wedding that it was a very frightening day. Being 1944, there was no films, no photographs taken; at that stage private photography was impossible. But my mother had somehow organised food.

Suzanne Samson

A lot of us teamed up and got married from Kingsley Hall. I started going with Eddie when I was twenty-seven, but I was thirty-three before we got married because the war came, and we both had commitments to our family, and my family was all injured, and Eddie's mum was ill so we just couldn't get married. The war broke it all up.

Violet Kentsbeer

My friend had been let down by her fiancé. She'd been engaged for fifteen years, and her mother was a widow, and there was a fuss each time there was any suggestion that she should get married. And her fiancé went into hospital to have his appendix done, and he was in there a fortnight and came out and married the nurse.

Doris Salt

We got married in 1942 and my mother-in-law managed to get some things together. My friend and I got engaged the same week. My in-laws made a little engagement party at the house, just for relatives and family; that was in December time. Then on the August bank holiday, I got married, and my friend got married on the Monday – I got married in the Philpot Street synagogue; he got married in the Nelson Street synagogue, but we had the reception in the same hall, and on the Tuesday we went away and had our honeymoon in Babbacombe, which is just near Torquay, and we went together.

Joe Morris

We spent a week on honeymoon on a boat in Richmond, which wasn't allowed to move, because there was no petrol, but it was anchored on the wrong side of the river as far as amenities were concerned, so in order to go shopping or anything, we had to get into the dinghy and row across the Thames. It was a lovely week, except for the doodlebugs that kept flying over us, and one or two in fact dropped very close by, and the only time the boat really moved was when it was shaken by one of these things that dropped a very short way from us. But we were unhurt. And when we got back to London two days later, he was off in the air force.

Suzanne Samson

We didn't have a proper honeymoon, but we spent our first night in London at the Bonnington Hotel. The next day, my husband liked greyhound racing, and there was greyhound racing at West Ham, and my husband thought it would be nice to go and do that. I had never been to a greyhound race in my life, but we went off to the races, and then we went off to Wales and had about a week, I think, with his people in Wales. Then of course, he was back in the army, and I was back at home waiting for the time the war should finish.

Elsie Edwards

For six or eight weeks that autumn, he was stationed in London, but that was the only time we had together before he got demobbed in 1947. So all our married life between the first of July 1944 and the end of October 1947, that was the only consistent six weeks that we had together. We had holidays together; we had leaves together eventually, but that was the longest spell. I was playing my part of keeping home and cooking and that was very strange because I'd never learned to cook, so that was a great novelty.

Suzanne Samson

My son was born in September, that's the year the war ended, but his dad was right over the other side of the world when he was born so he received the message by going on to different ships; the message went right along from one ship to another and they all added their congratulations. By the time he came home, the war had ended and then we had to start sorting ourselves out into civilian life.

Anne Griffiths

I came back on a tanker and I got a telegram to say that my wife had a baby and I had a daughter. I got compassionate leave for that.

Leslie Hoe

When he came out of the army, we had to look for somewhere to live. I was staying with my mother by then. Well, of course, there'd been so much bombing, and everything was in a state of chaos. Housing was very difficult. Fortunately, along from the police station, just past the hospital which had been bombed, in East India Dock Road, was a row of houses, Victorian houses. And in it was the offices of a coal merchant. Well, because they had offices there but they lived out in Essex, and they wanted someone responsible to be

Long after the war was over, many families continued to live and bring up children in bomb-damaged houses that lacked hot water, electricity or modern appliances, many relying on wood- and coal-burning ranges instead of cookers. Henry Grant, 1958

living in the building. So he advertised in the police station, and Walter got hold of me and I came down to look, and we took the flat for seventeen and sixpence per week.

Elsie Edwards

After the war, we found ourselves living in one room, with a landing outside and on it was a gas cooker on a paving slab. That's the way people used to live years ago. We were lucky to get that from a friend of the wife's mother – there were other ex-servicemen who had to live with their parents. And when we applied eventually for the local authority to house us, they wanted to see me in uniform to prove that I was an ex-service-man, because they were given preferential treatment.

Leslie Hoe

When we got married in 1942, we lived with my mother-in-law for three years, in her house in Turner Street. The week the war was over, I said to my wife, 'We've got to move now.' Although I always got on with my in-laws and all that, we always wanted our own place. So my mother-in-law found us a flat. It was a nice little flat – of course, not modern, like today, we never had a bathroom or anything like that. In fact, the one reason I didn't want to take it was we had to share a toilet outside with the tenants opposite us; you see, there were two flats on each floor, which was only two floors above, so there was six flats in the whole block. But we had to share a toilet. And we were stuck there for seventeen years.

Joe Morris

When we got married, I lived in north London. I lived with the mother-in-law for thirteen years while we saved money to go in for a house, and the only way we could buy one was south London, 'cos it was cheaper. That was when I crossed the Thames, and I felt like a fish out of water. Still do. That feeling of not being right. I suppose as a child, you never crossed the river.

John Beattie

The East End's Housing Challenge

The Blitz had obliterated about 110,000 houses in London with a further two million suffering damage. The East End had taken the brunt of the direct hits from bombs and incendiaries and its predominantly older housing stock had been badly affected by shockwaves from bomb blasts. Even before the end of the war, London County Council was preparing maps for each area showing the extent of the bomb damage, colouring in buildings in black (total destruction), purple (damaged beyond repair), dark red (repair doubtful), light red (repairable at cost), orange/yellow (general/light blast damage), and light blue and green (clearance areas). The picture was not good: the area that makes up present-day Tower Hamlets – from the Isle of Dogs up to Blackwall, South Bromley, Bow and Victoria Park, across through Bethnal Green and Spitalfields taking in Mile End, Stepney and Whitechapel, then along the river to Tower, Wapping, Shadwell and Limehouse – had 46,482 houses destroyed and 47,574 damaged. Stepney had lost a third of its housing stock. Although building repairs began as early as 1944, and by 1947 most houses that could be repaired were at least habitable, the darker areas of the maps were a bleak reminder of how much still needed to be done.

———

The aftermath of bombing made it worse; it made us less slums to live in. A slum was somewhere to live, but we had nowhere to live.

Maurice Foley

Me first memories are basically of a bombing or the bomb damage in the area – Roman Road, Shoreditch, Bethnal Green in particular were flattened. Vast areas were flattened, and a lot of the buildings were dangerous – but of course, as children, you love to get into them. Particularly the Jews' houses. I've got recollections of the Jews, going through the Jews' houses when we was young, and on the side of the doors, on the frame of the doors, was little metal containers that had some sort of Jewish manuscript in. What it was, I don't know – it was in Jewish – but I can remember every Jewish house you went into, it must have been some sort of religious testament of some kind.

School holidays was six weeks where you just was let out to roam wherever you want and we roamed from Bow, Bethnal Green, Shoreditch, Liverpool Street, the Brick Lane area – vast areas of debris.

Brian Lane

There was enormous damage to the East End, although it was more towards the docks; there was tremendous damage in the Stepney area and the Mile End. In my street, our roof had gone, but that was repaired, and my sister who had been married at the beginning of the war had her house completely destroyed, her flat – my nephew showed me recently a document that showed they paid £360 compensation; the government at that time paid compensation. But my sister went to live with my mother for a while.

Jack Miller

I was born in Mead's Place, in Hackney, east London. My mother had a little cottage that's been pulled down – flats are there now – but it used to back on to a factory. We had this small cottage and a garden and my old dad had a chicken shed. Didn't have any front garden, I think it was sort of one

Much of the East End consisted of vast areas of rubble – an urban adventure playground for children, but a headache for the authorities who needed to provide homes, schools and shops. The scale of the challenge led to new ideas about housing and communities. Henry Grant, c1951

bedroom and a little diddy box room, a downstairs, a kitchen and then this garden. The flats have been built, it's been bombed around there, all kinds of things, and yet there's now a grass verge and this factory wall is still there, and it's still painted, the outline of a chicken shed, in whitewash, even to this day.

Bob Silver

North Woolwich and Silvertown, when I was a kid, the houses were always condemned. How long they was condemned for, you know, I don't know – twenty or thirty years or something. But people were still living in them.

Eddie Corbett

People would move from across the road rather than move their streets. Even with their houses down, they'd move to one and say, 'Well, at least it's got a roof on it.' They used to board the windows up and go and live in it. A lot of people get a funny idea of the cockney – he's a funny bloke, he's like the ships, sometimes he'll go back to the green pastures, but he's always pining to come back. And this place, which as you realise was the heaviest bombed area in Great Britain, people just wouldn't bloody move. Particularly the elderly people.

Maurice Foley

We found another house in Cordelia Street, which had a very posh name. It was a street that hadn't... well, it had been knocked about a bit. One side of it had gone, but the other side wasn't too bad. So we moved in one of them. And we stayed in there until we got a notice from the borough that they was all going to be demolished.

Joanna Roberts

When I came out of the army, the labour exchange said, 'Right, you're going on bomb repair work.' And across to Upminster

I had to go. In those days, our builder at Upminster employed about sixty men, some old boys that you wouldn't employ, painting and decorating, putting sash cords in, repairing French doors, doing a bit of brick work, bomb damage. Right, he sent me to room stores one day, which is the big stores at Upminster, and he met me and he said, 'What are you going for?' I said, 'I'm gonna get a sash cord.' He said, 'You don't get one sash cord.' He said, 'You get twelve.' He said, 'You can sling the other eleven. And when you get a bit of green paint or brown paint, you don't buy a little tin, you buy a gallon.' See, after the war, the people on the government scheme was paid, I think, twenty per cent on the men's labour and so much per cent on the materials, so the more materials he booked, the more money he made. He took us by lorry every day across to Enfield; we was building new houses that we would book to bomb repair work to Upminster. He was paying us well, so we didn't care a damn, as long as we got the money. This is how the world was run after the war. There was little builders everywhere, springing up everywhere, that's because of cost plus. The more you employed, the more you earned. Yeah.

Walter Dunsford

They sent in gangs of the most awful men, rough and ready, who were quite frightening. We were eventually told that they were prisoners who were sent out to these houses and they did things like light a fire on the tiles of the fireplace instead of in the fire grate itself and burnt all the tiles. And there were mahogany and oak mantelpieces downstairs and they cut bits out, just wantonly, and banged a nail in the door just to hang a coat up. The repairs were so awful it was just heartbreaking. They simply took bits out of other houses and banged them up with heavy nails in your house, and in no room did the skirting boards match – some were only planks where mine were all moulded – and there'd be one half an inch higher than the other. The lavatory door wouldn't shut because it was taken from somewhere else and was too big, and in the box room, the door swung through because it was too small.

Eileen Brome

Basically, the area was never emptied. People still lived, and streets and streets were derelict, but if you see one house that had a roof on, you can always bet there was someone living there.

Maurice Foley

London Goes Back to Work

Having learned from the lessons of the First World War, when returning soldiers found almost no arrangements to help them return to civilian life, the government were determined that following the Second World War, the process of demobilisation would be quick and efficient. Thanks to guarantees of jobs held open, and the provision of training camps for younger members of the armed forces, four and a half million men and women went back to work in 1945, with no great fall in employment.

The East End's largest employer remained the London docks. During the war, these had been the most heavily bombed civilian target in Britain, hit by nearly a thousand bombs, causing the loss of nearly a third of the warehouses and sheds, and half of the storage areas. The East India Export Dock had been drained for the construction of the Mulberry Harbours and it was never refilled; eventually, Brunswick Wharf Power Station was built on the site. The river had not been dredged for six years and there had been a big build-up of silt. But straight after the war, the Port of London was working as hard as ever. In 1949, Britain's exports were fifty-five per cent higher than immediately before the war, and by 1958, London's docks were handling greater volumes of trade than at any time in their history.

I spent most of 1945 and 1946 teaching carpentry and joinery to returning soldiers. They'd obviously planned it fantastically well – somebody had been responsible for planning for the returning soldiers and training them up in these government training centres. Many of the instructors were men of fifty to sixty, in that age group, and they were people who had learned their trade. Though they weren't, obviously, academic people, they were sheet-metal workers, artificial limb makers – highly qualified people. They produced these books and so on so you had a complete six-month course, itemising week-by-week what they would be doing.

Charles Megnin

They had a branch what they called the ten ninety-eight, which meant that though you was a union member, any soldier coming back could claim your job – he belonged to the four seven-eight branch, and he had the right to take your job away, because you was classed as a ten ninety-eight – which was considered fair in those days. But I worked in family business and they lost a son in the war, so nobody really came back to the firm I worked for.

John Beattie

Up till 1945, there was full employment. But apart from having full employment, the fact of having people like Ernest Bevin and Herbert Morrison in government, it was realised that people will work better if they're treated better. And you had things like music while you worked. And holidays with pay – one week's

© PLA Collection/Museum of London

A giant leap forward: two years after the end of the war, Ajax, one of the Port of London's massive 250-ton floating cranes moored in the West India Export Dock, lifts a London bus on to a ship bound for the newly independent Ceylon (now Sri Lanka). 1947 holiday a year. Now, these things were unheard of prior to 1938 – the only holidays you got were when you got the sack. So there's no doubt that from that period onwards, conditions were vastly improved.

Charles Megnin

Once the war was over, the tailoring improved because the unions put their foot down and said you've only got to work so many hours a day. 'Cos in the period I was working, in a busy time you had to work through till eight or nine in the evening to carry you through the slack periods when you weren't working – I had to do that myself. My brother and I made a rule, 'no later than eight o'clock', so we used to finish work, go out and have a bite to eat and then go to the cinema, because in those days the cinema started later on, after half-past eight, nine o'clock – you used to get a three-hour show for sixpence. There was about four or five cinemas in this vicinity alone.

Joe Morris

When I first went to work at the Alaska factory, it was a fairly dim place and all wooden paddles and great big lifting gears that lifted the paddles up and down in the air – it was still from pre-war days, they hadn't re-equipped it. They re-equipped it with all the stainless steel equipment that they use today a year after I started there, in 1947 – and then it was supposed to have been the most up-to-date dyeing process in Europe at that time.

Bernard Alger

Most of the restrictions had been lifted from the war, a lot more licences had been granted, it was export, export, export. And this meant to say that there was an awful lot of ships coming in and out of London docks, bringing raw materials in and exporting the finished goods. At the busiest times they were working at night with floodlights down there, loading and unloading. Of course this meant extra money from the point of view of the dockers, and I suppose it was around this time that the unions really started to get quite a strict hold on the docks.

Gordon Beecham

A and B sheds handled export cargo for Mediterranean berths – this department actually replaced what was known as the old rum quay, which was literally burnt out during the war – being a rum quay, it didn't resist bombing very well, and it was reduced to ashes and the whole quay was modernised by 1959, and a very thriving fruit and vegetable trade developed, particularly with Israel, the Middle East, some Canadian apples, and South African oranges, and fruit in general.

Dick Butler

The River Thames was very busy, I would say perhaps at its busiest for a number of years, and this pertained for several years after I joined. For instance, the Pool of London, and both downriver and upriver from there, was a hive of riverside wharves, with ships coming and going endlessly, and a lot of traffic by barge was still active, and the river was really used in the way that seemed most sensible at the time.

P Satow

Shortages, Scams and Social Change

Despite full employment, continuing shortages meant that the end of rationing did not start until 1948, three years after the end of hostilities. Flour was the first rationed item to come off the list, followed by clothes in 1949; in 1950, it became possible

An inspector checks a fishmonger's scales for accuracy, to comply with the Weights and Measures Act. The sheer hard work of finding enough sufficiently varied food to feed a family on rations was a huge burden for housewives in the post-war period. Henry Grant, c1950

once more to gorge yourself on dried fruit, chocolate biscuits, treacle, syrup, jellies and mincemeat; supplies of petrol and soap also loosened up this year.

It was two long years more before tea became freely available, in 1952. The next year, sweets, eggs, butter and sugar came off rations. Finally, in 1954, restrictions on the sale of meat and bacon were lifted and Smithfield Market was allowed to open at midnight as it had before the war, instead of at 6 am. Members of the London Housewives' Association held a ceremony in Trafalgar Square to mark the end of rationing.

Like the effect of prohibition in America, rationing provided unlimited opportunities for profiteering. A black market selling everything from freshly caught rabbits to imported goods operated fairly freely and the opportunities and potential for profits created by this may have contributed to the rise in organised crime which was such a feature of the East End after the war. During the 1950s and Sixties, close-knit criminal families operated in a number of fields, from protection rackets to betting scams, nightclubs, housing and brothels. It was in this post-war world that criminals such as the Kray twins, and their close associate Peter Rachman were able to flourish. In the case of the Krays, the effect of post-war National Service, the compulsory two-year military training that was supposed to transform potential thugs into disciplined citizens, actually exacerbated their violent tendencies, bolstering their sense of grievance against society, and leaving them with a criminal record for desertion and assault.

There were a lot of shortages – we made sausages do for all sorts of things. The shortages went on for quite a long while; there were still shortages when I got married, and that was in 1952. You had to queue up for food. Oxtail and things like that, you couldn't get things; they were still on ration, and this was quite a long way after.

Jean Cunningham

I remember the coupons after the war and two ounces of cheese for the week, and Angela and I were teenagers and always hungry, and having a piece off it that was probably one day's ration. There was a bag of shredded coconut in Granny's cupboard and my Aunt Joan and I ate most of it; this was a terrible thing.

Freda Hammerton

In the canteens, we only got a bit of tea, because it was rationed – we only got a little bit on a plate. We never had any handling of that; it was dished out to us, from the stores. I mean, the rationing went on for donkey's years, about nine years, wasn't it? After the war. We wanted any extra, we'd have to buy it on the black market. Which I did, very often. Our milkman used to come round with a bit of tea. Well, you had to live, didn't you? I mean, you couldn't buy much, but a bit of tea, you had to. Never had any coffee.

Eileen Gibbons

After the war, rations didn't increase for a long, long time. Then all of a sudden, it just came off. And of course, things went up in price then. In the biggest shop in our area, you had to queue up at each counter. You queued up for your butter, and then you queued up for your bacon, and everything else, so what would have taken about fifteen minutes in these days used to take you about an hour.

Jean Cunningham

Food started going a bit better – things like rabbits would turn up – illegally, because they were supposed to go through ministry sources, but it used to be governed by price and some used to turn up on what you'd call the black market, I suppose, and they were sold to tradesmen in the market. All sorts of things started going through the market – clothes and that, they were on ration, things like that somehow started to appear; anything to do with women's clothing you always bought, 'cos your girlfriend or your wife never got a chance to buy them.

John Beattie

Of course things were rationed then; you didn't have a great deal of food, no luxuries as such. I got a seaman's rations which gave me the equivalent of double rations for being afloat, but as far as the luxuries are concerned, you know, your cigarettes and things like that, they were, you know, non-existent, unless you was in the right circles.

So one of my jobs the skipper used to give me was the job of climbing up the ladder, going aboard the ship and having the towing order signed. Now you can imagine, a young sixteen- to seventeen-year-old lad, going up there and seeing the Americans, everything there. Ice-cold water fountain in the galleys, ice cream, seeing the master and saying 'Sign the order, please'. Up comes the steward, who happens always to be coloured, strangely enough, and he said, 'What are you going to have for breakfast, this morning, skipper?' He says, 'I think I'll have three eggs this morning.' Seeing the notice board on the companion way, the crew are complaining they're getting lemon waffles too many times, about three times a day or something. Of course, I used to come down with a carton of Lucky Strikes, a couple of American doughnuts, Hershey bars, candy...

Dick Allington

You got to remember we're dealing with a period when there'd been five or six years of rationing, and now things was coming over the boats and so certain accidents happened down the ship's hold or in the shed and there would be a little bit of merchandise had to be taken home. We were honest thieves, we'd only wait till the case was broken up. The Port of London authority, they had their watchers and when there was a special consignment coming aboard, if it was very, very special, they'd increase the number of watchers. For instance, there was two watchers to a hatch, and they would be sitting down on cases or whatever, and seeing that you didn't open a case and help yourself, or break open a bottle and start drinking. The axiom of corruption is there for everybody, and many of the watchers got corrupted, you know – they'd been sitting down there five or six hours a day, and if there was a case of chocolate broken open, they made sure they got their bar of chocolate. That's working-class life, isn't it – we're the greatest at that. Well, after all, we only learned to thieve from the upper class because they'd been the biggest thieves of all. They taught us it.

Jack Dash

My mate Padge said to me, 'This game's finished, it's clapped out.' I said, 'Why's that, Padge?' and he told me that one night during the war, he went up to Lisle Street, parked his cab in Lisle Street and he took seventeen quid in one night and never started the engine up. He was using it as a brothel, with the Yanks. This was during the war – I was at sea for a pound a week, and he took seventeen quid in one night.

John Cleary

Also, there was a black market going on: some of my cousins did things like stockings, silk stockings. Amazing how suddenly they would appear. There was a lot of corruption going on. The people coming in on merchant ships would bring stuff in from America, and I remember one case where these silk stockings went from man, to man, to man, to man – and it was all engineered and organised by the police. And when it had done its round, they would fall on the person with the stuff and arrest all the people who were in that little circle. And a group of police were instigating it.

There was always stuff you could buy, if you had the money. There were people who never even used their rations, they preferred the money, so these things were also put up for sale.

Bernard Kops

My husband used to go round to the Westminster Bank in Silvertown and get the money on his own, often two thousand pounds at a time, which is an immense amount of money in those days. But there was never any attack or trouble, no problems whatsoever, and he was greatly respected. But after the war, it began to be very dangerous to be the wages clerk. Where he had carried the money about by himself in a bag, they then had to have two men always to go to the bank in a car with a policeman, and the bags began to be chained to their wrists, which was very frightening. Some of these wages clerks were jumped on between sheds and coshed, and the money stolen. So they had to eventually stop paying the men off at the ships and build little offices, which were made secure.

Eileen Brome

There were no betting shops then, and of course there were runners, which were illegal, and the police used to have to try to catch them out – they used to do spells of a few weeks at a time, 'on bookies' as they called it, which would have been in plain clothes – to try to get these bookies. Then the betting shops came in the late Fifties, I think it was.

Elsie Edwards

I was there supervising a lot of purchase tax, a certain amount of general excise, where one met strange people at times. The dog track used to occupy our minds because entertainments duty became excise duty on dogs. And on betting. So we were looking after the bookmakers – rather, watching the book-makers – and they needed some watching.

Eric Cropper

When houses were very difficult to come by, there was this awful man called Rachman, and he used to buy up council flats and let them at extortionate rates, and throw people out if he could find someone who could pay more rent and that became an awful racket.

Elsie Edwards

The rougher lot – I mean, I'm talking about the rough old lot, they mixed with the Kray brothers and people like that. So, everything they touched, they pinched. I think I was a bit of a novelty, but they trusted me because they knew I'd never shop 'em. My father used to say to us, as little kids, 'Keep your ears and eyes open, keep your mouth shut.'

Charles Beck

CHAPTER 13

Out With the Old

A New Government for a New Era

'The principles of our policy are based on the brotherhood of man.'

– CLEMENT ATTLEE, 26 JULY 1945

Wars can prompt great social change. Many of the soldiers who died in the trenches in the First World War were not eligible to vote, as property qualifications denied this right to the poorest forty per cent. As the soldiers were returning home, the government quickly passed an act giving the vote to all men at the age of twenty-one (and, at last, to women, although only those over the age of thirty).

An equally dramatic social change came about after the Second World War when in 1945, for the first time, a Labour government swept into power. Despite Winston Churchill's war-time popularity, the people chose Clement Attlee, who had run a club for poor boys in Limehouse, been politicised by Toynbee Hall and, as Mayor of Stepney, supported the Poplar Rates Rebellion when George Lansbury and twenty-two councillors were jailed. After representing Limehouse as an MP, Attlee landed his first ministerial post when Oswald Mosley deserted Labour for the wilder fringes of the fascist movement. At the outbreak of war, when George Lansbury – by then leader of the Labour Party – resigned over his pacifist views, Attlee took over as party leader and became Churchill's deputy in the war-time coalition government, his job being to run the country while Churchill ran the war. He was not an orator in the Churchillian mode – a popular story has it that on his first meeting with the tongue-tied George VI, the two men stood in awkward silence for some minutes, before Attlee volunteered the remark, 'I've won the election.' The King replied, 'I know. I heard it on the six o'clock news.'

Attlee was firmly behind the Beveridge report that proposed setting up a Welfare State and a National Health Service. He told the electorate, 'The Labour Party is a socialist party, and proud of it. Its ultimate purpose at home is the establishment of the socialist commonwealth of Great Britain – free, democratic, efficient, progressive, public-spirited.'

Early on in his career, Winston Churchill spoke at the greyhound track in Walthamstow, and I'm pretty certain that if you check you'll find he got a black eye when he attended. But obviously, he'd become a hero during the war. Yet in spite of that, he'd rather made a mistake in that for the Tory Party propaganda, they'd had this 'Reds under the bed' – if we voted Labour, we was gonna get Communism, and so on – well, that couldn't go down too well, because after all, he'd had Bevin and Attlee and all those in his government. So to suddenly turn round and try and paint Attlee as some kind of left-wing Communist was rather ridiculous really.

Charles Megnin

All the soldiers were coming home, and they'd had enough of it; they were looking for a better life and it was just natural that the ordinary man on the street knew that Labour would triumph.

John Beattie

At the 1951 Festival of Britain, Churchill (seated) was the grand old man of British politics, but young people no longer saw themselves as part of a Victorian empire. Although lacking Churchill's charisma, Attlee (right) held views which chimed with new thinking about society. Henry Grant, 1951

The close-knit communities of docklands – you can include Bermondsey and areas such as that – were always great supporters of the Labour movement, and they was always great supporters of the trade unions, irrespective of whether they work in the factories, whether they work in the ship repairers or if they worked in the docks. And we were promised by central government, by Clem Attlee, that in fact the worst bombed area in Great Britain was going to get priorities.

Maurice Foley

When it came up to the election, and the war finished, well, it's not generally realised that people like me that was born in 1915, well 1945, that was the first time that you voted. So when they did vote, they realised that though Churchill was no doubt a great war leader, he would have wanted to have held on to the empire in India and various places like that – they realised that their best chances of getting out of the forces reasonably quickly was to elect a Labour government. And this is what they did.

Charles Megnin

My father was a Labour supporter and my mother was a very staunch Labour supporter and George Lansbury – and Clement Attlee, several times – George Lansbury quite often would come to our home.

Lucy Collard

I remember meeting Attlee once, when he was on a tour, and he was like a professor of a college – so quiet and unassuming, whereas Churchill was thump-the-tub and plenty of rhetoric. He was on an election tour around the city. I thought what a wonderful person he was. He couldn't put himself over, but nevertheless, everybody went mad for Labour – and what Attlee didn't put over, Bevin did.

John Beattie

We used to put on these 'Wings for Victory' weeks, and all these sort of things, and Attlee would come and speak – he had a very weak voice and he was no orator. He might have been a brilliant man as a committee chairman, but he wouldn't have inspired anybody to do anything very much.

Charles Megnin

I remember meeting my husband's sister, in 1941, and I said that I really couldn't sum up much enthusiasm for politics. 'Well, you should,' she said, very wisely, 'You should.'

Elsie Edwards

After the war, in the East End, they believed that Churchill was the villain of the piece – despite being a hero – and there had to be a change to the whole caboodle. There was that feeling that things were gonna get better – that the working man was gonna come into his own. We favoured Labour because we wanted things done that hadn't been done before.

Bill Crook

I remember the election because we had some correspondents from *The Times* or *The Telegraph*, which we regarded as sort of a very high-class press, and they came round the market asking who we thought would win the election, although in their minds, there was only one winner, and that was Churchill. Churchill was God, and now the coalition had come to an end, there was no point them asking really; no one else would win the election except the Conservatives. But having my ear to the ground, sort of thing, everybody was looking forward to a new deal, and they thought that after the war, everything would change to their benefit. Therefore they wanted a Labour government – a government of the people, as we thought. And I said to this *Times* correspondent that Attlee would be our next prime minister. And he said, 'Son, get your brain examined.' Those words have always stuck in my mind – to think that I turned out right, and here was people at the foremost of the news media who'd got it wrong.

John Beattie

Cleaning Up London's Air

If there is one enduring image that conjures up post-war London, it is that of a thick blanket of fog. London's pea-soupers had been regular events throughout the nineteenth and early twentieth century; every docker and seaman knew the dangers of working on the river when fog rolled in. Even while cursing its effect, households would take advantage of thick fog for a little illicit chimney-cleaning – fires which added to the growing problem of pollution.

The fogs got dramatically worse after the war when, in the need to stimulate growth, Britain began to export all its clean coal, keeping the sulphur-laden dirty coal for home consumption. With more homes being able to afford to burn coal, and industry going at full tilt, the fogs kept getting worse until the government was forced to act by the Great Smog of 1952. For five days in December, London ground to a halt. The freezing fog left people unable to see even their own feet, greyhounds could not see the hare on dog tracks, opera-goers could not see the stage, and the cattle at Smithfield Market dropped dead where they stood. More than four thousand people died of the fog's immediate effects, and many more, possibly up to twelve thousand, in the weeks and months that followed. In an echo of the 'gas explosion' fabrications that hid the truth about V-2 rockets at the end of the war, the Ministry of Health invented an influenza epidemic to cover up the high death toll. The Clean Air Act, which become law in 1956, put an end to open-hearth coal fires and thus the worst of the smogs, although

Even after the high death toll that 'coincided' with the Great Smog of 1952, the government were reluctant to stifle industry with regulations about emissions. Eventually, the 1956 Clean Air Act was passed, and pea-soupers like this became a thing of the past. Henry Grant, 1956

they continued to occur in the late 1950s and early 1960s, adding more layers to the soot-blackened buildings that were such a feature of post-war London.

———•———

The London pea-souper: a thick yellow fog, which occurred usually from November onwards. Besides its usual vapour base, its main constituents came from factories and household chimneys, all burning Derby brights, or nuts, the two forms of coal then available. This noxious effluvium could be smelled, tasted and even felt between the teeth as a fine sort of grit.

Louis Dore

We'd missed the tide, so we couldn't sail until early the next morning. Unfortunately, during the night a thick fog settled down over London – I think it was the thickest fog I ever saw – a real pea-souper. The fog lasted the whole of the next day and nothing moved on the river at all. It was the most eerie feeling, I can remember it now – the eerie feeling with that thick fog. You couldn't hear a sound. Nothing could move, nothing at all. There was almost not a sound to be heard. This fog lasted the whole of the day, so we didn't get away the next morning; it was not until the next night that the fog began to disperse, and we sailed on the next morning tide.

Captain A R Williamson

You know, you used to say, 'Fog coming up,' and I'm on two-to-ten shift, and there's all the men dashing home from work at five o'clock, all the stevedores, but of course, I'd got to wait on till ten, hadn't I, and down is coming the old fog – no, it used to be very worrying in those days. Did away with it, didn't they, as soon as they stopped all the fires, you know, the coal fires that was doing it. You was just blind, you know – if you got to the dock to come on and the policeman was there, the policeman had to accompany you to where you was going, and he had a lifebelt on. That was orders.

William Mather

The policemen were issued with long canes about ten feet long so in foggy days or nights, they could go along the dock quay and put the poles on the side and they could feel their way along. And it was also useful if anybody fell in; they could be pulled out.

Alexander Gander

The docks scared me a lot when it was foggy – when we used to go along and you'd see the water down below, and you'd go ring around the edge – you know, it really frightened you.

Eileen Gibbons

Winter times, when it was dark, and particularly if it was foggy, we'd have our chimney 'swept'. Father used to catch it alight, 'cos if the fire brigade caught you, I think it used to cost them two bob. They used to come and put it out, so everybody used to wait till they got a fog so nobody could see it and set the chimney alight. Used to go outside and watch it all burning, you know. Of course, you had it regularly swept, nobody ever caught their chimney alight – but we were always in the fog, so that helped, didn't it?

Dennis Pike

When I took my wife out, 1949 to '50 it must have been – sweets were still rationed, strangely enough. We both never had a great deal of money and most of our time was spent walking up the West End and round the City. Nobody ever molested you or abused you – you could go to the West End, all this naughty square mile as they called it – nobody approached you, nothing like that. During the great smog I used to walk my wife home – I got lost one particular night, it was so thick. People were dying of bronchitis.

Dick Allington

It was really so bad that the buses, while still running, had to be led in front by the conductor waving a torch. And when I got off the bus at my home stop, I still had about a ten-minute walk, and I couldn't see my own hand in front of me – I could just see the sodium street lamp, and I had to feel my way by touching people's hedges as I went by to realise that I had come to the end of a road, and now I had to count twenty paces to cross over before I would be on the other side of the street. You really couldn't see anything. It wasn't scary; all the time I was conscious that I would be able to say that I had experienced a London pea-souper. Then after the Clean Air Act came about, there's been no such thick fogs since.

Abraham Lue

In my opinion, two of the greatest things that have ever happened to this country was the National Health Service and the old Clean Air Act, because the smog, when it did come down in those particular areas, you absolutely couldn't see a hand in front of your face. I've seen bus conductors walking in front of buses. Even with their headlights on, they couldn't see nothing. You've heard of pea-soupers, but it was the colour of pea soup. If you did have a handkerchief and you was in somewhere after you come out of the fog, whatever you blew from your nose or mouth was absolutely covered in black. Terrible.

Albert Patten

I was horrified at how dirty London was – we passed Great Russell Street in front of the British Museum and the young man from the British Council pointed to that and said, 'That's the great British Museum,' and all I could see was a large building, totally black and totally white. The black was centuries of accumulated soot, and the white was the contribution from London's pigeons. And most of the public buildings in London looked like that – starkly contrasting black and white. Only after a few years, when the government passed the Clean Air Act and London air quality changed, then the buildings were cleaned up and you found they were quite beautiful stone in some instances slightly pink, instead of this stark black and white.

Abraham Lue

All Change at the London Docks

Even as the London docks returned to working at full strength, a number of significant changes were taking place, both at a management level and within the workforce. Towards the end of the war, anticipating a shortage of labour, the National Dock Labour Board had begun to consider greater mechanisation. Some innovations had been suggested by the equipment and working practices of the American forces during the war.

As part of the post-war changes in employment, the old dockside casual labour contracts, with gangs selected by foremen, were replaced by a more centralised system with a guaranteed minimum wage. The dockers, like workers in many other professions, were resistant to change, despite at last being able to exercise some negotiating power with the strength of a trade union behind them. Relations between the dockers and the management did not start off well in the post-war period; they began with a strike, followed by a lockout over the proposed Dockers' Charter, which asked for a guaranteed wage of twenty-five shillings, pensions and an end to casual work.

Striking dockers at a rally in Victoria Park in 1951. The world-beating success of the London docks was due to many elements, the loyalty of dockers to one another being one of them. By this time, however, solidarity seemed to be contributing to the end of their working lives. Henry Grant, 1951

The principle of solidarity applied not only to one's own union, but to other unions, even those from overseas. In 1949 the dockers walked out after being ordered to unload the *Beaverbrae*, a Canadian ship whose seamen were involved in a strike back in Canada. So from the early post-war years, a pattern of confrontation was set, and as the dockers sought to increase their say in working practices, the management continued to find ways to exclude them.

The unions started to come to the front – everybody in those days was affiliated to a union; the dockers were union men, the market men were union men, and if you belonged to any sort of profession you were in the unions, and this is what you thought was best to vote for. You was pleased as punch to get a union card when you were eighteen.

John Beattie

The port workers' unofficial committee came as a result in 1945 where the lads coming back from the forces, and having defeated the greatest enemy of trades unionism, now wants to make a better industry. They're not coming back as pussy cats, they'd been commandos, they'd been trained to kill and fight for the world democracy, so when they come back, they wanted to change the conditions of their industry. Immediately after the war, most of us was coming back from the armed forces. We had the old boys, as we call them, that had stayed behind and kept the fort. First thing we got involved in was a Dockers' Charter. It was drawn up, it was moved and that's what we wanted. And this was laid down by the old boys before we got back – this was our 'Welcome home' gift.

Jack Dash

About this time, the head office had a study of cargo handling and a number of the officers had been with port operating units in the army and had seen forklift trucks being used on some of these jobs, particularly by the Americans. And some of these trucks had been left behind by the American forces and so they decided to use, as an experiment, forklift trucks on the handling of export cargo.

Dick Butler

Those of us who'd travelled abroad during the war had seen the introduction of mechanisation in the handling of goods – palletisation, containerisation – the Yanks had been using it in their armed forces.

Maurice Foley

When I rejoined at Surrey Docks after the war, I found out there was something strange happening. It was so different to what I had been used to before the war. The cacophony of all the winches running, before the war, and the hooting of the tugs, wasn't there any more. Some of the tugs were still running around, but the steam-driven winches seemed to be giving way to electric winches, and luffing cranes that were driven by electricity. There seemed only half the noise.

De-casualisation was in the air. And I had a strange feeling that we were not going to accept it in that form, you see, because before the war we were so free. We could go to work when we liked and go to work for who we liked. If we didn't like the thought of going home with the smell of fish clinging on our clothes, or guano droppings, we wouldn't go on those jobs.

Norman Grigg

Cargo, before this, had been handled entirely by hand trucks, and what were called dooley trucks which were large platforms on wheels which you would put heavy loads on and push around, either with a tractor or by hand, and also mobile cranes were used. But most of the work was done by manual gangs using hand trucks; they would unload the lorries, pile the cargoes to ports in the shed, and then, when the stevedore wanted to load them on the ship, other gangs would come along and remove them from the shed to the ship's side, where stevedores put them in slings or whatever and took them into the ship for stowage.

Dick Butler

They wasn't on the stones no more. They had to report to an office. It was between the two docks down there, between the Victoria Dock and the Albert Dock, but it was a great big office and they had to book on there and they'd get sent from there to a job. They was allocated. The other way, they had to stand on the stones and be sorted out. So, in a way, it was best to be sorted out because the good men was known and you picked out a good man. But if you got allocated, you might get the laziest geezer under the sun, see? So I think, meself, that started the rot. When I was in the West India Dock, there was always that incentive to go faster, to do more, to get more money, to beat the other gang; you know, you looked at him like a bleeding rival. You were going to beat him, see. And this is competition, and this is what made the dock industry.

Alfred Green

It was a Canadian ship called the *Beaverbrae* – we refused to work it and the employers locked us out. And it wasn't long before not only the whole of London, but the whole of the bloody country come out in support, on the issue of our rights to support other workers.

Maurice Foley

It's only just after six years of a bitter war where the Canadian lads and lassies had been fighting side by side with our own to defeat fascism, so they sent for their general secretary and he told the employers, 'We'll load and discharge any ship we've got in this port, but we will not touch the *Beaverbrae* because we will not lend ourselves to break another man's struggle for bread.' When we presented ourselves for work on Monday, the employers walked over: 'Are you going to discharge the *Beaverbrae*?' We said, 'No, we work any ship, unload it or load it, but the *Beaverbrae* stays where she is.'

So we had a situation where the whole of the British registered port workers' industry was locked out. Housewives all round the dock area of London docks and up in Liverpool, housewives joined in and took the Canadian seamen off the ships because now the employers wouldn't allow them to sleep any longer on the ship. So the wives of dockers and stevedores took them in and they become sons of the family and built up this tremendous loyalty – as far as East Ham, Stepney, Poplar, over in Rotherhithe, the housewives there was calling for food parcels, and food parcels came in, and clothing, all to keep the Canadian seamen going in their struggle with their employer. After about three weeks, they conceded, the Canadian employers, gave in, and victory was won.

Jack Dash

It was brought home to me, I suppose in the late 1940s, that some sort of malaise was affecting our ports. This was only a matter of four or five years after the finish of the war, and yet other countries seemed to be building, refurbishing – bombed docks were being cleared, and in fresh fields, new docks were being constructed. The turnarounds were much quicker than ours, the workforce seemed to come down looking much more superior – they seemed to be well dressed, they seemed to have an attitude. It was rather depressing to do such a trip and get back to our own ports which were either on strike or some go-slow or some hassle was going on with one of the transportation systems upon which the ships relied. The same was true of the shipbuilding side and the ship repairing.

George Shaw

The operations were simply unloading from road and rail vehicles into the shed and later picking up and taking to the ship's side. And of course, both operations could go on simultaneously. Well, we started off and we got very high outputs, before the men realised what we actually did – we didn't pay them piecework, we paid them high upstanding wages. I'm talking now about 1951. And I believe that the maximum figure I had of men employed on that operation was twenty-four men. And normally that would have been done by a minimum of seventy-two men. So you can see what a drastic change this was to cargo handling in the Port of London.

Dick Butler

After the war, meetings were taking place in the superintendent's office, and all the lads from the various shipping companies would come in every day, and they knew it had got to come, and they knew it was going to mean one almighty big change within the authority. Because, staff-wise, containerisation meant quay staff would diminish, tally clerks would no longer be wanted to count all the cargo, police would not be required, customs would be cut down, bonded warehouses would no longer be necessary. Everything would be pushed into a container, locked, sealed, and just put on a ship. That's when it began, oh dear, and I moved on to head office where they were daydreaming about all this.

Elizabeth Garrett

One often tries to think of what were the root causes of the problems affecting the docks. I think one thing seemed to be different on the Continent, in that the towns – say, a place like Hamburg or Rotterdam – there was much more of an involvement on the part of the town authorities with their docks than there was here. The Port of London Authority was a bureaucratic set-up which ran these docks on behalf of the users – they employed a lot of labour – they seemed to look after a lot of the services on a more or less bureaucratic set-up, outside the local authority. I think this peculiar set-up of this very large organisation, having very large tracts of land and an enclosed water system, seemed to work against the general community and efficiency of the place.

George Shaw

Being a barge builder at that time was gradually dropping off – the work on the river was getting slacker and slacker. Dockers were causing a lot of trouble, and containers started to come in – it was the beginning of the container trade. Since then, I've met numerous barge builders I knew, and none have remained in the trade. In fact, I think the trade now is extinct.

Bill Pyne

Slowly it began to change, but before the big changes happened, they were talking about them, and the widening of roads and the building of roads for all the container traffic to come through.

Elizabeth Garrett

With the advent of containerisation, slowly – or comparatively slowly – the whole pattern of traffic changed, and so the docks, from being fully used, with ships waiting outside, and ships berthed two abreast or more, changed to becoming what one might almost describe as derelict. Instead, the place had been taken by these container-carrying ships which were able to move such enormous quantities of cargo that much more quickly. The effect of this, of course, was that it became uneconomic to keep the enclosed docks open, and in the course of the years, the upriver docks were slowly closed down, ending in the authority keeping only Tilbury open. This created some very difficult times where labour relations were concerned, and to some extent, the reluctance of labour to accept this change accelerated the process.

James Quick

There was a very long, bitter seamen's strike in 1966, which caused ships to be in London for much, much longer than they should have been. In fact, a ship called the *Rangatani*, I think it was there from something like July to December.

George Shaw

The bone of contention was that they would not handle container traffic. I don't know why, because all the equipment was there, cranes to lift it off, but they would not, and then Tilbury Docks was made into the super container operating docks, and the unions would not allow it to be used. It was kept inoperative for two years, as far as I recall. At the same time, they were not allowing the container goods to come into the London docks. And gradually it all faded away. It became a place of bitter contention, of everybody fighting for paltry little rights.

Eileen Brome

When voluntary severance came in, things started to move somewhat different. This is the strange thing with the Port of London – when you first went there, the money was very low, but you felt pride there, although you probably didn't realise it. But a sort of 'couldn't care less' attitude happened.

Dick Allington

What it really meant is that the river traffic changed in that bigger and bigger ships began to use the river. They could not get as far upriver as their predecessors, or needed more deep water to lie at the particular berths they were using, and so the extent of upriver traffic fell away. The effect of this was, of course, to make more and more riverside wharves to go out of active use, and with the passage of time, sadly the upper Thames – and by that, I mean from Woolwich upwards – began to look more and more sad and empty.

James Quick

With the new roll-on, roll-off stuff, they don't even have to unload it as such from containers, and fit it on the ships, apart from the long-distance stuff, but all the cross-Channel stuff, they just roll it straight on, with your container on the lorry, on to the ferry.

Gordon Beecham

I know that I've stressed the certain amount of militancy and the problems of dock workers, and the people who took ships to sea, but to a great extent, they were no doubt doing their best, and they were loyal and, I think, patriotic, people, who saw – and I guess I'm in this category – some sort of exclusiveness in our working area. We all worked in a secretive world, behind the high dock fencing; we thought we were dealing with the basic world – it wasn't a world like other people's, who seemed to go up to the City and pass their days pushing paper – we seemed to think of it as a job which had to be done, that was important to the country.

George Shaw

The big thing about dockers was their loyalty to anything. Their loyalty to particularly their own people. They'd been brought up in Depression, they'd lived in slums, and they'd seen a pretty rough life. And as a result of that, that built a sense of loyalty between all of them, and this, in my view, was cleverly exploited by the people who were politically motivated. Unfortunately that gained a hold, particularly in the Fifties, and people would go round: 'Come on, everybody. Off the ship. We're all out.' Nobody gave a reason why they were all out, and they followed off like sheep. But I must say that my life was greatly improved, I think, for knowing such people. They taught me a hell of a lot about handling men, and respectability.

Dick Butler

Planning a Brighter, Higher Future

Back in the 1920s, the London County Council had put into practice a plan to provide 'a land fit for heroes' for returning soldiers from the First World War. The result was the Becontree Estate, the first of the LCC's 'cottage' estates outside London, with 27,000 houses built on four square miles of farm and heathland in Ilford, Dagenham and Barking. Most of the early residents were relocated after slum clearance in Limehouse; many continued to commute back to work in the East End, although the new Ford motor factory in Dagenham provided jobs for forty thousand workers at its peak.

The team chosen to transform London for the heroes of the Second World War was headed by Lord Abercrombie, at the London County Council. He was not a Londoner but he was up to date with contemporary planning ideas. 'London grew up without plan or order,' he remarks in a contemporary newsreel, 'that's why there are all those old and ugly things that we hope to do away with if this plan of ours is carried out.' Not all his ideas were accepted, but in 1948, one of the first large post-war building projects was proposed for a triangle of land between East India Dock Road and Limehouse Cut. In an early planning enquiry about the new scheme, a resident challenged the programme of demolition, saying, 'It seems that we who were fortunate enough to escape Hitler's bombs, did so only to have our houses knocked down by the LCC.' The planning officer admitted, 'There's no suggestion these are slum property,' but added, 'We do feel it's an area which should be developed.'

The scheme replaced old houses with low-rise flats, along with shops, churches, schools and two small parks. The Victorian Chrisp Street Market, so long a key East End shopping street, gave way to Britain's first purpose-built pedestrianised shopping centre with a central square and decorative clock tower – this innovation was exhibited as a showpiece for the 'living architecture' element of the 1951 Festival of Britain. Named in honour of local politician George Lansbury, the estate was well thought out and generally liked, but its construction proceeded at a snail's pace, with some of it still being built in the 1980s.

In the 1950s, London also saw the emergence of a building of an even more modern design: the tower block. These vertical versions of the old-fashioned, closely packed streets were hailed as the way forward, offering light and air for everyone, with the latest modern fittings. Because high-rise buildings used less land, metropolitan boroughs were offered larger subsidies for building higher flats. Some were built around the now dwarfed Lansbury Estate, others proliferated in East and West Ham, which was blessed with 125 high-rise blocks in the Fifties and Sixties, the trend only subsiding after a gas explosion at Ronan Point killed five people as the tower block partially collapsed.

New homes
rise from
London's
ruins...

LANSBURY · POPLAR

The future arrived in the East End in the form of the Lansbury Estate, a highlight of the Festival of Britain and the embodiment of all the latest thinking in town planning. However, it took years to complete and in the meantime, tower blocks began to provide much-needed housing.
HMSO, 1951

We lived in Poplar and what had happened was after the war they were building 'a brave new Britain' and we were going to get Lansbury Town, Lansbury it was called, 'cos he was our MP.

Joanna Roberts

And they started knocking the old debris into shape. Building these four- or five-storey blocks of flats with inside toilets, bathrooms, hot and cold running water. And women at the time were used to sort of like boiling their washing up in a bucket, or in a copper. And they see these flats going up and they didn't give them a choice, really, they just said, 'We're gonna rehouse you up in a flat. You can have this flat or that flat. Not an house – that flat or that flat.' And all the women went 'Yeah! It's got a toilet inside'. And they went up and they had a look at them, they had show flats and all that, and they're all, 'Yeah, we'll go up there.' They all jumped at them.

Eddie Corbett

Brownfield Street, it was at one time called Grundy Street, and this was mainly small houses, side by side, with an upstairs flat and a downstairs flat, with a back door leading into the yard, which was called in some cases, the garden, but more often than not it was composed of a scullery or wash house, where people used to do their washing. At the end of the road there was an old-fashioned dairy where the people used to see the cows being taken in of an early morning and late evening. Now the whole area is covered in maisonettes, which people are very happy with because they've got all the amenities – indoor toilets and bathrooms.

Pat Thompson

The fashionable thinking of the time, it was a post-war reaction. Hitler's done a jolly good job, he's cleared a lot of these rotten old houses – let's finish the job. Let's get rid of all the rest. And you see the results in some parts of the East End now. It's not attractive and it's not conducive to the building of communities. The communities that existed in those little streets may have been poor and not particularly well provided for, but they were communities.

You were living at a time when the view was – and you didn't even argue it, it was like the weather – that everything was eventually going to go. One gets caught up in the feeling 'it's going to be a wonderful future and it's going to be different from now'. You still want to register the things that are now and may not be in the future, but it's only as the time goes by and you see what happens, when you lose those places, that you begin to think, I think we should have kept them.

John Earl

There was new flats going up all the time. And the old houses were being knocked down – Swedenborg Square was completely demolished, and all new flats were there now. And also Cable Street – Cable Street was all like little houses and that was completely demolished and there was only a few houses at the end, near Royal Mint Street, that are left.

Julie Hunt

They tore a lot down which they shouldn't have torn down, 'cos a lot of Victorian stuff went which was quite buildable, kept, you know. The area had taken a terrible pasting during the war with the bombing.

Joanna Roberts

They had prefabs and I remember going to visit Tubby Rosen across the Mile End Road, and across Globe Road, there was a host of prefabs around. Then bit by bit, they began shooting up these big, monstrous buildings.

Jack Miller

And then of course all these big high-rise blocks of flats started to be built, and it disfigured the whole area.

Elsie Edwards

It's certainly hurt the character of the area – I'd say the building of the flats were a major factor in destroying the communities that existed. I can't think of any reason why they should build them, really. I mean, everybody had some kind of garden – some kind of side gate that led to an alley, that led to next door's side gate, that led to a garden of some sort.

Eddie Corbett

I had the top half of a house I had to share with an old lady so all I was interested in was me own front door. So when they offered it, it was great. And it was nice, for the first couple of years, but course, as you start getting children and that, you realise what a mistake you've made by moving into a tower block. They can't get out, they're shut in all the time. I was pretty lucky, my mum lived round the corner so I used to take them round to play in her garden. But the children that were shut in those flats – they were sort of, I dunno, they didn't know how to play with other people.

Lynne Warne

When the kids started school, they didn't know how to mix with people. Like when you're brought up with kids, you learn how to play with kids, but they don't, they really don't. You didn't know them as people, like you do down a street, you know. You just see them – oh, I know that person in the lift. That's it. You don't know them to speak to, their name – if they had a problem, you wouldn't know about it. Especially in these sort, because the evens floors got different lifts to the odd floor, so where they was two separate floors, odds and evens, they never have met in a lift. Until you met in a lift you didn't know who was in those blocks at all.

Pat Vicks

Nobody wanted to really move into them, the high-rise tower blocks. It's a case of, the majority of the people that got them were on the housing list and they had nowhere to go – they had to live somewhere, so it's there or nowhere. Bearing in mind that most of them were GLC and GLC of the day were a lot quicker in getting you somewhere to live rather than if you were on Newham council which took a lot longer. The GLC were just sort of filling these white elephants up with people, not really caring that much, just fill them up, get them in, get them off our housing list.

Eddie Corbett

There was a tower block when I was at school and the only reason I remember it is 'cos it fell down. So I remember, like, you know, the kids coming in saying 'block of flats is fell down', and waking up at seven o'clock when it fell down. You heard it for about two miles, I think it was.

Pat Vicks

We moved into this tower block in 1964. After I'd been here about six months I decided to form a tenants' association. I went round to each door and I put notices in the lift, and as people tore them down I put another one up. We had meetings and outings and got a very good community spirit – people going on outings got to know one another in the block and they would go in each other's flats and they formed friendships, that's where the community spirit came in. That's what's missing in all these blocks – 'Hello, I live in number 49,' and you get them together and they have a few beers, and that's the secret of community spirit. These tower blocks are very good, but it's after you've been in here then the problems come with this – you only meet in the lift and you just have time to say hello and ta-ta; some talk, some don't, and you close your door and that's finished. You can live here years and not know who is the person next door.

Stan Rose

You never got to know the other people really; it was like a prison. I met a school friend in the street one day, I said, 'Oh, where you living?' She said, 'Westland House,' and I said, 'Oh, you live underneath me.' You know, she'd lived there for ages and we didn't know.

Lynne Warne

They all moved in and they found out after if they'd stuck it out with all the kids they had and everything, if they'd stuck it out, they'd have got a house somewhere else. But they said at the time, 'Oh, we're not building houses, we're only building flats.' So they all moved out of these old condemned slums into high-rise sort of boxes, and now they're all regretting it. They all wish they had their houses back and all the rest of it. Then after that they started building the real high-rise flats – the eighteen- and twenty-storey blocks. Which were a complete shambles right from the start. The lifts never worked. If something went wrong, they couldn't get it repaired. I seen women carry shopping, her children and a pushchair up six flights of stairs to get to her flat when the lift's been out. And then back down again. They're living up there in solitude, they were. Living up there in solitude from when the old man went out to work till he come home again at night.

Eddie Corbett

Who do you talk to in the high-rise block? Who do you ever sit outside on your window sills of a summer's night, chatting with?

Maurice Foley

Dispersal Beyond the Green Belt

It was also Lord Abercrombie who came up with the notion of a Green Belt to stop the sprawl of outer London, and he planned to relieve urban congestion by building new towns beyond it. His survey of 1944 recommended building eight new satellite towns, where 300,000 Londoners should be encouraged to settle. The towns were Stevenage, Crawley, Hemel Hempstead, Harlow, Hatfield, Welwyn, Basildon and Bracknell. Movement to these new towns was entirely voluntary, but the slow pace of rebuilding, and London County Council enthusiasm for relocation meant many East End families took the opportunity to leave behind the rubble and the memories of the Blitz. Another factor in the post-war dispersal of the East End was the psychological effects of evacuation during war time. This meant a generation of children grew up lacking the strong ties that linked the older generation to their local streets. Overall, population totals for the boroughs of Bethnal Green, Poplar, Stepney, and East and West Ham fell from nearly a million in 1931, to just over half a million in the 1951 census.

The Jewish community of the East End was subject to a more gradual but constant dispersal, with second- and third-generation immigrants keen to escape the poverty of their parents' life as circumstances improved. Accelerated by the heavy bombing of Whitechapel during the war, their migration took them northwards through Hackney to Stamford Hill, and westwards to Golders Green, Brondesbury, Wembley, Finchley and Harrow.

Once catering solely to immigrant sailors, Chinese restaurants boomed in the post-war period and proprietors left Limehouse to set up all over London, eventually congregating in Soho. This eating house called The East and West was a rare survivor in Pennyfields in the mid-1950s.
Henry Grant, 1955

By the end of the Second World War, the houses in Pennyfields, at the heart of East End's Chinese community, were in very poor condition and were compulsorily purchased by the LCC. A few elderly Chinese stayed on, but by 1960, Pennyfields was demolished to make way for the Birchfield Estate. Already there had been a drift outwards from the East End, partly because Chinese food was becoming more popular, entering a boom period in the mid 1950s. New restaurants catering for people outside the Chinese community were set up by immigrants from Hong Kong, eventually concentrating in Soho in the early 1970s.

We had a great plan for London to be surrounded by Green Belts which was a part of the Abercrombie scheme to make our environment better. But it never even touched the fringes of the East End of London, except those small areas which they classify as parks and built particularly within Tower Hamlets, Stepney and Newham.

Maurice Foley

There were certain trends leading up to the war and after the war, that some of the master tailors and master furriers were beginning to move out, going to Hackney and Stamford Hill, where you found, oddly enough, that they founded synagogues, particularly in Stamford Hill, where they became more and more orthodox in their observance. The East End was always more of a mixture, ideologically, amongst Jews, young and old.

Jack Miller

After the war, Jewish life in the East End started to peter our. Because of the massive bombing, people were forced to move away and so it was not a Jewish district any more, as it was before the war. And with it, the Yiddish theatre started to peter out – whereas we had two Yiddish theatres before the war, Adler Hall and the Grand Palais, now there was just the Grand Palais. We carried on bringing in guest stars – not from Europe any more, alas, because they all perished in the Holocaust, but from Israel and America. But in the 1960s, the Grand Palais had to close down for lack of an audience. The population from the East End of London had to move – north, south, east and west – and we lost them all.

Anna Tzelniker

During the war, lots of the Jewish children were evacuated and many parents left then. That made a great change in the life of the buildings. I remember some friends moved out to Kingsland Road and that seemed marvellous: Kingsland Road, Amhurst Road – like a hierarchy – I think people aimed at getting out of the buildings because they must have associated them with poverty.

Miss M

A lot of people had fled from the East End when the bombing got very bad, and some began to move towards Ilford and Forest Gate; there was a certain population drift away from the East End, particularly amongst Jewish people. From that moment on it diminished rather rapidly. By about 1955, vast areas began to be filled with these big buildings.

Jack Miller

Now we look at the line stretching along the river course from Tower Hill – and it was supposedly the heaviest industrialised area in Europe – and it's come to a situation because of wartime measures, some of it was moved away, but by far the greatest percentage was flattened during the stage of 1940 up to around 1943 by very heavy bombing. And as you can see, very little of it was ever replaced. And in consequence of this, immediately after the war, rather than the people moving back, hundreds of families that would normally have resided or continued to reside in the East End of London left – firstly because of the housing shortage which had been caused by bombing wasn't being replaced speedily enough to rehouse the people. Secondly, the planners were now building overspill towns and taking the people into the fields of Essex, hoping that they would enjoy some better environment.

Maurice Foley

Obviously, if someone said to you, 'All right, we'll build a new town at Basildon, we gotta get a job there, the docks are shutting down in two years' time; use your loaf, get out now, get another job,' and all the rest of it, people just move out. They go with the jobs, or after a job. So you had a lot of people moving out of the community, and a lot of new people moving in. Not necessarily to get a job, but moving in anyway. From, say, the other end of London or somewhere. They doesn't know anything about the area and they're just sort of living round here, hoping to get a job somewhere, whether it's sweeping or whatever.

Eddie Corbett

They started scattering during the war – whereas once a bloke would have married a girl out of Canning Town, he finished up marrying a bird out of Newcastle, or vice versa, and when he came back home, she didn't want to know too much about a way of life here. And a lot of them people they moved out in Essex, some went into Kent – some, in fact, never came back.

Maurice Foley

When I started work, there was very few immigrants there, very few, there were hardly any. It was almost all men that

were born and bred in those parts of London, actually. Course
of lot of them, once they got married, moved a little bit further
out, but it was after the war, youngsters got married and they
didn't want to stay in the East End – they all moved out. The
parents either died or they moved out to be with their children. The character of the East End was not like it used to be
– it really changed.

Joe Morris

In the 1950s, the employers and unions got together and they
went to a professional film-making company to make a dock
safety film. And the film crew, while we were making it, they
decided they would like to go to Chinatown for a meal, and
all that was left of Chinatown was about one or two small
houses which were dishing up Chinese food.

Dick Butler

Well, I believe that family life has gone – there's very few areas
now where you can go down within four streets and visit all
your relations, including your grandmother, sometimes your
great-grandmother. It's gone.

Maurice Foley

CHAPTER 14

That Which Fades; That Which Endures

The End of the Busy Years

Although in 1951 employment in London was as high as it was in 1931, the type of work had changed, and in the East End, the range and variety of jobs never returned to pre-war levels. Many East End firms had voluntarily evacuated or been bombed out, and large numbers chose not to return after re-establishing themselves elsewhere. Even if they did want to return, they were often unable to do so, because of post-war residential zoning where industry was not allowed. Small businesses were also at a disadvantage in an economy that became dependent on access for heavy lorries; the old cobbled yards and small turnings that were fine in the days of the horse and cart were now at a considerable disadvantage. The East End's furniture trade, for example, lost more than half of its workshops between 1939 and 1958. Through the 1950s and early Sixties, which were boom years for the economy as a whole, the trend away from manufacturing hit the East End hard, and there was little to take its place.

At the beginning of the 1960s, the East India, St Katharine and London Docks were still open, but none would see out the decade, and the following fifteen years spelled the beginning of the end for ships coming into the Isle of Dogs, the

Royal Docks and West Ham. When the docks thrived, all manner of related industries had grown up alongside them, but these all fell away without their central means of support. By the time of Sir Winston Churchill's solemn funeral procession along the Thames in 1965, the busy years of the East End were, like the memory of the Blitz, a part of history.

***

The funeral of Sir Winston Churchill included a passage from Tower Pier to the pier near Waterloo. The arrangements for the riverside part of the funeral included having the Port of London Authority vessels available – one of the survey vessels took the coffin aboard and a second vessel carried the family mourners, including Lady Churchill, and other vessels provided escort. At the same time, the river was closed while this passage took place; the cranes of the wharf on the south side of the river opposite Tower Pier all together lowered their jibs in salute as they went past, which was very impressive, and aircraft of the Royal Air Force flew overhead soon afterwards.

P Satow

On many occasions that I went with my father when he was mayor, it made me realise that there's much more to living in the borough than just being a person. You've got to understand how the borough needed refurbishing, and how the docklands needed replenishing, because the work was finishing and the cranes were standing idle, you know, particularly along the East India Dock wall. They were standing there like sentinels, waiting for work, and most of the dockers had moved further down the river to work because there wasn't anything coming in to the Pool of London for them.

Pat Thompson

Cargo ships were being displaced because of the enormous upsurge in containerisation, in spheres and geographical areas which had never been contemplated, say, ten years before. But it was found that with expertise, trades could be containerised in quite a short time. It meant displacing an enormous number of personnel – the sea staff suffered badly, the dockers, of course – the need for them kept on receding, receding, because of the rationalisation of the numbers of employers such as Scruttons, Maltby's, Thames Stevedoring – they became smaller and smaller, and they were faced with the problem of taking all the labour left over from the other companies, and it was not a particularly happy time.

George Shaw

In my young days in the docks, a man with a horse and cart used to get a living out of carrying about a ton or two ton at most. He got a living out of that. Only about £2.50 a week, but it was a living, brought up the wife and family on that. One man today drives a container or van weighing about forty ton, he only gets a living wage, see? And all these men have lost their jobs. They say you can't stop progress – possibly you can't – but it doesn't benefit mankind. It's an easier living, yes, but is it progress?

William Abbott

The pool then was alongside a pub called the Connaught, which you had to go around a very sharp right-handed bend over a railway crossing, and at that particular period of time that area was an absolute hive of industry, with PLA shunting yards, all the factories, all sorts of industries down there. I know of about fifteen, twenty transport firms down there, other factories like Tate & Lyle's were busy trying to catch up with people's demand after lack of sugar and stuff after the war. The whole place was alive. The docks, well, very saddening for me now to see what's happened. I can remember ships in those docks two, three abreast and not a berth to spare. Every crane going.

Albert Patten

The time we're talking about in the 1950s, there must have been about twenty-five, thirty thousand people coming round that docks in the morning. And the trolley buses used to queue up along the dock road there to go into the terminus, and there'd be thousands of these – you'd not only get dockers, but the factory workers all used to go in at the same time, and cleaners, and they'd all sort of fight to hurry up to get on the bus.

Mrs Lester

Every job, every labourer's job, has got a skill to it. Never anyone thought about inventing machinery in those days – not that men wanted machinery 'cos they foresaw that once that had machinery, their jobs were in peril. They tried to avoid using machinery as much as they could, because they knew their jobs would go. In the end, it did happen that way.

William Abbott

I went down to see one of the large ship repairers that used to be there, Nicholson's, that had two massive factories and used to employ somewhere upwards of two thousand, three thousand people. It was very sad to see the old business had virtually disintegrated. The total staff when I went there was the manager, a woman who came in cleaning and an old sail maker, and that was the total staff out of two, three thousand.

Gordon Beecham

They had places like Harland and Wolff, right, the ship repairers, and all the rest of it. I mean, they just shut them places down. One at Silvertown, one at Woolwich. Two dirty great

You can't fight mechanisation: the war is over and it looks like the machines have won. By 1970, Tilbury had been transformed into the most successful container port in Britain, handling more than 230,000 containers a year. 1970

big factories. Just shut them down, because of the decline in the docks. The Standard Telephones and Cables – they moved them to Basildon. The people they used to employ are round here. Thousands. And they just moved out to Basildon. Didn't care about the people that lived round here. Just moved them out.

Eddie Corbett

Most of the people round that area, Bow and Poplar, it was a dock area, and you either built boats or repaired ships, or you were a docker or you was a seaman. Limehouse was where some of the greatest ships were built.

John Cleary

You could hear work being done on the docks – I mean you could actually hear the riveters with hydraulic or air-driven rivet hammers, the noise absolutely rebounds, you could hear it in West Ham, East Ham, Upton Park. When there's any major repair work done in the dock, it was a very noisy place – and a very busy place. But noise didn't seem to bother us in those days.

Gordon Beecham

All the time, the sort of work we were doing was being curtailed, withdrawn – staff withdrawn – and after I left, instead of the four surveyors when I arrived, they were down to two, and finally down to one after I retired. Because firms were moving out and our work was no longer required. Things like export rebate had gone, and things like that.

Eric Cropper

If you had the docks you had coffee shops, you had chandlers, you had engineers, you had transport, and it was all from within the borough. And of course that's all gone – all gone entirely. None of my children can get property. Of course, there was no such thing as private property to buy in the borough in them days, not like today. Houses and flats and mansions are going up around here all along the river which used to be the dockers, a million pound and that sort of business. So the whole of the borough will change utterly and completely in the last sixty or seventy years from a very slummish, er, hard-working community, I suppose, to a very affluent one. And that means the entire ending of anybody that used to live here once upon a time.

Bernard Alger

Quite nearby was the Manganese Bronze and Brass Works, and we would see ships' propellers on horse-drawn vehicles being taken away. There was the Lock, Lancaster's lead works; there was timber yards – Sir William Burnett's and John Linanden's, which I remember quite well. A few hundred yards down the road was Hawkins and Tipson's manila rope works – they were a very busy and quite a famous firm in their day; apparently one of the achievements was to produce a rope to pull a ship off the Goodwins, and that seemed to make their name. There was also Binks's wire rope works. There were varying ships' chandlers, chain makers, barge breakers, barge builders. Millwall was encircled by all these little draw docks with all their little trades. If it came to provisioning, there were of course McConnaghys and Moreton's, jam-makers and canners and such.

Laurie Landick

Stratford, there used to be a lot of firms – there used to be a big chemists place, then there used to be Yardley's, all scent; Silvertown was all factories, West Ham was full of them, and Stratford, it was all factory work.

Charles Beck

The area in Bermondsey was the leather area – I mean, you got the leather market down the roads; if you look round the streets you got Tanner Street, you got Morocco Street, even the public house is Simon the Tanner. It was all here in this area because of the docks, obviously. The skins come up the docks.

It's a very interesting job. You never get bored with it because every day there's something new or something different to do. Mainly our people, especially the fashions, are in the East End of London, in Hackney, Shoreditch area, the Jewish community – nearly all the Jewish community, the fur trade. If you took the Jewish people out of the fur trade, I mean, well, there'd be no fur trade. I'm not Jewish myself – but I'm saving up.

Terry Loveday

At that time, there were timber yards all over the place. Take it from Shoreditch Church; you had Mallinson's, your two up where the old Penny Bank used to be, and one further up on the corner of Temple Street, and that was only in one road. They was all round the back turnings. Little yards would go and buy job lots, and sell it to the makers. According to what kind of wood you wanted, you could spend a couple of hours walking round them all.

George Wood

I retired as the market closed – our family business just couldn't trade any more, and that was it. The emergence of supermarkets – they'd started to come into being – and once they got the knack of trading outside of markets, and not going to markets, then this sort of trade got less. So instead of my father sending all his mushrooms to the market and taking a chance on what he realised, price-wise, the supermarkets, emerging, would give him a fixed price before they'd even grown, so he knew he was on to a safe wicket by dealing with them. So he started rather dealing with them than with traders in the market, even though he'd dealt with them all his life.

John Beattie

While I was there, more breweries closed – I seem to have been superintending the closing of breweries left, right and centre: Mann, Crossman's and Whitbread's closed – a great shame that, the last brewery within the City, Whitbread's – for so-called economy, but really for development. When Charrington's closed, they invited me down to a party at the end and the brew they made for the party was never sold and no one ever put a hydrometer in it to find out how strong it was, but it was very strong – quite illegal.

Eric Cropper

Well, there's seventy thousand jobs gone out of the borough in the last few years. I mean, all the docks have gone and most of the dockers have either moved down to Tilbury or retired, you know, with severance pays. A lot of them have still got some working life left and have got jobs in various places, but most people have to travel out of Bermondsey nowadays. For forty-one years I've worked in Bermondsey – I've never been farther than walking distance from home.

Bernard Alger

For me, I was witnessing a tragedy. It was like walking into an old cowboy Western ghost town. When I think, or I visualise, eight thousand men that was registered dock workers of different docks – Victoria, Albert and King George – I can visualise them all in motion, their language, their swearing, their humour, the speed in which they had to work because they was piece workers, and I have to pinch myself again when I am looking at it now as I look out the window. It's like an old Western ghost town. I'd equate it with financial vandalism. All right, people say it's the march of time and you can't stop progress, but then what qualifies as progress? Eight thousand wage packets gone, and of course if you take the accompanying industries that served the docks, the engineers, the ship repair workers, the lightermen, the warehousemen; it must have run into about fifteen thousand men, and they're no longer here earning their livelihood, and that means fifteen thousand wage packets are no longer being spent in the borough.

Jack Dash

I get very sad and nostalgic when I go around that area and see the whole docks covered in, no cranes. One good thing about it, a lot of the slums have been cleared. But there's a lot of greed, I think, with these, for want of a better word, fat cats, these land developers. I'd still like to see the ships coming in and out and the basis of some good employment down there. Being an ex-seaman, I feel very, very nostalgic about it.

Albert Patten

I don't think you could get a row boat in between the craft that was on the river. It seems very sad that today the river is absolutely dead. Back then, in the Pool of London on the east side and on the north side and the south side, you just had one cargo boat after another coming in, unloading and going off. I feel very sad when I see the river today, just the pleasure craft occasionally or the police launch. That's just about all you see.

Lucy Collard

I used to walk through the inside of the railway bridge over the dock, and it was lovely on sunny days to see right down to the dock and the water sparkled, you know, and all these ships bobbing and the cranes ever so busy, and crowds of people walking about all the time.

Eileen Brome

On the docks, there was nothing going on, grass growing over all the railway tracks, nobody in the docks, no ships, no cranes working, no noise, no nothing, absolute devastation.

Gordon Beecham

I think they could do something with the river. You look there, I mean, there's nothing on there. That's fetched livelihood to London for centuries.

Mr Lester

Windrush and Beyond

Much of the East End's early twentieth-century reputation came from the exoticism of its Chinese and Indian communities. At a time before widespread travel, visitors were genuinely astonished to see people with different skin colours wearing strange clothes and buying unfamiliar goods and foods.

In 1951, only one in twenty Londoners had been born outside the United Kingdom. After the Second World War, most of the existing communities dispersed, but new ones arrived to take their place. Famously, the *SS Empire Windrush* docked at Tilbury in 1948, bringing the first large group of post-colonial migrants to the UK. The short-lived economic boom of the 1950s brought more visitors, many of whom were overqualified but who took low-paid, low-status jobs in the National Health Service, transport, and service industries. Cypriots settled mostly in North Islington, Hackney and Stoke Newington and former residents of Hong Kong helped establish Soho's new Chinatown. The biggest group, arriving from the mid-1950s onwards, were the Sylhetis from what is now Bangladesh, who settled around Spitalfields, particularly Brick Lane.

With the problems of housing and the decline of the old working-class industries, these new immigrants were not always accepted, but although some East Enders were drawn to the far right groups such as the National Front Party, many others joined opposing groups, including the Anti-Nazi League and Rock Against Racism.

———•———

When you live so many years together among foreigners – my wife's family lived round the docks, you see, before the war and there was many nationalities mixed there; it was not like today, there was no racialism, no hatred, nothing. It was just accepted. Because when you were in the docks, there was Irish, Scots, Chinese, Jews, all mixed, there were all nationalities. It is only recently the prejudice, because they have different religions, different cultures now, and all the foreigners who come here, they build their own mosque or church or something and they all want to be independent and they will never succeed. Because if you come to this country to experience it, you must integrate and you must follow the law of the country.

Zygmund Izycki

Of course, by about 1955, vast areas began to be filled with these big blocks of buildings, as you're seeing in this area. Then of course, a process developed which was a very strange one; at first there was Jews, and a few Cypriots who had come here, and then, bit by bit, till about the Sixties, there began to come in – about the time of Enoch Powell fulminating about it – the immigrants. And more and more Bangladeshis and Pakistanis began to fill the area up. I don't think at first there was animosity – it was only when it became too... you might say, seemingly excessive, to have upset completely the homogeneity of the area, that the reaction began to take place. In fact, there's a great deal of resentment, but it's not... except for a few fascist types that resort to violence against them, but there's a great deal of resentment among elderly people who feel they're favoured. They're big families, and they seem to do a hell of a lot of shopping and the men are all smoking good brands of cigarettes – there's all sorts of rumours that fly around about the amount of welfare money they get and the welfare they get in all directions for their children and their rent and whatnot.

Jack Miller

I went to St Mary's and St Michael's School, and there was all different types of people who lived in the area. They were mainly Irish, Maltese and a few Scottish. The Irish were like O'Sullivans, Collins, O'Brien. The Scottish were like Fullerton, and the English were like Lloyd, Murray and Smith, and the Maltese, they were Spitari, Borg, Benicci, Sapiano. We all mucked in together and we had a time, but it was a very religious school, run by nuns. At that time, the English didn't have a lot in their families, there was only about two or three, might be four at the most, but the Maltese and the Irish had big families, sometimes up to nine children, and these big families, they were mainly living sort of in two, three rooms, because they'd come here from their country in the 1950s and they didn't have a lot of work to do – they were sort of hunting around looking for places to live and any work that became available.

Julie Hunt

We had a lot of problems with the children who'd come in on *Windrush*. Ours was a catchment area, so we got them. And it was really difficult because the parents had been brought up in Jamaica – or the West Indies – so things were completely different education-wise. So we had a lot of kids at the school who weren't good; caused lots and lots of trouble. So they devised this scheme whereby you took out the children who were disruptive and you put them into a unit *en masse*. There was a teacher and there was a mother, and I was the mother.

Joanna Roberts

In 1961, we moved to Christian Street, and it was a completely different area. It was mainly Jews – it was only five minutes away, but it was like moving into a new world, because where we had been mixing with English and Irish and Maltese, now we was mixing with the Jewish nationalities, and the Greeks and the coloureds, and the Turkish. But they were all right, they weren't bad. And we knew everyone in the building, same as we did in Shadwell Gardens.

Julie Hunt

I think prejudice started when the Jamaicans came over. It wasn't so much against the people, I think it was the way they took over the houses, and there was so many of them in 'em. The prejudice built up over the years because there was too many come in, and too fast.

Jean Cunningham

I remember in the 1950s, after the war, a lot of people stay behind – there was no trouble. Nobody called each other names, they just worked together and rebuild the country. It's all the hatred now; one black, one white, one pink, all in their little groups, they want to fight each other.

Zygmund Izycki

As the population sort of moved, it wasn't moving as fast as people think it was, it was moving over a slow period. 'Cos when Hessel Street closed, the Indians started taking over a few shops from the Jewish people, and eventually, they came in, taking over the different shops. It was over a period of about five or six years, and also their families started coming over. And this is how they moved in. Then they started taking over the Jewish companies – the company I worked for moved to Kingsland High Road, and a few other companies moved out of the area. Of course, they sold their businesses to these Sikhs, or Indians, and also our local picture house – that turned into an Indian cinema.

Julie Hunt

When the Ocean Estate was built, it was quite an elated feeling and quite a good deal of neighbourliness, the women would come and sit out and chat on the stoops. The flats were quite reasonable – we did discover late on that it was asbestos-lined and we made a campaign about that. Sometimes the lifts would break down. But by about the Sixties, some people, I think, didn't like it when they saw inroads being made by the Asian families and they began to go elsewhere. Some of them used to take in work, you know, and use their rooms as workshops, and when relatives came, they would often put them up, whether it was legal or illegal. I remember once canvassing for a meeting of the tenants' association on the fourth floor. And the door opened – and at night, they changed their clothing, and they were all in sort of night attire – and the whole place was packed with people, young and old, probably about thirty people were in that two-bedroom flat up on the fourth floor.

Jack Miller

Rathbone Street Market, the atmosphere down there was entirely different somehow or other, until this nation started to become more cosmopolitan than it has been. Now you've got an influx of Indians and West Indian flavours down there. I don't know, some people can be in favour of it, some are not, I don't know what to think about it. The way I look at it, it don't matter whether you're green, black, white – if you bleed, you bleed red. I've always found I've got on all right with that particular type of nationality. I look at it this way – if I fell overboard at sea and there was a hand reached out to pull me on board, I wouldn't care particularly what sort of colour it was. I'd certainly grab it.

Albert Patten

On Being an East Ender

For most of the twentieth century, having your roots in the East End was hardly something to boast of – it was more like something you'd want to hide. It was a place of great poverty and low expectations, of fighting men and tough women, of smells and dirt and noise. It bred many inward-looking people with narrow horizons, whose lives revolved around work, family and the pub – but that hardship also fostered a proud independence of spirit. East Enders have always known what others thought of them, but they knew their own lives and the opinions of outsiders were largely irrelevant. Those things that had held communities together through good times and bad included an ability to share and understand the same stories, hardships and celebrations.

If East Enders lacked respect for the law, that didn't make them all criminals; they simply had different rules – the basic laws of hospitality, helpfulness and friendliness were understood and common to all. Perhaps the most valuable thing East Enders possessed was a sense of identity. That identity embraced a variety of cultural backgrounds and influences, but the ideals of solidarity, of 'all for one; one for all' were paramount. Especially in the early years of the twentieth century, East Enders grew up in a world that lacked material possessions and comforts, but it offered instead a life of experiences. It was a world of vivid encounters, passionate debates, strongly held beliefs and stronger language, a world peopled by larger-than-life characters and tellers of tall tales.

———•———

They reckoned 'cos you lived in the East End, you lived in slums. It didn't feel like a slum. Even now, if you say you live in the East End, in Bethnal Green, they look at you as if you were dirt, beneath them, if you know what I mean. Even now, they say, 'Where do you come from? Bethnal Green? Oh, I couldn't live there.' I say, 'Well, I live there and it suits me.' There's good and bad everywhere, isn't it. I mean, the majority of people, they moved out, moved to Loughton, but it's just as bad at Loughton as what it is here. I mean, all the East Enders moved down there, so what's the difference?

Dolly Cooper

When my husband was being interviewed to be made a major, his colonel looked through all his papers and said to him, 'Not exactly out of the top drawer, are you?' This was having read where he was educated, you see. And my husband said, 'No, I'm not interested in which drawer anybody comes out of, but if I'm in the bottom drawer, I'll do a good job while I'm in it.'

Eileen Brome

I did miss the friendliness when I came to Highgate. United Dairies had a shop just a few doors along from where I lived and I was in there talking and there was a lady came in and I think there had been a fight or something in the papers about the East End and she said, 'Oh, how dreadful to live amongst the scum of the East End.' And of course, I really went for her. She said, 'Well, what do you know about the East End – you don't speak as though you come from the East End.' I said, 'Well, what am I supposed to say then – gawd blimey after every sentence?' She said, 'I don't suppose you know a thing about the East End.' I said, 'Well, I do – because I happen to come from the East End,' and I said, 'And if there's any scum around, it's obviously people like you – people that really don't know East Enders.'

Lucy Collard

My first tug was the *Sunrise*; the skipper was Charles Thomas and the engineer was Mike Hatch – to hear the two of them in an argument was an education, because I've never heard language flow so easily and so foully at the same time.

John Henry Arnold

We've always been cosmopolitan; we've had Irish, Jews, we had bleeding French, Belgiques, we had a sprinkling of Chinamen and we had a few West Indians that was left from the 1914–18 war that lived in the area. We had Poles; if you look at the Silvertown area, they weren't basically Poles, they was poor sods that was driven out of Latvia and Estonia because of the political situation. The same collective one thing – injury to one was injury to all.

Maurice Foley

Today, I found for the first time in years, well over a decade, what we called at sea '*dhobi* soap'. It's like white, hard soap that we used to wash our clobber with. I found it in Harry Street, Walthamstow, in a little Indian shop, plus they had that hard red Lifebuoy soap that used to have a nice pungent smell to it. I bought eight bars of it because I like that soap, it's very good. The Indian woman said to me, 'Why do you want all that amount?' I said, 'Oh, I'm a *dhobi wallah*.' She understood what I meant – *dhobi*, meaning washing, and *wallah* meaning the person who does the washing.

Albert Patten

I've got a list at home of every person in that street, from one all the way down, from the odd side to the even side, and I can remember every single one. And there was people who, if you come home from school and you was a bit early and Mum wasn't in, Mrs Donovan, the woman next door – 'Come in, you can have tea with us,' you know. I had, honestly, an idyllic childhood, I would not swap one bit, not one little bit. Even the hard bits I wouldn't swap because most of it was lovely. I could play in the street – I was allowed to do things.

Joanna Roberts

When our children was younger, nearly every house there was PLA houses, and nearly every house was let, downstairs and upstairs, two families. They'd have to share the scullery once a week, share the toilet, because the toilet was out in the yard, you didn't have a bathroom, you had an old tin bath in front of the fire, they never had central heating or nothing. I suppose we'd have still been in there now if they hadn't come along and said we'd all got to get out – I liked it there.

Mrs Lester

Everybody helped each other, you shared your troubles. For instance, if there was an unfortunate occurrence in a family, a death or an illness, and somebody was in trouble through it over money, the list used to go round the door, there'd be a penny or tuppence put on the list. Shopkeepers were very good at helping out. When times were hard, people would get tick; in other words, they'd go on the slate. They'd get stuff from the shop and it would be put on the slate then, when times improved, they'd pay it back.

Jack Banfield

There was a club I belonged to in those days, called the Cambridge and Bethnal Green Boys Club, and if you belonged to a club, that club was the best club in the world – there was no other club to touch it, you know. There was pride, real pride. Same as with the grown-up people, the gangster types I met, they had pride in themselves, and pride of their birth and area they came from.

Harry Silverston

There was always lots of people about and an air of bustle and there was none of this shutting the door and shutting yourselves in; doors were open all day and all night and in the summer nights the women used to sit outside the doors on their stools because it was so hot they couldn't go to sleep. Anyway, there was always something going on. Plus they had a marvellous sense of humour.

Although there was poverty, terrific poverty, everyone laughed, everyone could tell a joke, everyone could make light of life. Nobody had anything so therefore if you suddenly found yourselves with a penny in your pocket you thought you were rich, and you were – and you felt it was marvellous.

Mary Partlett

I think it was the war that broke up the community. You see, during the bombing, people were cared for – when they were bombed out, the people went to the rest centre service who said, 'Where were you living; what did you have there? Well, we can give you this, that and the other.' And then they began to have a taste for good furniture, for bedding, which perhaps they'd never had before; they had a thousand and one things given to them.

Florrie Passman

Of a summer evening or a weekend, Dick and his friends would get together and they would go for a row up or down the river as the tide indicated, and some of the lads would take along a mandolin or two, and Dick was the most perfect mouth-organ player. They would slip up or down the river, and when it got dusk and we were waiting at Blackwall Stairs, you would suddenly hear the sound of the mandolins and the mouth organ and it was just as romantic as when you talk about Venice.

Tom Stothard

I always remember when I hear anywhere, the song *Abide With Me*. Because, I've forgotten the exact time, but after tea, everybody would be rushing around, playing games or chasing each other, all running around in our nightshirts, then there'd be a long G on the bugle, and wherever you were, all the boys had to sing *Abide With Me* – '*Fast falls the eventide...*'. I always remember this lovely sound – of course, I didn't realise it then, all we wanted was to get it over, and jump in our hammocks – we were given ten minutes after that, last boy in, you know. But I hear that and I picture and hear all this, six hundred kids plus, all over the ship, upper deck, lower deck, all had to sleep in different decks, so many of us, and lashed up.

George Barnes

When Friday came round, one could smell and feel the impending Sabbath. We used to go and buy a penny hearth-stone – that was my job when I came home from school – and every Jewish woman would scrub just in front of the door and the doorstep and make it white. And all the curtains were changed. Friday night's meal was a sacred meal; Father used to go to the synagogue and come home and make an evening blessing for the Sabbath. Mother would make a most glori-ous meal, which always consisted of not the cuts that you would have today, but the cheapest cuts – offal, bits of lung, liver, melts – all full of carrots and onions, sort of a casserole. If we were lucky, we might get a chicken, some old boiler, to make soup for the Sabbath meal the following day. One could feel the atmosphere.

Mr U

I sometimes go to bed and dream that I'm back there. I do. I'll tell you something else, when my sister died, and I moved from the East End to Chingford, I used to have an urge to go back, and it took about eighteen months before I lost that urge. I did used to go back – I used to find any excuse to go back. After all, I spent my life there. I grew up there.

Mrs G

There was real poverty but people weren't self-consciously unhappy. People would sit outside the front door, you see, when they'd done whatever it is they could do in the house. And if the weather wasn't too bad, they'd sit on the doorstep, outside the front door, just talk or just sit there if the sun was shining and there was an acceptance. Everybody would look at each other and go 'You all right today?' ''er next door, she's a bit...' 'Have you been in?' 'No, I'll go in later.'

Alfie Bass

Still sitting on doorsteps, still cheerfully engaged with the world passing by, a new generation of East End children are better shod and fed than those of half a century before – but what are the prospects for their community's future? Henry Grant, 1954

Biographies

Mrs A was born in 1891 in Austria and came to London in 1897. Her family lived in Rothschild Buildings, Whitechapel, and her father worked as a cabinetmaker. *2008.102*

William Abbott was born in Poplar in 1911 and worked in the docks all his life as a labourer unloading cargoes such as cheese, sugar and meat. *86.352*

George Adams was descended from a long line of lightermen, born in 1924, in Poplar. He worked as a stevedore in the Royal group of docks. *86.13*

Alfred Alexander was born in 1908 in Russia and arrived in Spitalfields as a baby. He worked as a cabinetmaker and was an active trade unionist. *LHW 65.5*

Bernard Alger was born in 1924 and worked as a fur dyer in the Alaska Factory, which first opened in Bermondsey in 1869 to process seal fur. *DK88.5*

*Dick Allington was born in 1927 in Poplar and worked on tugboats in the docks during the Blitz, before becoming an engineer. *85.362*

John Ardley was born in 1932 in Stepney and followed his father into the coopering trade, making barrels to hold port, brandy, iodine and other cargoes. *DK89.24*

John Henry Arnold was born in 1915 in Plaistow and worked as a tugboat skipper on the Sun tugs which operated out of Wapping. *DK89.50*

Mrs B was born in Whitechapel, in 1893, one of eight children. Her father died young and two brothers were sent to West Norwood orphanage when her mother could not cope. *2008.114*

Jack Banfield was born in 1907 in Wapping. Like his father, he worked in the docks where he became a trade union shop steward. *85.597*

George Barnes was born in 1909 and orphaned by the age of twelve. He was sent to a training ship run by the Metropolitan Asylums Board and later became a merchant seaman. *85.360*

Alfie Bass was born Abraham Basalinisky, in 1916, in Bethnal Green. He had a successful career as an actor, starring in films and a 1960s TV series called *Bootsie and Snudge*. *2010.48/237*

Rose Bater was born in 1923 and worked as a typist at the Port of London during the war. *86.349*

John Beattie was the son of a costermonger from Islington, born in 1926. He worked as a market trader at Chapel Market and Borough Market. *CC 96/42*

Charles Beck was born about 1910, in Custom House, and worked as a delivery boy with a horse and cart, then as a railway porter operating the trains at Poplar Dock. *DK89.18*

Gordon Beecham was born in 1919 in Plaistow. He worked as an upholsterer alongside some of the last of Spitalfield's Huguenot weavers. *DK88.9*

Sidney Bell was one of a family of ten children, born in Wapping, in 1906. He was a newspaper delivery boy and later worked in the docks. *DK88.77*

Philip Bernstein was born in 1910 in Mile End. He became a full-time violinist at a cinema in Bermondsey at the age of fourteen. He married the actress Anna Tzelniker. *92.150*

Eileen Brome was born in 1916 in Leytonstone. She worked as a typist at the Port of London before she married a wage clerk who worked in the same office. *86.359*

Stan Bryan was born in 1922. He trained as a joiner, served in the air force during the war, and worked at the ship repair firm Green, Silley and Weir, close to Albert Dock. *DK88.57*

Hilda Bunyon was born in 1904 in Hoxton to an unemployed father, and a mother who worked from home on piecework, making boxes. *2010.48/52*

Dick Butler was born in 1920, in Bow; his father worked for the dock companies and Dick became a director of the PLA. He married Elizabeth Butler. *DK88.56*

Elizabeth Butler was born in 1905. Her father and brothers were dockers and she worked at the dock's canteen before marrying Dick Butler. *86.348*

Kevin Chandler was born in 1902 in Bow, the son of a freemason. He worked as a clerk for the Port of London Authority. *86.273*

John Cleary was born in 1916 in Bow, the son of a merchant seaman. He worked on ships during the war and then became a cab driver. *CC 92.151*

Ivy Cobbald was born in Wandsworth in 1913 and grew up in an orphanage. She married a Thames river policeman. *DK88.58*

Lucy Collard was born in Stepney in 1915 and was the daughter of a lighterman, descended from the Huguenot silk weavers of Spitalfields. *DK88.96*

Dolly Cooper was born in 1910 in Bethnal Green and followed her father into the upholstery trade. *2010.48/230*

Eddie Corbett grew up in the East End around North Woolwich and Silvertown just after the war and witnessed the decline of the docks. *2010.48/30*

Henry Corke was born near Caledonian Road Market, in 1912, and was one of a family of fourteen. As a child he played truant to travel the country as a stowaway on lorries. *2010.48/47*

Bill Crook was born in 1905 in Bethnal Green. His father was a woodcarver and he served eight years in the army before working for the library service. *2010.48/233*

Eric Cropper was born in Essex in 1915 and became a customs officer at the Port of London. After the war, he inspected and collected duty from East End breweries. *DK87.4*

Jean Cunningham was born in 1930 in Whitechapel. She was an only child, and she lost her father and stepfather during the war. *CC 97/64*

Jack Dash was born in 1907 and worked in the docks. He was a lifelong Communist and a leading trade unionist. Jack Dash House on the Isle of Dogs is named after him. *DK87.85*

Cyril Demarne OBE was born in 1905 in Poplar and joined the West Ham Fire Brigade. He was the inspiration behind the Blitz Memorial statue of firemen by St Paul's Cathedral. *CC 2004.13*

Louis Dore was born in 1908. His grandfather sailed in the *Cutty Sark* and he worked on the docks. As a Quaker, he joined for the Friends' Ambulance Unit in the war. *DK90.3*

Walter Dunsford was born in 1910 in Canning Town and worked as a carpenter in the docks. He helped build the 200-ton floating derrick known as the London Mammoth. *85.593*

John Earl was born in 1928 on the Becontree estate. He worked for LCC Historic Buildings and was instrumental in saving Wilton's Music Hall from demolition. *CC 2005.24*

Elsie Edwards was born in 1918 in Derbyshire and came to London to work as a nurse in Poplar, just before the war. She married a local policeman. *CC 96.40*

Len Faram was born in 1936, in Poplar. Descended from a long line of lightermen, he served his apprenticeship with the Union Lighterage Company. *DK89.57*

Maurice Foley was born in 1923 in Canning Town and was an active trade unionist during his fifty years working at the Royal Docks. *DK87.76 and 2010.48*

Harry Foss was born in 1912 in Custom House. His father was a lighterman and his mother a factory worker, and he worked as a plumber in the docks. *DK88.57*

Mrs G was born in Russia in 1899 and came to England in 1913. Her father, brother and sisters were all tailors in the East End, and one of her nephews was Arnold Wesker. *2008.113*

Alexander Gander was born in 1911 in Shadwell and worked in a Whitechapel brewery. He was on an oil tanker during the war, before becoming a docker. *86.364*

Elizabeth Garrett grew up at Tilbury Dock where her father worked. She started work as a secretary there at nineteen, just before the war. After the war she joined the PLA head office. *DK87.62*

Eileen Gibbons was born in 1922 in Canning Town. Her father was blind and worked in the docks. She worked in factories, and in a mobile canteen in the docks during the war. *DK89.48*

Alfred Green was born in 1909 in East Ham and worked as a messenger boy in the docks and as a docker in the West India Dock and the Royal Docks during and after the war. *DK88.101*

George Green was born in 1919 in Canning Town and worked as a river pilot. *DK89.39*

Vicki Green was born in 1916 in Whitechapel. Her parents were Jewish immigrants from Russia. She had to pretend to be unmarried to keep her job during the war. *CC 99/32*

Anne Griffiths was born in 1918 in Mile End. She grew up in Poplar in a family of dockers and worked at the Tate & Lyle factory and the Royal Mint. *DK88.66*

Norman Grigg was born in 1915, one of a family of eleven children in Rotherhithe, near the Surrey Commercial Docks. He worked as a stevedore on the docks. *DK89.77*

Charlie Gubbins was born in 1906 in Leytonstone and was a chemist at Associated Lead Manufacturers. He enjoyed playing practical jokes with small quantities of explosives. *86.360*

Miss H was born in Austria in 1900 and arrived in London two years later. Her father died in 1911, leaving her mother with six children. She became a dress machinist at fourteen. *2008.112*

Freda Hammerton was born in 1930 into a family of watermen who had been working on the River Thames for three centuries. Her father was killed in the Blitz. *DK89.9*

Henry Harington was born about 1905 and lived in Silvertown. He worked for a paint factory and then as a cooper in the Victoria Dock. *86.350*

Winifred Herbert was born in 1892 in Manchester and came to London as a laundry maid. Her husband was in the navy and she became a canteen cook in the Surrey Docks. *DK87.49*

Leslie Hoe was born in 1919 in Poplar to a Chinese father and Irish mother. He joined the Merchant Navy in the war and married Connie Hoe while she was an evacuee in Oxford. *CC 92/116*

Connie Hoe was born in 1922. Her father returned to Hong Kong and after her mother died, she was brought up by a family friend in Limehouse. She married Leslie Hoe. *CC 92/116*

Herbert Hollingsbee was born in 1899 and was an audit clerk at the Port of London working in Tilbury and West India Docks. He was a signal clerk in the First World War. *DK87.81*

Alice Humm was born in Bow. Her father was the manager of a chocolate factory; after he died, her family lived with an uncle who ran a shop near the dock in Bermondsey. *CC 96/29*

Edwin Hunt was born in Camden in 1920; both his grandfather and father were lightermen. He was apprenticed to his father and became a Thames barge master. *DK88.99*

Julie Hunt was born in 1954 in Stepney; her father was a docker at St Katharine Docks and she later ran a pie and mash shop. *DK88.94*

Zygmund Izycki was born in Latvia. His father disappeared on a business trip in 1939 and he then escaped on a ship to England. He served in the army and married an East Ender. *CC 92/175*

Joe and Wally James grew up in a Roman Catholic family in Stepney near to the West India Dock, before the war. Their family had been lightermen for several generations. *2010.48/36*

Violet Kentsbeer was born in 1919. After her mother and sisters were injured by shrapnel in the war, she left nursing to be a full-time carer. She met her husband at Kingsley Hall. *CC 2004/11*

Bernard Kops was born into a Dutch Jewish family in Stepney Green in 1926 and scored a success with his first play, *The Hamlet of Stepney Green* in 1957. He is an acclaimed poet, playwright and author of novels and memoirs. *2011.103*

Mrs L was born in 1900 in Whitechapel to parents from Poland. Her father had a market barrow. She worked in a cigarette factory, then later set up a shop with her sister. *2008.117*

Laurie Landick was born in 1908 on the Isle of Dogs. He joined the Port of London as a messenger at the age of fifteen and later worked as a timber measurer in the Surrey Docks. *DK87.44*

Brian Lane was born in 1941, in Hertfordshire where his mother was evacuated. He first met his father at the age of three, back in Bow. He worked as a plater on the docks. *DK88.128*

Victor Leigh grew up in an observant Jewish household in the East End with Polish parents. He became a Communist and worked as an actor and in the textile industry. *CC 2009/60*

Mr and Mrs Lester were born in the 1920s. He was at sea during the Second World War and became a docker in 1952. They lived near the Royal Docks. *2010.48/39*

Julia Lewis was born in Bow in 1930 and evacuated to Banbury during the early years of the war, returning to London in time for the doodlebugs. *CC 96/28*

Sissy Lewis was born in 1914 in Tottenham and, like her parents, worked for furniture firm Harris Lebus, where she met her husband. She was the firm's only female shop steward. *LHW 65.5*

Charles Lisle was born in 1899 in Stepney and was a clerk at the Port of London Authority. He was a fire warden in the First World War. *85.590*

Emanuel Litvinoff was born in 1915 in Whitechapel to Russian Jewish parents. A prolific writer and poet, he once publicly castigated T S Eliot for an anti-Semitic poem. *CC 99/29*

Terry Loveday was born in 1934 in Stratford and was one of the third generation of his family to go into the fur trade, working in Hackney and Bermondsey. *DK88.3*

Abraham Lue was born in Jamaica in 1939 to Chinese parents. He came to London in the 1950s to study mathematics at University College. *CC 93/42*

Miss M was born in Whitechapel in 1900 to Lithuanian parents. Her father worked as a peddler, selling household goods from a pack on his back in the suburbs of London. *2008.118*

William Mather was born in 1911 in West Ham, the son of a docker. He served in the air force during the war and then worked in dry docks on ship repair until retirement. *DK87.52*

Charles Megnin was born in Walthamstow in 1915 and made propellers for planes in the First World War. As a carpenter, he retrained soldiers in 1945, then worked on liners. *CC 96.41*

Joseph Milchard was born in Stepney about 1900. His mother supported the family through tailoring after his father was committed to an institution. He worked as a docker. *85.366*

Jack Miller was born in 1912 in Whitechapel to Latvian and Polish parents. He was in the army in Coventry just after it was bombed and guarded aliens interned in the Isle of Man. *CC 92/177*

Joe Morris was born in 1917 in Whitechapel to Russian and Polish parents. He worked as a tailor and used to make all his wife's and mother-in-law's clothes. *CC 93/43*

Florence Mugridge was born in 1908 and was an office worker at the Port of London. She met her husband when he worked in the office beneath hers. *85.591*

Pat O'Sullivan was born in 1898 in Dublin. She came to Poplar in 1934 to work as a nun in the East End where she ran children's clubs and visited poor families. *DK88.20*

Mr P was born in 1905 in Rothschild Buildings, Whitechapel. He was a cabinetmaker. Mrs P grew up in Cable Street and her father was employed by her husband's father. *2008.98*

Mary Partlett was born in 1928 in Limehouse. Her father was badly gassed in the First World War and unable to work. She worked at Hough's paper mill. *DK88.125*

Florrie Passman was born in Leeds in 1888 and moved to Rothschild Buildings in Whitechapel as a child. She ran a Jewish Girls' Club from 1913 to 1953. *2008.98*

Albert Patten was born in 1929 in Bow. He joined the navy during the war and worked on boats until 1955, and then in the docks. *DK88.76*

Jim Penn was born in 1931 in Canning Town. Like his father, he was a lighterman, and his father stopped him from going to sea on a boat that sank on its next voyage. *86/117*

Dennis Pike was born in 1924 in Rotherhithe into a large local family. He worked as a stevedore in Surrey Dock and married a docker's daughter. *DK89.83*

*Harry Plum was born in 1894 in Bethnal Green, the son of a Smithfield meat porter. He was an amateur boxer and later worked as a foreman at the docks. *85.361*

Annie Pope was born about 1905 in Cubitt Town and worked at Burrells Paint Works at Burrells Wharf on the Isle of Dogs throughout the Second World War. *DK87.84*

Charles Poulson was born in 1911 in Stepney Green to Russian parents. His father was a photographer, and he worked in the fur trade and was a fireman during the war. *CC 92/153*

Bill Pyne was born in 1919; his parents ran pubs. He trained as a barge builder, was in the navy during the war, and later worked for Courage's Brewery. *DK87.90*

James Quick was born about 1904. His father made wooden ships' propellers and he worked as a porter on the Surrey and Royal Docks. *DK87.61*

Mary Ridgeon was born in Hackney in 1916 into a family of publicans. Her father ran the Lord Palmerston pub in Bethnal Green and she later ran her own pub. *CC 96.43*

Joanna Roberts was born in Poplar in 1924, into a family with deep East End roots. In 2004, she was awarded an MBE for her work in local primary schools in Hackney. *File at British Library*

Stan Rose was born in 1910 and grew up in Bow. At fourteen, he was a pageboy at a club in Piccadilly; he was later a professional boxer and then worked as a dock labourer. *86.345*

Graham Rutherford was born in Gateshead in 1910 and joined the Metropolitan Police in 1928, choosing to work in the East End. He policed the Battle of Cable Street. *CC 2000.30*

Doris Salt was born in 1904 in East Ham. After her father died she spent some years in an orphanage while her mother went out to work. She was a typist at the Port of London. *DK87.53*

Suzanne Samson was born in 1924 in Berlin. Her mother brought her to London with a group of Jewish children from Mussolini's Italy, and they were taken in by an East End doctor. *CC 93.56*

P Satow served on the HMS *Belfast* during the war and became Assistant Harbour Master for the PLA in 1965. *DK88.126*

George and Joan Shaw were married in 1945, when she was an office worker at the Port of London, volunteering for the ARP, and he was serving in the navy. *DK88.91*

Dorothy Shipp was born in 1912 in Kent, and worked as a typist at Snowdon's oil lubrication factory in Millwall during the war. *DK87.14*

Bob Silver was born in 1931 in Hackney and worked as a mariner. He was involved in the deployment of Mulberry Harbours during the war. *87.11*

Harry Silverston was born in 1915 into a Jewish family in Whitechapel. He married Sylvia, who was born in Bethnal Green in 1920. *CC 92/179*

John Sleap was born in Clapton about 1898 in Bethnal Green and worked as a clerk for a textile trading firm. His wife was born in Bethnal Green, about 1896, and was a secretary. *2010.48/25*

Gracie Smith was born in 1912 into a family of pearly kings and queens. She and her husband both worked as costermongers. *DK 89.81*

Jane Smith was born in 1900 in Stepney, one of ten children, with Russian Jewish parents. Her father was a costermonger and she worked in a relative's tailoring business. *DK89.91*

Alan Spong was born in 1920 and was in charge of the *Queen Boadicea*, which was one of the boats that rescued men from the beaches at Dunkirk. *DK88.22*

Robert Stapleton was born in 1920 in Whitechapel and grew up on the Isle of Dogs. His dad was a stoker and his mother died when he was young. He worked as an engineer. *85/370*

Tom Stothard was born in Blackwall in 1908. His father worked for a ship repairer and the family lived in the midst of one of the East End's Irish communities. *86/269* and *DK89.40*

Pat Thompson was born in 1920 in Poplar; her parents both had Irish roots. Her father served as mayor of Poplar and she later became mayor of Tower Hamlets. *DK88.19*

Stanley Tooth was born in 1899 and was an administrator for the Port of London Authority, working in Millwall Dock, among others, during the Blitz. *85/371*

Anna Tzelniker was born in 1922 in Romania and her family came to England in 1933. The daughter of an actor, she became a well-known actress in Yiddish theatre, on TV and in films, including *Yentl*. She married Philip Bernstein. *92/150*

Mr U was born in Rothschild Buildings, Whitechapel to Russian parents in 1916. His father ran a stall in Petticoat Lane Market. *2008.101*

Pat Vicks grew up in Custom House just after the war. Together with Lynne Warne, she led a campaign to improve conditions in post-war tower blocks in Dagenham. *2010.48/30*

Lynne Warne grew up in Woolwich just after the war. Together with Pat Vicks, she led a campaign to improve conditions in post-war tower blocks in Dagenham. *2010.48/30*

Captain A R Williamson OBE was born in 1891. In 1909 he first left the Port of London on a three-master bound for Australia. He sailed on the *Discovery* six years after Scott. *DK87.54*

George Wood was born in 1903 in Bethnal Green. He and his two brothers both followed his father into the cabinetmaking trade. *LHW 65.7*

* Denotes names have been replaced, at interviewee's request, with a pseudonym.

Acknowledgements

Without the initial encouragement and ongoing critical support of Charlotte Cole at Ebury Press, this book would not exist. I suspect first books – like first children – suffer from an excess of nurturing, and Charlotte's firm and wise guidance has been a help and a spur every step of the way. At the Museum of London, Alex Werner recognised the book's potential and gave me free rein to use the museum's incredible oral history collection, as well as correcting errors in the final draft. The help, humour and unfeigned enthusiasm of oral history curator Sarah Gudgin has shaped my ideas, and lifted my spirits more times than she will ever know. I also learned a huge amount from my conversations with Hilary Young, who has been a wonderful sounding board throughout. I owe a debt of gratitude to picture library manager Sean Waterman for finding such excellent images and enduring my constant demands with exemplary patience.

For detailed background reading, I cannot recommend too highly Jerry White's meticulous accounts of *London in the 19th Century* and *London in the 20th Century*. For atmosphere, Jack London's *People of the Abyss* was the volume that introduced me to the East End. However, all credit for the lively evocation of communities, streets, workplaces and families rests with the East Enders whose accounts make up this book. To listen to them was a privilege and an education.

Finally, thank you to my lovely teenage sons, Alfie and Arthur.

Harriet Salisbury
November 2011

Index

People Index

About the Author

Harriet Salisbury has been a writer and editor for twenty years and has a special interest in the history of East London. She lives in Hackney. *The War on Our Doorstep* is her first book.

The Museum of London oral history collection contains more than 5,000 hours of recorded life story interviews with a wide variety of people who have lived and worked in London and who talk about their lives and everyday experiences.